THE POLITICAL ECONOMY OF NIGERIA

THE POLITICAL ECONOMY OF NIGERIA

Edited by
I. William Zartman

A SAIS Study on Africa

PRAEGER

PRAEGER SPECIAL STUDIES • PRAEGER SCIENTIFIC

Library of Congress Cataloging in Publication Data

Main entry under title:

The political economy of Nigeria.

Bibliography: p.
Includes index.
Contents: Introduction / I. William Zartman with Sayre Schatz – Social change and political conflict in Nigeria's Second Republic / by Larry Diamond – Income distribution and politics in Nigeria / by Henry Bienen.
1. Nigeria–Economic conditions–1970- –Addresses, essays, lectures. 2. Nigeria–Economic policy–Addresses, essays, lectures. 3. Nigeria –Politics and government–1975- –Addresses, essays, lectures. 4. Nigeria–Foreign economic relations–Addresses, essays, lectures. I. Zartman, I. William.
HC1055.P638 1983 330.9669'05 82-19064
ISBN 0-03-061476-7
ISBN 0-03-061827-4 (pbk.)

Published in 1983 by Praeger Publishers
CBS Educational and Professional Publishing
A Division of CBS, Inc.
521 Fifth Avenue, New York, New York 10175 U.S.A.

3456789 052 987654321
Printed in the United States of America

Contents

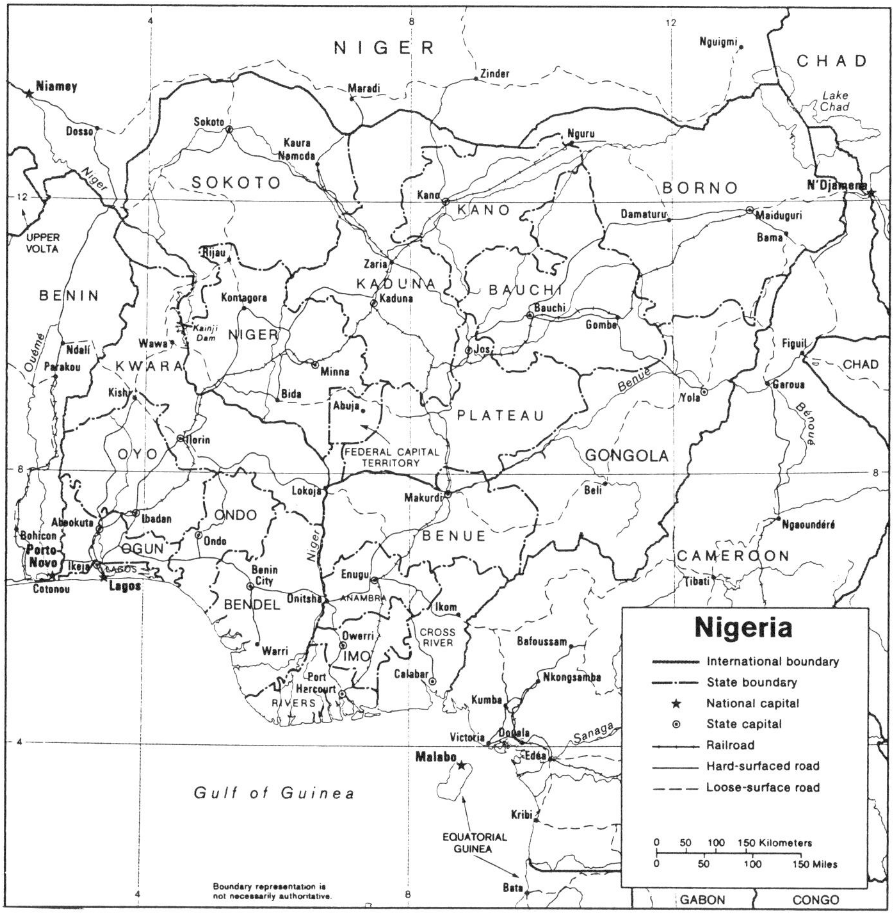
Nigeria
International boundary
State boundary
National capital
State capital
Railroad
Hard-surfaced road
Loose-surface road
0 50 100 150 Kilometers
0 50 100 150 Miles
Boundary representation is not necessarily authoritative.
NIGER
CHAD
Lake Chad
BENIN
UPPER VOLTA
CAMEROON
EQUATORIAL GUINEA
GABON
CONGO
Gulf of Guinea
SOKOTO
KANO
BORNO
KADUNA
BAUCHI
NIGER
KWARA
PLATEAU
GONGOLA
OYO
ONDO
OGUN
LAGOS
BENDEL
BENUE
ANAMBRA
IMO
CROSS RIVER
RIVERS
FEDERAL CAPITAL TERRITORY
Niamey
Dosso
Maradi
Zinder
Nguigmi
N'Djamena
Sokoto
Kaura Namoda
Nguru
Kano
Damaturu
Maiduguri
Bama
Zaria
Kaduna
Bauchi
Gombe
Jos
Rijau
Kontagora
Kainji Dam
Wawa
Minna
Bida
Abuja
Ndali
Parakou
Kishi
Ilorin
Figuil
Garoua
Yola
Lokoja
Makurdi
Beli
Ngaoundéré
Abeokuta
Ibadan
Ondo
Bohicon
Porto-Novo
Ikeja
Lagos
Cotonou
Benin City
Enugu
Onitsha
Ikom
Tibati
Owerri
Warri
Calabar
Port Harcourt
Bafoussam
Nkongsamba
Kumba
Victoria
Douala
Edéa
Malabo
Kribi
Bata
Niger
Benue
Bénoué
Ouémé
Sanaga
4
8
12

1
INTRODUCTION
I. William Zartman with Sayre Schatz

Nigeria has been born again. The war is over, the reconciliation has been accomplished, the military government has withdrawn, political life has been renewed. By some coincidence, just as the new political structures were being set in place, a new economy began to flourish as oil revenues flowed in quantity through the veins of the country. Perhaps it is too much to say that social structures have been revised as well, but the horizontal effects of modernistic class formation shake the vertical structures of traditional ethnicity.

Yet these changes were not sudden. They have been the product of decades of experiment and evolution. Strains slowly accumulating beneath the surface of society produce ostensibly sudden shifts representing years of pent up pressures. Political decisions to handle problems in one way rather than another set up logical sequences of events and channel new decisions. The new Nigeria is therefore merely an outgrowth of the old, rising from roots reaching deep into the colonial and even precolonial past. To trace back all these roots is beyond the scope of this presentation. But to understand the changes that are taking place in the interrelations of economics and politics in Nigeria in the 1980s, one must first look at changes in various structures in the 1960s and 1970s, during the first two decades of independence. This introduction will describe such

---

This chapter is by I. William Zartman except for the section "Structures of Spending and Structures of Earning," which was contributed by Sayre Schatz.

structural changes – in politics, leadership, demography, residence, expenditures, revenues, and international context – to set the stage for the subsequent analysis of the political economy of the Second Republic.

CHANGING POLITICAL AND SOCIAL STRUCTURES

In its *political structures*, Nigeria was born in a search for an organization to contain its large territory and huge population in governable units. This evolution can be compared best to an experiment in the form of international relations systems in rapid succession before finally landing on the particular form of federalism outlined in the 1979 Constitution. In the African context, Nigeria is practically a subregional international organization in itself, with more than twice the population and more than twice as many federal states as the territorially larger federation of French West Africa (or the Mali Federation, as it was scheduled to have been named) would have had if it had held together after independence. The state organization of this Nigerian federation was originally so loose as to be almost confederal, but the political structure of the three federal states was that of a balance of power system. In 1957, a strong ethnically based political party had won elections in each of the regions; two years later, following federal elections in preparation for independence in 1960, the Northern and the Eastern regions had made an alliance against the Western region through their respective political parties: the Northern People's Congress (NPC) and the National Council of Nigerian Citizens (NCNC) against the Action Group (AG). But the particular balance of power alliance was unstable, for it united the two strongest parties rather than the two weakest parties against the strongest as balance of power theory would indicate. The 1962 census, upon which state representation was to be based, gave the North an absolute majority of the 53 million population and so was rejected by the East and West. A careful rerun the following year confirmed the results but was no better accepted. At the same time, a new region was created out of the West to further weaken the opposition and the new Midwest region was won by the NCNC. But an unnecessarily large coalition will split, and a balance of power system pushed to extremes will become bipolar. In the 1964 elections two rearranged coalitions faced each other: the NCNC allied with the persecuted national wing of the Eastern region, the AG, forming the United Progressive Grand Alliance (UPGA), against the NPC allied with the regional wing of the Eastern party, the Nigerian National Democratic Party (NNDP), forming the Nigerian National Alliance (NNA). The UPGA boycotted the elections and the other side of the bipolar confrontation won by default. It then broke the rules of the confederal system by illegally trying to consolidate its national victory through destruction of the opposition's regional base. In 1965, the Western elections were rigged to allow the NNDP to win, and the system collapsed in general strike, rebellion and war by the following year.

The first reaction to collapse of a multiparty system was a unipolar system inaugurated in May 1966 by the first military government of General Aguiyi-Ironsi. It did not last for the same reasons that the federation had never been much more than a confederation: the central government was not strong enough, the state governments were the centers of power, and loyalty, identity and allegiance were attached to the parts, not to the whole. The unitary system was abolished in September 1966 by General Yakubu Gowon, chief of the second military government, and in May 1967 was replaced by a new federal system of 12 states, a number large enough to permit a working federalism and to avoid the trap of bipolarity. Its first effect, however, was to trigger a different kind of interaction among states: the independence of Biafra and war. The war reinforced the power of the central government for the first time and brought a greater sense of national identification to Nigerians; but it also left the nine states remaining in the federation under the autonomous powers of military barons. Once the war was over, in January 1970, Gowon was indecisive in changing this system to an integrated civilian-run federation and so was deposed, in July 1975, by younger military leaders – first General Murtala Muhammed and then, after he lost his life in an abortive coup, General Olusegun Obasanjo. Obasanjo created 19 states in February 1976 and supervised General Muhammed's timetable for arriving at a federal constitutional democracy by October 1, 1979.

Political collapse, war, military government and the process of constitutional return all contributed to the consolidation of the Nigerian state and the evolution of its structure from successive experiments in interstate relations to a possible working model for federal, intrastate politics, analyzed by Larry Diamond in the following chapter. No state in Africa – including those such as Cameroon, Zaire, Libya, Ethiopia, Tanzania and Uganda, which have abolished their federal-type systems – has gone through such a broad range of alternatives in such a violent exercise of politics before arriving at a workable framework for national politics. Not only is the result a feasible arrangement, but the process of trial and error that led to it may work in favor of its success. For Nigeria's path has differed both from the stable single-party states with bureaucratic politics such as Tunisia, Cameroon, Ivory Coast, Kenya and Tanzania and the military regimes with no clear future such as Togo, Benin, Upper Volta, Mali, Niger, CAR and many others. Both have established a pattern of politics during their first brief decades of independence, the first providing a basis for a stable institutionalized polity and the second offering a history of unsatisfactory institutions, extralegal succession and reduced politics. Nigeria is unusual in that its first independent decades may appear to follow the second pattern but, in fact, carry some of the results of the first. Instead of setting up an alternate pattern of extralegal politics, Nigeria's experimentations have effectively discredited alternatives and brought the polity by negative example to a commitment to making the new state work. Nothing predicts that this commitment is absolute, of course, and it is likely to be tested on occasion by those whose attachment to it is weak. But demands for the formation of new states – as have been on the federal agenda since the beginning of the second Republic – no longer pose a challenge to the nature of the system, and threats of military conspiracy – as were discovered once in early 1982 – have to overcome a much more complex structure than under the previous structures.

Changes in political structures have been reflected in the *structures of the political elites.* The two generational characteristics of the political elite are notable. The first is the major generational shift that occurred in the military coup, when, in a now typical African pattern, the military intervened to throw out an Independence Generation that was not up to the tasks it had won for itself. The second is the half-generational step backward that characterized the return to civilian government as a new Post-Independence Generation of civilian politicians replaced the younger army officers. The average birthdate of 1916 of the political elite at independence was slightly older than the African average (the Class of 1918), indicating a long history of engagement in politics and preparation for independence. The average birthdate of 1927 for the Gowon military government in 1967 showed a jump of a political generation, and the government of Obasanjo in 1976 was born over a quarter of a century after the original Independence Generation. These men went back to the barracks or to other nonpolitical pursuits, but the elite who succeeded them were not only born nearly a decade earlier than they but at 48 were actually older than any elite who came to power in Nigeria. Geographically, the new elite was of dispersed origins, with more even representation of the provinces than any before it. Education levels in the political elite have risen as well in the two independent decades. Education has become the necessary condition for entry into the political elite, and an ever increasing proportion of the leaders have gone beyond college (or military higher education) to advanced degrees. Increasingly, too, elite members received their higher degrees outside of Nigeria, in England or, also increasingly, in the United States, although many of them first went to college in Nigeria. Elite backgrounds are divided between the public and private sectors, with the public sector (civil service, including schoolteachers) in a minority in the new civilian government for the first time; both the growing economy and the military monopolization of power for a decade gave a boost to the private professions (business, law, academic and liberal professions) as a place where the elite could grow while awaiting its return to politics and then to government. (See Table 1.1.)

TABLE 1.1
Dimensions of Nigerian Elites
(Head of State, Ministers, Governors, Party Chairmen, Parliamentary Presidents)

Year	*1960*	*1967*	*1976*	*1980*
N	*26*	*27*	*48*	*51*
Carryovers				
Mean Age (Birth Year)	*44 (1916)*	*40 (1927)*	*35 (1941)*	*48 (1932)*
Standard Deviation	*7.1*	*10.5*	*6.4*	*8.8*
Origins: North				
Sokoto (%)	8	4	6	6
Niger (%)	4	0	4	2
Kaduna (%)	4	7	13	8

continued

TABLE 1.1, continued

Year	*1960*	*1967*	*1976*	*1980*
N	*26*	*27*	*48*	*51*
Carryovers				
Mean Age (Birth Year)	*44 (1916)*	*40 (1927)*	*35 (1941)*	*48 (1932)*
Standard Deviation	*7.1*	*10.5*	*6.4*	*8.8*
Kano (%)	12	4	4	6
Bauchi (%)	4	4	0	4
Borno (%)	8	7	2	6
Kwara (%)	0	7	4	6
Benue (%)	0	4	2	2
Plateau (%)	4	7	4	2
Gongola (%)	4	0	10	4
West				
Oyo (%)	4	4	0	4
Ogun (%)	8	4	2	6
Ondo (%)	4	0	2	8
Lagos (%)	12	11	4	4
Midwest				
Bendel (%)	12	7	6	4
East				
Anambra (%)	4	4	2	6
Imo (%)	0	0	4	4
Rivers (%)	0	11	0	6
Cross Rivers (%)	4	4	2	4
Unknown (%)	8	4	29	8
Education (highest level)				
Secondary (%)	15	7	0	0
College (%)	38	22	16	36
Military/Police School (%)	0	44	57	0
LLB (%)	27	11	4	26
MA (%)	8	0	2	12
MD (%)	8	4	2	14
PhD (%)	4	11	8	16
Unknown (%)	0	0	16	8
Education (last place)				
Nigeria (%)	53	30	13	38
Other Africa (%)	0	4	6	2

continued

Year	*1960*	*1967*	*1976*	*1980*
N	*26*	*27*	*48*	*51*
Carryovers				
Mean Age (Birth Year)	*44 (1916)*	*40 (1927)*	*35 (1941)*	*48 (1932)*
Standard Deviation	*7.1*	*10.5*	*6.4*	*8.8*
UK (%)	42	67	43	42
USA (%)	4	0	4	16
Other (%)	0	0	6	0
Unknown (%)	0	0	29	4
Profession				
Teacher/Government (%)	50	25	2	38
Journalism/Business (%)	15	7	4	16
Lawyer (%)	19	7	2	18
Academic/Professional (%)	8	11	6	22
Medical (%)	8	4	2	4
Military/Police (%)	0	56	77	0
Unknown (%)	0	0	6	14

Data compiled by Roxanne Rogers DeSola.

Thanks to efforts of some diligent scholars (Beckett and O'Connell 1977), a good deal is known about the attitudes of the Class of 1945, the young generation born about that year, growing up at the time of independence and finishing their higher education as the Biafran War was drawing to a close, and forming the rising leadership of the 1980s. Consistent with the political socialization provided by these experiences, this generation is nationalistic and idealistic, concerned with some of the basic problems of their country but struggling in an attempt to combine notions of democracy (which were seen to be perverted under civilian government and suppressed by the military) with strong central leadership. An understanding of these views and tensions is necessary for an understanding not only of the way in which their predecessors' actions were perceived but also of the way in which the new generation will act as political leaders.

The first set of tensions arises from nationalism. While students of the new generation saw national identification becoming more important and felt themselves to be "nationalized" by the experience of the Biafran war, there was continuing competition for primacy among home community, home state, broader ethnic, and Nigerian national identity. "Each level means *something* to the individual, even if not *everything*," conclude Beckett and O'Connell (p. 71); ". . . most students are potential 'tribalists,' . . . [but] never more than 'reluctant tribalists' " (p. 79). Similarly, regarding attitudes toward others, "contempt" and "respect" and "envy" and "hostility" held equal rankings (the two pair separated by "ambivalence") on views toward Westerners and Western culture, but the highest ranking was registered by "imitation." Opinions split evenly about whether colonialism brought more advantages than disadvantages to Africa and whether Third World poverty was the result of exploitation of underdevelopment. Data do not show the direction in which these attitudinal contradictions are moving, but the contradictions themselves show concern for ideological debate. At the same time, attitudes showed high personal motivation and dedication, even idealism, pointing to political and personal engagement (ibid., pp. 79, 89, 68-71, 100, 92).

The new generation overwhelmingly felt that academic qualifications, effort, and competence (much more so than ethnic factors or "pull") were the guarantors of success, that present sacrifice was necessary so that future generations might enjoy economic development, and that they would be able to make a significant personal contribution to Nigeria's future. On the other hand, future career choices strongly emphasized security over risk, even when security in civil service was clearly seen as going hand in hand with lack of challenge, lower salary, and lesser importance in affecting economic development. This too reflects tension and a serious contradiction between national aspirations and the means versus the ends of personal commitment (ibid., pp. 127, 76, 87, 90, 129).

A third set of tensions concerns the eternal contradiction between democracy and strong leadership; again, the very presence of contradictions in the political attitudes of the Class of 1945 shows a healthy mixture of realism and idealism even if its resolution can lead in a number of directions. A situation in which the human requirements for development (stable leadership, national unity, patriotism, technical skills, efficiency, honesty and integrity, in that order) were the opposite of the characteristics of early civilian and military governments (corruption, sectarianism, ignorance, in the first case, and mistakes, venality, and irresponsible authoritarianism, in the second), but in which the mass of voters was unlikely to make rational choices but rather would be swayed by ethnicity and personalities, it was difficult to find the appropriate political system. More than any other, this issue split the new generation into regional groups, according to student responses of the early 1970s. Northerners (in Ahmadu Bello University) felt that an authoritarian, technocratic government was a better guarantor of development than a democratic one, and that competence, development, stability and unity were all preferable to democracy. Westerners, Mid-Westerners and Mid-Easterners (in Ibadan University) felt the contrary on all points except the preferability of stability and unity to democracy, but students of the same regional origins (in Lagos University) and Easterners (in Nsukka University) were more evenly divided on all questions except the preferability of unity to democracy. Translated into the practical terms of institutions, this mean that the Westerners (in Ibadan) had come to terms with democratic exercise ("in a democratic system we must take the risk of letting the people choose") whereas Northerners and Easterners were evenly split between that option and a search for some indirect system of selection ("so that the final electors are sensible and informed") (ibid., pp. 69, 111, 155f, 28, 154-163).

Throughout these details of emerging elite opinion over the proper form and exercise of government, a general trend of discussion – even if not a firm consensus – is evident. The Class of 1945 favors neither unbridled democracy nor irresponsible authoritarianism; rather, it is concerned with combining the better features of both with an awareness of the need for democratic controls on leadership but also for leadership direction for democracy. This generation is neither one of technocrats nor of politicians, which means that the stereotypes of the first two decades are no longer accepted. The more difficult task of working out effective roles remains. That posture is cautiously favorable for the stability and progress of the Second Republic, whatever other indications may show.

For the population as a whole, Nigeria's *education structures* are not outstanding, even for Africa. In 1964, Nigeria ranked twenty-ninth in Africa by educational enrollment with 5 percent of the population in primary school, nineteenth in secondary education with less than .5 percent of the population enrolled, and (with some others) fifteenth in higher education. In 1970 (a bad year because of the Biafran War), by a different measure, 34 percent of the primary age group was in school, 4 percent of the secondary school age group, and less than .5 percent of the higher education age group. A decade later these percentages had doubled, meaning that the absolute figures had almost tripled (Figures from World Bank). By 1982, there were 22 universities with 77,000 students.

Despite this increase, universal primary education was a long way off. Not only are these figures relatively low by African standards (twenty-eighth in Africa in 1980), but they cover some serious imbalances. In the southern states, school enrollment at all levels has been as high as the best of the African states, but enrollments in the northern states vary from a third to a tenth of the southern average for any grade or level. Furthermore, without being able to cite even statistical indicators, it is clear that urban dwellers and children of parents with some education have a better chance of entering a university than rural dwellers or children of uneducated parents. Parents' education is a better predictor of children's higher education than is wealth or profession, and the more advanced the parents' education the better predictor it is. Otherwise stated, educated families reproduce themselves. There is, however, another side to the same coin. Nigeria university surveys in 1970-73 showed that approximately 40 percent of the student population came from families of farmers, 40 percent to 50 percent came from families with illiterate fathers and another 27 percent to 31 percent from families with father educated only in primary or Qoranic schools (Beckett and O'Connell 1977). Thus, education not only reproduces but also improves itself and is powerfully attractive to all social levels. Furthermore, comparison of education with class or profession in students' backgrounds indicates that education is a key but not a guarantor of occupation and income. Education is neither sufficient nor even necessary for wealth and status. Social mobility is galloping in Nigeria, breaking up both old and new criteria for social and economic status, although doing so more rapidly in the south than in the north (where traditional structures are more rigid).

It is even more difficult to be precise about these *traditional structures*. This results, in part, because of their nature since segmentary or hierarchical social organizations diagram easily but become more elusive when it comes to assigning names and numbers to the levels in the diagrams. In part, however, the difficulty arises because "traditional" structures are growing and consolidating, and national politics is growing out of communal politics by becoming ethnic – and divisively sub-national – first. Thus, Western Yorubas, Eastern Igbos, and Northern Hausa-Fulanis were divisions that were meaningless at the beginning of the century, became caricaturally meaningful through the politics of independence and the breakdown of politics in the civil war, and are still resilient underneath political and social relations in the new republic.

Nobody knows how many Nigerians there are within the new democracy and therefore there is little precise information on other *demographic structures*. By official counts, the population was 87.5 million in 1981, a fifth of the people of the African continent, between Pakistan and Bangladesh in size of population. But participation in the 1979 elections suggested a population of 100 million, bringing Nigeria closer to Japan as the eighth largest country of the world, with nearly twice the population shown in the contested censuses of 1962 and 1963. Population growth has shown little change over the first two decades of independence, however, increasing at a steady rate of 2.5 percent. In the early 1950s, half the population was under 17 years old; by the time of the second republic at the end of the 1970s, half the population had been born under Nigerian independence. Such age structures promise a large working population for the future but a heavy burden of social costs and political expectations for the present (Figures from UN Economic Commission for Africa).

The quality of life of this population is poor but probably slowly improving, although one of the characteristics of its underdevelopment is the absence of any reliable measure of its condition or its improvement. Attempts at statistical evidence show that the composite measure of the Physical Quality of Life Index (from Overseas Development Commission *Agenda 1982* & World Bank 1981) stood at 31 in the 1970s, comparable to the poorest of the poor with much lower per capita incomes than Nigeria, but without enough data to measure the Rate of Reduction of Disparities (DRR) with other nations. By the end of the 1970s, however, life expectancy had risen from 39 to 48 years since independence, child death rate dropped from 38 to 24 per million, population per physician dropped from 56,000 to 15,800 (still by far the highest in the middle income category and higher than most low income countries), but calorie intake dropped from 91 percent to 83 percent of requirements. However, interesting as it would be to have reliable data on these matters, the more interesting questions concern the way in which change is felt and perceived. For ultimately, the stimulation and continuation of improvement depends on whether expectations are aroused and satisfied, and in relation to which reference point – one's own past, others' present, or the future.

STRUCTURES OF SPENDING AND STRUCTURES OF EARNING

The major attempt to bring about a change in its *economic structures* has been Nigeria's effort since the first great oil price increase in 1973-74 to convert its oil wells into "a solid foundation for self-sustaining growth and development in the shortest time possible" (Fourth National Development Plan 1981-85, p. 6). The immediate reaction to the surge in oil revenues – the Udoji wage increases and the euphoric planning (Schatz 1977) that encouraged waste and corruption – was intemperate, but a less extravagant approach was then adopted.

Nigeria's use of its resources can be divided into three broad categories: private consumption, government consumption, and investment (both private and government), i.e., the creation of additions to the country's stock of capital goods. Private consumption has been growing briskly by conventional standards. Its rate of increase in the four years after the oil revenue surge was more than thirteen times its rate of increase in the pre-civil war 1960s (more than 8 percent per annum for 1973-77 compared to 0.6 percent per annum for 1960-66). The lion's share of the increase went to the relatively affluent. Although few data are available, it seems clear that the lower 40 percent of the population economically benefited relatively little.

Nevertheless, private consumption has been increasing *relatively* slowly and is sharply shrinking as a percent of gross domestic product (GDP). Under the first civilian government in the 1960s, private consumption constituted 82 percent of GDP whereas under the military government in the 1970s (data for 1970-77), it was down to 58 percent. Thus, despite the excesses of the rich – the imported champagne and lace – and the consumption gains of some other relatively affluent groups, in the aggregate there has been commendable restraint in private consumption.

With respect to government consumption, however, there was no belt tightening (i.e., government expenditures for purposes other than capital formation). This portion of GDP has always grown rapidly – at an annual rate of 10.6 percent during the 1950s and 6.4 percent during the pre-civil war 1960s. Then after the first big oil price increases it soared, tripling (to 29.7 percent) in the four years from 1973 to 1977. As a result of the growth in the rate of increase, the proportion of GDP devoted to government consumption also grew significantly: it was 4.9 percent in 1950-60; 6.1 percent in 1960-66; 13.8 percent in 1970-77; 15.9 percent in 1977; and 10 percent in 1979. Thus Nigeria manifested a much greater degree of indulgence in its government consumption than in its private consumption.

Despite this indulgence, gross domestic investment (which can be considered the most fundamental requisite for economic development) also increased rapidly. (Curiously, its growth since 1950 has closely paralleled that of government consumption except for the first half of the 1960s.) Investment increased briskly during the 1950s and 1960s, at roughly 11 percent per annum and then took off after the oil price hike, tripling (30.1 percent) between 1973 and 1977. As a percent of GDP, it shot up from 11.7 percent in the 1950s and 15.7 percent in the pre-civil war 1960s to 31 percent at the end of the 1970s.

These figures suggest a diligent development effort by Nigeria, but some interpretation is required. On the one hand, the investment figures understate the development effort in that some government consumption expenditures can be considered as productive investment in human capital (e.g., recurrent expenditures on education). On the other hand, this is more than outweighed by two other factors. First, we can distinguish conceptually between productive investment and investment for the purpose of consumption (e.g., investments in parliamentary buildings, theaters or stadia and, partially, in roads in Lagos or in the construction of Abuja). This investment-for-consumption probably exceeds the human capital adjustment mentioned above. Second, effective productive investment has been reduced by waste and corruption.

All things considered, the intensity of Nigeria's development effort is moderate. On the one hand, a gross domestic investment rate of 31 percent is certainly substantial. It significantly exceeds the 23 percent rate of the industrial market economies as a group. On the other hand, Nigerian investment is about equal to that of the rest of the group of countries in which the World Bank places Nigeria (the oil exporting, mid-income developing countries), and a significant portion of that investment has not been productive.

Economic growth has clearly accelerated. Nigerian investment has generated or contributed to a number of developments in the economy. In appraising the economy's growth-generating performance, it is best to leave aside oil production and revenues, for these represent a windfall. GDP growth from oil, adjusted for inflation, accelerated from 4.2 percent per annum in the pre-civil war period 1958-66 to more than 12 percent per annum in 1974-78, although it then slackened during the recession phase of the petropolitical fluctuation. The per capita annual increase rose from about 1.4 percent (1958-66) to 9.3 percent (1973/74-1978/79), which would result in a doubling of average income in less than eight years. The World Bank has moved Nigeria from the low to the mid-income category of developing nations. Its 1979 GNP per capita was $670, slightly less than Morocco and Peru, about the same as El Salvador, a bit above Congo, Philippines and Thailand, and higher than any other Black African country except Gabon and Ivory Coast.

The general standard of living has improved much less than the GDP figures would suggest. There are several reasons, the first two already mentioned: individual consumption has grown much more slowly than GDP, and the income distribution has become more unequal. Third, official GDP data are unreliable and the figures tend consistently to exaggerate growth. (To prevent the long-run figures from getting blatantly out of touch with reality, retroactive corrections – which go completely unnoticed – are made some years later. For example, official Nigerian data for 1956-66 showed a 6.1 percent annual increase in GDP. Now, the most recent World Bank figures show a 4.3 percent growth rate for that period.) Fourth, the very nature of national income accounting, which tends to undercount nonmarket contributions to true GDP in any given base year, and then counts fully the market economy increments in GDP, builds in an exaggeration of GDP growth.

While a normal development pattern unfolded in most sectors, there was sudden, even spasmodic, structural change in three major sectors of the Nigerian economy: (1) construction's share of the GDP almost doubled in five years (going from 5.8 percent in 1972 to 10.9 percent in 1977); (2) the portion of GDP attributable to public administration and the military almost tripled in the same period (going from 4.5 percent in 1972 to 12.1 percent in 1977); and (3) a slow decline in the relative importance of agriculture is to be expected, but the agricultural contribution to GDP simply plummeted. Agricultural production fell from 60 percent to 30 percent of GDP (including oil) between 1960-65 and the last half of the 1970s. Agriculture provided 81 percent of export receipts in 1960 and fell to 6 percent in 1977. These figures perhaps overdramatize the decline because they result, in part, from the rise in the petroleum sector, but even more sober figures showing the agricultural portion of GDP excluding oil show a sharp drop, from 58 percent in 1960-65 to 36 percent in 1977.

Each phase of the spasmodic change has involved problems. The government sector expansion neglected to ask whether substantial increases in government consumption and military expenditures were what Nigerians most want or Nigerian society most needs. The increase in construction was accompanied by great waste and corruption. The decline in agriculture was associated with considerable discontent among the many in simple farming and also with balance-of-payments problems and the enormous costs and pressures of urbanization.

Agricultural output has decreased not only relatively but absolutely, falling 1.5 percent per annum (1970-77). Food production per person declined 13 percent in the past decade. The portion of the labor force in agriculture also decreased (from 71 percent in 1960 to 55 percent in 1979) but not nearly as sharply as the agricultural share of output (58 percent of GDP excluding oil in 1960-65 to 36 percent in 1977). Together, these signify a relative productivity decline in agriculture from 82 percent of the national average productivity (excluding oil) in 1960 to 66 percent in 1977-79. The rural-urban income differential widened substantially. Average rural income, only 38 percent of urban income in 1960, fell to 24 percent by 1977.

In response, the government has initiated a new program dubbed the Green Revolution. One can be hopeful, but past history enjoins skepticism. In every new plan for more than 25 years, there has been a rhetorical emphasis on agriculture that has in practice had little effect. Just before the new Green Revolution, there was Operation Feed the Nation; to some it was known as Operation Fool the Nation.

The enlarged oil revenues spurred persistent inflation. The price level increased by as much as one-third during 1975. The rate of inflation slowed during the 1978-79 recession but has accelerated since. Data on inflation are particularly unreliable. The official urban retail price index shows 1980 prices 8.9 percent higher than 1979 prices. The increase according to the Lagos business community average estimate was 25 percent. Moreover, there are different measures of inflation – the GDP deflator and various consumer price indexes.

It is generally agreed that the inflation rate topped 30 percent in 1981. A substantial increase in the national minimum wage in September 1981 (to ₦ 125 a month) was both response to and stimulant of inflation. (Two years earlier the federal government monthly minimum had been increased from ₦ 60 to ₦ 100.)

The figures are less important than understanding that oil revenues generate a persistent inflationary tendency unless Nigeria increases its production responsiveness to domestic demand (i.e., increases its elasticity of supply). A substantial portion of oil revenues are spent in the domestic economy. These expenditures augment aggregate domestic demand, e.g., for foodstuffs. If domestic production responds only sluggishly, prices increase.

For reasons relating to government management of oil prices and revenues, Nigeria has experienced recurring economic fluctuations since the oil price increases of 1973-74. There was a "petro-political fluctuation" (Schatz in Whitaker, ed. 1981) during the period 1973-79 that had many characteristics of the business cycle of a more developed economy. The recovery after 1979 was aborted by a severe decrease in oil sales caused by Nigerian persistence in charging a high premium price for its petroleum.

Nigeria's economic development orientation may be characterized as nurture-capitalism. Development in the directly productive sphere of the economy is to be the province of private enterprise and particularly indigenous private enterprise, as discussed in the chapter by Akinsanya. The vision is one of a viable capitalist economy powered to an ever increasing degree by Nigerian businessmen. A wide range of measures have been implemented to assist indigenous business.

However, nurture-capitalism is limping. Private investment remains small. Solid data are lacking and widely different estimates can be made. President Shagari's Fourth Plan projection is that all private investment, domestic and foreign, will amount to only 14 percent of gross domestic investment for the period 1981-85. Some World Bank data can be interpreted as suggesting that the private share of gross domestic investment is 30 percent. Even the latter figure indicates that indigenous private investment hardly has been an important engine of growth.

A NATION IN A WORLD ORDER

A Nigeria undergoing these changes and developments is itself part of changing *international structures* with an evolving notion of its own role. The most hotly debated question among Nigerians since independence on the subject of foreign affairs is how the country should respond to its own considerable weight. Some feel that Nigeria needs first and for a while to pull its own house together and leave the world alone, shying away from any major external role and seeing that its very size makes its neighbors wary the more it tries to throw its weight around. Others feel that Nigeria is called by its size, position and development to play a leading role in Africa and beyond. This debate raged among the political parties at the time of independence and took its first official form in the All-Nigerian Peoples' Conference in 1961; twenty years later it has taken a more ideological and economically based form of reasoning, as Timothy Shaw's chapter shows. Under the first civilian regime, the first argument was predominant. The first military governments were too concerned with internal cohesion to stray from it, but by the time of the Muhammed-Obasanjo regimes the second argument was dominant. The second civilian government has reverted to greater caution.

These attitudes were responses to Nigeria's location in a geopolitical structure that underwent its own changes over the two decades. Nigeria was born isolated and surrounded by wary French-speaking territory and with a great gap in mutual understanding between the two. France has long been viewed as the most dangerous external power, not only threatening but profoundly foreign, and "its Africans" are frequently viewed as inferior and dominated (mutually reinforcing characteristics). Incidents with France – the atomic tests in Algeria in 1961, the tacit and indirect support for Biafra in 1967-69, and the role in Chad viewed as tricky and neocolonial in 1979 – have reinforced the gap, even when they attempted to bridge it. The real effort to bridge the gap did not occur until 1973 when Nigeria and the French-speaking Associates of the European Common Market began to bring their positions together on the subject of closer economic relations with the European Community. The African Declaration of Cooperation, Development and Economic Independence issued by an OAU Summit at Lagos that month was followed by negotiations leading to the Lome Convention with the EC, signed in February 1975, and to the Economic Community of West African States (ECOWAS), signed in May of the same year. ECOWAS (which developed a mutual defense commitment) was only the second African alliance that Nigeria had ever joined, the first being the defunct Monrovia Group of 1961-62 that led to the creation of the continental OAU. Thus, with time, Nigeria has moved from a postcolonial linguistic structure of relations to a regional structure in its African relations.

Nigeria has also moved into a more active role in West Africa and in the continent more broadly. Nigeria's troops went to Congo for the UN in 1960 and were offered to Tanzania in 1964. Also in 1964 it mediated between French-speaking Africans and Ghana. But after the end of the Biafran War Nigeria suddenly emerged as a major African mediator: in the Ethiopian-Somalian border dispute, as a member of the OAU presidents' commission to offer proposals for the Middle East dispute in 1971, as a member of the OAU Wisemen on the Western Sahara after 1978, as a mediator between Zaire and Angola at the time of the Shaba crises in 1977-78, as the major African contact state outside of the Frontline States in the Angola-American initiative on Zimbabwe in 1977-78 and the Western Five mediation on Namibia after 1977, and as the diplomatic host and military participant in the round tables and peace-keeping forces in Chad after 1979. It also used some of its clout by nationalizing BP to move Britain toward a more favorable position on South Africa and Rhodesia in 1979 and cutting off oil supplies to Chad and Ghana the same year in response to unfavorable events, swinging African recognition behind the MPLA government in Angola in response to the South African invasion in consort with other Angolan movements, and by responding heavy-handedly to border incidents with Benin and Cameroon in 1981. Yet most of these actions were taken under the younger military; under the older civilians, Nigeria showed less drive and decisiveness. The trend has been toward a larger role in regional and African affairs, but Nigeria's growth into that role has been uneven.

Within the world structures of international relations, Nigeria's position has evolved more slowly. It has joined the Non-Aligned Movement, the Group of 77, and the Organization of Petroleum-Exporting Countries (OPEC), but it is a leader in none of these. Yet Nigeria is fiercely independent and is no one's agent. It has a history of ties with England but resents being called a neocolonial society. It enjoyed Soviet aid at a crucial time during the Biafran War, but Russia has no influence over it. It desires better relations with the United States because of its size, exports and African role and because it uses America as a constitutional model; but it is no ally. Nigeria's comparison with American history is interesting for some parallels that relate similarities to differences. Having gone through both a confederal dissolution and a secessionist civil war, Nigeria has appeared to have compressed 80 years of American historical experience between the Articles of Confederation (1781-87) and the Civil War (1861-65) into less than a decade. Its political events evoke more the rise of business and the taming of the West in the America of the late 1800s than the rise of the farmer and the taming of the East in the America of the late 1700s. But in foreign affairs, it has to a large extent emulated the first century of American experience by expressing its concern about its own continent but holding itself aloof from global conflict and politics. In the fast world of the late twentieth century, the 1980s will tell whether such aloofness is long possible.

CONCEPTS AND QUESTIONS OF ANALYSIS

In all these aspects, Nigeria is interesting in and of itself. Its size alone makes it the most important country in Africa, and the other elements of national power – its GNP, raw materials, army and location – reinforce its importance. But of far greater importance is the model that Nigeria provides for understanding the process of development and the policy choices that further that process. Nigeria in the 1980s finds itself squarely astride at least three sets of competing paradigms, and its experience will long be cited in future discussions over the inevitability of particular processes and the validity of particular choices. As with any concepts, these paradigms do not have sharp boundaries in reality and they overlap, but above a secondary level of debate over their fit on empirical events they represent the basic dimensions of the ongoing attempts to comprehend the phenomenon (or phenomena) of societal evolution in its social, economic and political aspects.

One such dimension runs from the tradition of ethnicity to the modernity of class. Modernization theories have indicated that the process of development involves both the breakdown of ethnic tradition and identity and the creation in its stead of class and class consciousness. Further investigation along this dimension has raised a number of questions about the inevitability of the shift of cleavages from vertical to horizontal strata. To begin with, it is not certain that ethnic divisions do break down, and some evidence indicates that modernization, to the contrary, only serves to reinforce horizontal divisions, at least in its early stages, as people cut adrift by its strains and changes seek a personal and social anchor in traditional identity and organization. Neotribalism in Nigeria is the result. Then, too, it begins to appear that ethnic breakdown and class formation are not a single linked process but in fact two with only a tenuous link. Vertical breakdown may or may not be followed by horizontal stratification. Horizontal stratification may or may not take the form of class consciousness, even if objectively, but not necessarily subjectively, identifiable social strata come into being. To be sure, from the beginning the class debate has focused on disagreement over the definitions of "class," including the necessity of real consciousness for its existence and the relationship between class, status and power. It is still unclear, however, whether "class" in both its subjective and objective manifestations is an inevitable concomitant of the modernization process. Obviously, too, if it is not, one is left with both conceptual and empirical questions about the successor or competitor to the ethnic identity and organization that was dominant in the traditional or precapitalist stage.

Nonetheless, the questions raised generally seem to be embellishments on an established process: the social differentiation and mobility that comes with industrialization and education outmodes the primacy of ethnic identification and organization – even if it reinforces it temporarily during initial stages of change – and brings about horizontal stratification that cuts across vertical divisions and creates the possibility of many new types of political interests, including – under particularly sharp conditions of socioeconomic cleavage – class interests as a basis for political organization. Such a formulation permits investigation and analysis of a process and above all of the differences in a particular society's conditions and evolutions that allow for variations on the general theme. But it also leaves room for policy decisions at crucial junctures as well. At some point, party leaders must decide whether ethnic appeals, class appeals, or something else provide the most promising basis of a platform. Constitutionalists and subsequent government decision makers must look for ways to minimize the disruptive effects of both vertical and horizontal cleavages and develop cross-cutting and overarching ties of interest and solidarity. Payoffs and the allocation of resources must be accomplished in such a way to increase solidarity and followership rather than conflict and division so that subnational identifications work for greater national identity and productivity. Nigeria provides examples of both efforts and errors in all these directions.

A second dimension ranges from planned direction to free competition. Organization theory clearly shows that centralization increases the chances of decision and direction and pluralization increases the chances of innovation and responsiveness; on the nation- and state-building level, concentration of power for the generation and allocation of resources is a necessary stage before the creation of a national modern economy and society. Yet there are exceptions. Although the classical statebuilding pattern is one of royal or state consolidation, other societies have been pluralist "from the bottom up" to the very top throughout the process of state formation.

A different form of the same argument in the context of Third World development is the debate over the inevitability or necessity of praetorianism as a path to national consolidation and the possibility of democracy under the same conditions. The democratic theory which holds – by definition – that political development is only possible when a polity continues to articulate, aggregate, and respond to demands raised by an increasingly pluralistic society may not correspond to the realities of the postcolonial era in the industrializing globe. The same theory would indicate that when resources are inadequate for a satisfactory response to inflated expectations, only a regime that suppresses or deflates demands, controls the demand articulation process of politics, and defers the payoffs of current effort and sacrifice can keep the polity running at all, much less consolidate it into an effective organization of governance. Thus the theory of democratic development can be construed as the basis for the inevitability of a nondemocratic interlude.

The same debate can be carried out on the nontheoretical level, whatever the imperatives of theory might provide for a proper or inevitable evolution. It is quite conceivable that praetorianism may be an alternative imposed by short-term opportunism rather than evolutionary necessity but no less inescapable as a result. If army officers can react unhindered (and indeed, encouraged by similar reactions in their own and neighboring countries' recent history) to the temporary dissatisfactions of resources allocation by taking over the allocation process themselves, the polity may enter the praetorian stage for very superficial reasons but may not be able to extricate itself for a very long time (as in Latin America). Pluralism can then grow in parts of the society and economy but be kept out of politics, along with liberty and freedom. On a more ideological level, the need and wisdom of centralized state planning has been questioned by free market pluralists as being not only economic but also as making the new economy more vulnerable by the institutionalization of mistakes. Thus centralization may be a choice rather than a process.

The broadest form of the debate over centralism versus pluralism is the global version of dependency theory, which interprets pluralism as the basis of national disarticulation and absorption by the industrialized North. Only national political, economic and social consolidation in the hands of centralized state control can keep elites and resources from being skimmed off in favor of an external attraction; centralism must come first for pluralism to be safe for the country. According to this interpretation, centralism must be a choice, against the theoretically indicated effects of pluralism. Thus the theoretical forms of the debate provide for the basis for the debate over policy. Again, Nigeria, because of its size and resources, is a strong test for the various theoretical forms of the debate as well as a site for the policy discussions.

The third dimension ranges from revolution to evolution, argued in terms of both inevitability and desirability. The revolutionary theory is the clearest because of the sharpness of the phenomenon itself. Through various schools runs the common insight that resources will concentrate into fewer and fewer hands until the deprived mass explodes, redistributes, and either begins some other process or begins all over again. Access to education, accumulation of wealth, and control of power are the various keys to the sharpening differences between the haves and have-nots that finally cause the roles to be reversed. Even the most cyclical interpretations see revolution as progressive in some sense rather than simply repetitive; old ways cannot be broken effectively by gradual change but must be destroyed by violence, eliminating their beneficiaries and uprooting their social and economic base.

Probably the weakest part of the revolutionary theory is its own cataclysmic nature. Revolutions cannot occur every Thursday or even every decade, and their very millenial nature puts them in doubt even when they purport to be happening. While waiting for Godot, something must be done in the meantime, and it is difficult to know whether to applaud the day-to-day events that bring on the distant inevitability or to fight them and delay the liberating cataclysm. The dilemma of action is persuasive argument for a sloppy process – if not a neat theory – of evolution. That revolutionary theory is inadequate for the analysis of developing countries in the short run does not mean that evolutionary theory is applicable in the long run. Simply because cataclysmic change does not appear is no guarantee *per se* that reformism or incrementalism is possible.

Furthermore, while the parameters of revolution have been generally established, there is little agreement on the determinants of evolution or even on the meaning of successful evolution. Guidelines are unclear. It is difficult to operationalize the criteria of routinization or determine the limits of proper institutional functioning. Perhaps a more identifiable condition of reformism or incrementalism is the constitution of a productive, open, expanding bourgeoisie. The other side of the same condition is the continual expansion of resources in order to satisfy the "ins" without alienating the "outs" in a context of growing societal pluralism. Nigeria is currently in an evolutionary state, although those who look for warning or promising signals of revolution are not disarmed. This dimension provides corresponding policy questions.

The following chapters cannot answer all the policy questions or pursue all the analytical questions that are applicable to the new Nigeria of the 1980s. They can address many of them and in the process investigate the general setting of all three concerns – ethnic versus class, centralized versus pluralistic, and revolutionary versus evolutionary. The concepts and the Nigerian case provide a fortuitous encounter, for these dimensions provide the current language of discourse about Nigeria's present and future, and Nigeria is an apt test tube and example of the conceptual debate.

NOTES

1. The majority of references in this chapter may be found in the section entitled, "Current Works on Nigeria – Politics and Society."

2. The data in this article are pieced together from many sources: the Central Bank of Nigeria, Nigeria's Federal Office of Statistics, the World Bank, Nigeria's development plans, various official statements by Nigerian government figures, news publications such as *West Africa* and *The Economist*, the authors' own works, and others. The source or sources for each figure are not cited in this paper because it would be exceedingly tedious to do so.

2

SOCIAL CHANGE AND POLITICAL CONFLICT IN NIGERIA'S SECOND REPUBLIC

Larry Diamond

> Nigeria is in the process of far-reaching social transformation. Two great forces face each other, and are locked in a grim struggle for survival and ascendancy. On the one side . . . are the conservatives, . . . their stand is to protect, retain and sustain the existing social order. On the other side . . . are the progressives, . . . their stand is to replace a system of oppression and exploitation with a new society. . . .
>
> Peoples Redemption Party
> General Programme
> (PRP, 1979:4-5)

> As things stand now, the Nigerian state appears to intervene everywhere and to own virtually everything including access to status and wealth. Inevitably a desperate struggle to win control of state power ensues since this control means for all practical purposes being all powerful and owning everything. Politics becomes warfare, a matter of life and death.
>
> Professor Claude Ake
> Presidential Address to the
> Nigerian Political Science
> Association (Ake 1981a)

I am indebted to the Vanderbilt University Research Council and the Institute for the Study of World Politics for funding my summer 1981 field research in Nigeria, from which this chapter draws extensively, and to Professor Richard Sklar for his assiduous reading of the manuscript and several crucial suggestions. Responsibility for the interpretations herein remains, however, mine alone.

For the past decade, the social structure and political economy of Nigeria have been in the grip of rapid and profound change. As Watts and Lubeck detail in this volume, the rapid development of the oil boom has distributed the vast amounts of new wealth in grotesquely uneven fashion, not only heightening the contradictions between the bourgeoisie and the lower classes, but reducing even in absolute terms the already miserable standard of living of large portions of the latter, and threatening to devour and displace large portions of the peasantry. Ostentatious display of the new (and often corruptly acquired) wealth has, particularly in the cities, exposed hideously stark contrasts between the splendor of the rich and the squalor of the poor, deepening considerably the resentment of the latter.

At the same time, development has been drawing the popular classes out of traditional social and economic relationships and into cities, classrooms, and factories. The proportion of the population living in cities has more than doubled since independence to roughly 30 percent (Sahota 1980, Table A2), the majority of whom are now concentrated in large cities of half a million or more (World Bank 1981, p. 172). Since 1970, the proportion of the school age population enrolled has increased from 36 to 62 percent for primary school and from 4 to 13 percent for secondary school (World Bank 1981, p. 178), whereas university enrollments have increased seven-fold (Osuntokun 1982, p. 24).[1] Since the early 1960s, the literacy rate among the general population has doubled to roughly 25 percent (Osuntokun 1982, p. 30), and the proportion of the labor force in the modern wage sector has tripled to 6 percent (Rimmer 1981, p. 106). Given Nigeria's rapid rate of population growth – which recent data suggest may be as high as 3.5 percent per year (*Washington Post*, May 9, 1982), implying a staggering doubling of the population virtually every two decades – these increasing proportions have also meant huge absolute increases: four times as many children in school, for example, as there were when the First Republic collapsed in 1966.[2]

Political changes have coincided with these social and economic changes. The dramatic expansion and centralization of the Nigerian state has been made evident by the increasing central control over national revenue, industry, produce marketing, college admissions, and much more, to the point where, "the Nigerian state appears to intervene everywhere and to own everything . . ." (Ake 1981a,

p. 1163). But this is just the consolidation of a process that has been unfolding since colonial rule. More novel have been the developments at the local level, where a 1976 initiative of the Federal Military Government significantly democratized the structure of government authority, especially from what had prevailed in the far north where local government had been dominated by the Emir and his appointed chiefs and council. Beyond the redistribution of formal power, these reforms have tended to undermine the cultural basis of traditional, hierarchical authority patterns (Aliyu 1978, 1978-79). These relations of clientage and deference are also being severed even more directly (again, especially in the north) by social and economic changes such as large-scale, capital-intensive agriculture and urban expansion, which are forcing peasants off the land (Lubeck and Walton 1979, p. 23).

Thus, the urban and rural popular classes have been becoming, simultaneously, more distanced and alienated from the dominant class, more "socially mobilized," and more independent from traditional, hierarchical authority relations. What do these changes imply for the politics of the Second Republic?

Theories of political development lead us to expect profound political changes as a result of the pattern of socioeconomic development Nigeria has experienced since the fall of the First Republic. Both Marxist and functionalist theories predict, in particular, a shift from communal to class based forms of political cleavage and conflict as a result of the increasing functional differentiation of the economy and society and the integration and differentiation of the polity. Such is the finding of Lipset and Rokkan in their classic functionalist interpretation of political development in Western democracies: "functional oppositions" emerged with territorial integration and social mobilization and displaced territorial-cultural divisions, as industrialization "tended to cut across . . . value communities . . . and to force the enfranchised citizenry to choose sides in terms of their *economic interests* . . ." (Lipset and Rokkan 1967, pp. 13, 19). Similarly for the contemporary Third World, Huntington and Nelson (1976, p. 79) found that increasing levels of socioeconomic development produce "broader, more diverse, and more autonomous patterns of political participation."

This hardly means the sudden disappearance of ethnic cleavage from social and political life. Indeed, the accumulation of theory and evidence has rendered positively untenable the functionalist prediction of an erosion of ethnic identity and conflict with modernization. Rather, socioeconomic development and state expansion widen and intensify ethnic identifications and stimulate pervasive competition on the basis of these enlarged cultural identities (Melson and Wolpe 1971; Bates 1974; Young 1976; Hannan 1979; Nagel and Olzak 1981). But at certain turning points in the modernization process – precisely those identified by the functionalists – ethnicity may be displaced from the polity as the primary organizing cleavage by functional, class-based cleavage. This does not mean that ethnic identity and conflict disappear or that ethnicity may not resurge once more as the primary basis of political division. It means that at a particular historical moment ethnicity is overtaken by a deeper contradiction. As the analysis of politics in the Second Republic will show, Nigeria stands at such a historical moment today.

Modernization does more than thrust forth new, functionally based cleavages. It also changes the way political cleavages articulate with popular political consciousness and activity. The multiple processes of social mobilization expand people's aspirations and expectations of government and consequently their propensity to read and think and act politically to achieve them (Deutsch 1961). Urbanization, education, literacy, and mass communication widen psychological horizons and tend to increase rationality, efficacy, and openness to change and new ideas (Lerner 1958; Inkeles and Smith 1974). Modern institutions, and education in particular, erode allegiance to parochial public authority, heighten interest in civic affairs, increase levels of political information, and generate not only more political participation but a more confident, rational, active and autonomous form of participation (Almond and Verba 1963; Inkeles 1969).

Hence, as Huntington and Nelson note, the nature of mass political participation changes with socioeconomic development from a form mobilized vertically through parochial loyalties and clientage relations to one motivated autonomously by functional interests. Changes in social structure further contribute to this pattern. The displacement of rural patron-client ties as a result of agricultural commercialization, socioeconomic development of the countryside and rural-urban migration removes the primary mechanism of vertical mobilization (Huntington and Nelson 1976, p. 56). The tendency for rural economic modernization (in the absence of dedicated land reform and redistributive policies) to heighten socioeconomic inequality and the sharpening contradictions between bourgeois and lower class interests further predispose marginalized lower classes toward mobilization by class-based parties, just at a time when political parties are becoming increasingly significant as bases of political identification and action (Huntington and Nelson, 1976, p. 59).

These socioeconomic changes imply changes in the nature of political conflict. In contrast with "Phase I" of development, where the conflict between "the emerging urban middle class" and "the declining rural peasantry" is muted by the political dominance of the nascent bourgeoisie and continuing political manipulation from above of lower class participation, "Phase II" finds lower classes mobilized autonomously into politics by rising levels of education, communications, and the like. Lower class demands for political participation and populist redistribution of wealth become prominent, conflicting with bourgeois interests in high rates of economic growth and concentrated distribution of income, characteristically achieved through a "technocratic" strategy of foreign investment and labor repression (Huntington and Nelson 1976, pp. 22-24). This conflict between established rural landholders and urban industrial elites on the one hand, and populist movements on the other, has been the archetypical cause of the chronic instability and widespread failure of Latin American and Asian democratic systems in the intermediate phase of development (Almond and Powell 1978, pp. 373-74).

If social mobilization does indeed thrust the peasantry, the urban proletariat and the small, independent producers and traders into politics as articulate and autonomous forces, class conflict would seem virtually predestined to become the decisive political cleavage during "Phase II" of development. In response to lower class political mobilization, the dominant class has a limited number of alternatives. It may seek to dissipate emergent lower class consciousness and mobilization by vertically mobilizing lower class groups along communal lines in its own internal competition for resources and state control. This was the strategy of the Nigerian elite during the first civilian regime (Diamond 1983). It may seek effectively to eliminate politics and lower class political mobilization through one-party or military rule, but thirteen years of military rule showed that in Nigeria the abolition of constitutional political competition eliminated neither politics nor lower class political agitation. It may seek to relieve lower class frustration through genuine reform and broad based development, multiplying opportunities for individual socioeconomic mobility and hence reducing anti-systemic pressure – the classic Hirschman trade-off between exit and voice (Huntington and Nelson 1976, pp. 51-52). Or it may choose to repress peasant and working class organization in an effort to maximize the extraction of surplus from their labor – the authoritarian technocratic alternative. Failure of these four dominant-class strategies for managing populist class pressure from below heightens the possibility of a wholly different political process – seizure of state control and transformation of class relations through socialist revolution.

As Nigeria moves rapidly into "Phase II" of development, with its high rates of social mobilization and social dislocation, these difficult choices press themselves ever more ineluctably upon the polity. The changes and contradictions of the oil boom, along with the innovations in federal and constitutional structure, are increasingly thrusting forth class cleavage as the organizing force in politics while precluding the ethnic mobilization strategy for containing lower class pressures and consolidating class dominance. Despite the continuing prominence of ethnicity in politics and the pervasive persistence of ethnic socioeconomic competition, the dominant class is no longer able to so manipulate ethnic consciousness as to organize political competition and conflict around it. The contradictions between classes and the social mobilization of lower class groups have progressed too far to enable class to be submerged politically in that fashion again.

In the midst of continuing ethnic political mobilization by competing communities and politicians, it is possible to overlook the transformation now taking place in the nature of political conflict in Nigeria. As popular classes mobilize for a more equitable distribution of resources and readier access to power, the polity is dividing between a reformist perspective that favors some kind of accommodation to these populist pressures and a conservative perspective more or less dedicated to preservation of the existing distribution of resources and rewards. This broad conflict over development strategy will dominate Nigerian politics through the 1983 elections and beyond. The intensity it would naturally inject into political competition will be magnified further by the enormity of what is at stake politically in a society in which the state bulks so large in social and economic life. It is by no means clear that the Second Republic can withstand the load. Nevertheless, whether the above conflict is played out within the democratic political arena or the military one, it can no longer be avoided. Its outcome will determine not only the viability of democracy in Nigeria but also whether, other strategies of conflict management no longer being viable, the core conflict of Phase II is resolved in Nigeria through reform, reaction or revolution.

THE BIRTH OF THE SECOND REPUBLIC

The Second Republic emerged out of a complicated and carefully staged process of transition from military to civilian rule, perhaps the most elaborate in modern political history, and one that will be closely studied by analysts and practitioners of Third World politics for many years to come. On the fifteenth anniversary of the nation's independence, October 1, 1975, two months after replacing General Yakubu Gowon as Head of State, Brigadier Murtala Mohammed announced a detailed and precise timetable for the restoration of civilian, democratic government. In five stages over a period of four years, a new constitutional and political foundation was to be laid. First, the issue of new states would be resolved (by April 1976), and a Constitutional Drafting Committee would be given 12 months to produce a draft constitution. Second, local government would be reorganized and new local governments elected, to be followed by election of a Constituent Assembly to consider, amend and approve the draft constitution. Stage 3 would lift the ban on political parties by October 1978. Stage 4 would elect state governments and Stage 5 a federal government in time to transfer power by October 1, 1979 (Kirk-Greene 1981, pp. 13-14).

Despite the tragic assassination of Murtala Mohammed in a failed coup attempt barely four months later and his replacement by Gen. Olusegun Obasanjo, and despite a bitter debate within the Constituent Assembly over a Federal Sharia Court of Appeal (within Islamic law) that threatened an explosive religious and regional polarization of politics (Laitin 1981),[3] the timetable was implemented with stunning exactitude.

There were many auspicious features of the process. The volatile issue of new states was tackled early and decisively with the creation of seven more states in April 1976 and the explicit expectation that the constitution should provide extremely demanding conditions for creation of any further states beyond this. This brought to 19 the total number of states, elaborating the federal system implemented by General Gowon nine years previously when he replaced the failed regional system of the first civilian regime with 12 states. This grant of still more autonomy to the nation's ethnic minorities and division of the three major ethnic groups (Yoruba, Igbo and Hausa-Fulani), each into two to four states, promised to thrust forth a fresh line of cleavage (state) into the politics of the new republic and break up the ethnic and regional solidarities that had so cursed the first democratic experience.

The creation of new states reflected a conscious effort to generate cross-cutting cleavage and, hence, a more fluid and complicated pattern of politics. This intention was evident in the new Constitution as well, which explicitly prohibited sectional parties and required broad ethnic representation in each party as a condition of recognition (Constitution 1979, p. 65). But these provisions only enshrined what the administration of General Obasanjo had mandated with its Electoral Decree of 1977, which required that a party demonstrate a viable presence (branch offices, officers, etc.) in two-thirds of the states (Koehn 1981, p. 24).[4]

These innovations in "institutional architecture" – including as well the executive presidency, the minimum requirement of breadth of electoral support for direct election to the presidency, and the creation of a strong Electoral Commission to certify political parties and candidates and regulate campaigning – may be seen as the most significant legacy of the transition process (Whitaker 1981; Phillips 1980). Also auspicious was the widespread popular participation in that process, not only in the various elections but in the free and vigorous debate that followed the presentation of the Draft Constitution. Between December 1976 and May 1977 the editorial pages of all the newspapers crackled with competing views on fundamental rights, press freedom, balance of powers, the role of the judiciary, the political party system, the economic proposals, and so forth (Ofonagoro et al. 1977). This spirited public debate continued through the deliberations of the largely elected Constituent Assembly. Although the military government did amend its final product in several particulars, "the thoroughness of the public debate, the freedom with which it was conducted, and the national consensus that has become manifest, together support the conclusion that Nigeria's Second Republic was established upon a genuinely popular foundation" (Sklar 1981, p. 14). It is probably not too much to conclude that "this deeply consultative process of political reconstruction" fulfilled what Whitaker (1981, p. 7) identified as its essential hope: "not so much of restoring legitimacy to national institutions as of creating it for the first time."

The process gave rise to at least one serious problem as well. Although the transition spanned four years, it was not to be until three of those years had passed that the ban on political parties would be lifted. From this moment, on September 21, 1978, aspiring political parties were given only three months to submit their registration forms to the Federal Electoral Commission (FEDECO). Given that political activities had been banned for 13 years and that the parties of the First Republic were to remain prohibited, this left very little time to found "wholly 'new' parties . . . , to establish followers throughout the country, and to satisfy the other stringent requirements . . . in the Constitution" (Phillips 1980, p. 15). In this brief period, national conventions had to be held, a roster of party officials elected, and a network of active state and local branches created.

The Federal Military Government's transition timetable reflected "the greater value and priority it placed on formal, legal change over institutional development" (Koehn 1981, p. 44), but it also revealed a more fundamental ambivalence about political parties and politicians altogether. This was apparent in the Supreme Military Council's terms of reference to the Constitutional Drafting Committee:

> In order to avoid the harmful effects of a proliferation of national parties, it will be desirable for you to work out specific criteria by which their number would be limited. Indeed, *if there were means to form government without parties, that will satisfy the Supreme Military Council.* (Quoted in Kirk-Greene 1981, pp. 18-19.)[5]

Paradoxically, the severe compression of the period for party development had precisely the consequences the military hoped to avoid: in the hurried, frantic pace, most truly fresh political formations either fractured into more familiar forms or died stillborn. Of the 50 parties reported in the press, 19 filed papers by the mid-December (1978) deadline, and only five of them were certified by FEDECO (Phillips 1980, p. 15). Those five were easily (if rather speciously) linked to the parties of the First Republic, each submitting as its presidential candidate a prominent party leader from that era. In the brevity of the period for party development and under the pressure of imminent elections, politicians tended to retreat into the convenient and familiar ethnic political alignments. This not only snapped some significant crosscutting alliances and individual alignments but also brought together politicians of such disparate ideological inclinations that their associations were bound to become sorely strained once the Second Republic settled into confronting the primary contradictions welling up in the society. Further party divisions and realignments were thus made inevitable by the hurried process, and these have, in fact, been central to the political turmoil the Second Republic has experienced so far.

The pressure on the parties – and especially the weaker of the five – was accentuated by the problem of disqualification of candidates. FEDECO was empowered by the military to disqualify candidates, in particular those who could not prove payment of income taxes over the preceding three years. Although tax evasion is believed to be common among the wealthy in Nigeria, the party most clearly associated with the affluent, the National Party of Nigeria, suffered by far the fewest disqualifications (6 percent), whereas its radical and much more humble challenger in the North, the Peoples Redemption Party, suffered the highest (49 percent).[6] Despite the large number of candidate disqualifications – amounting to almost half for the two parties that were poorest in finance and latest in getting organized and hence least able to rebound from this setback – the late date of the action (June 22, 1979) allowed the parties only a matter of days to find suitable replacements and then only a few weeks to campaign for them until the July balloting (Koehn 1981, pp. 30, 44). The PRP and NPP suffered in particular not only because they had the highest numbers of disqualifications but because their presidential candidates were not finally certified to run until less than three weeks before the election, after most of the campaign had transpired.

The Origins and Social Bases of the New Parties

If the transition process undervalued and stunted party development, it nevertheless did give birth to some significant structural advances over the regionally based party system of the First Republic.

Most significant was the emergence of the first truly national party in Nigerian political history – the NPN. Like the original NPP, the NPN emerged out of the politics of the Constituent Assembly during its eight months of deliberations in 1977-78. Indeed, party development is most appropriately traced from the start of these deliberations in that they "permitted preliminary soundings to be taken, approaches to be made, alliances to be projected and associations to be pencilled in by this fluid group or that shadowy caucus" (Kirk-Greene 1981, pp. 20-21). In perhaps the largest of these groupings and the original seed of the NPN, the "Committee of 111 MCAs," and in its successor, the National Movement, were prominent politicians from a breathtakingly diverse array of regional and ethnic origins.

The most common background of these NPN founders was Northern and Hausa-Fulani – many having aristocratic titles and prominent past roles in the dominant Northern Peoples' Congress of the First Republic.[7] Unofficial party power was still centered in the upper North (hence the NPC's decision that its first presidential nominee under its system of regional zoning would be a Northerner). Nonetheless, Yoruba, Igbo and minority political and business elites have played strategic roles in the NPN's formation, internal governance and command of state power – roles that would have been unimaginable in the old NPC and that decisively belie the interpretation of the NPN as a mere reincarnation of the NPC. Hence, the late Tiv Leader Chief Joseph Tarka (whose United Middle Belt Congress vigorously, and sometimes violently, fought the NPC during the 1950s and 1960s) and Dr. Sola Saraki of Kwara State (a Northern Yoruba) both contested vigorously for the NPN presidential nomination and went on to assume key positions in the party and in the Senate, where another minority member, Dr. Joseph Wayas of Cross River State, was elected Senate President, the third highest position in government. Under the NPN zoning arrangement, it was a wealthy Igbo architect, Dr. Alex Ekwueme, who joined Shehu Shagari on the national ticket and was elected Vice-President, and a Yoruba, Chief A. M. A. Akinloye, who was chosen party Chairman. Other Igbos, such as presidential legislative adviser Dr. K. O. Mbadiwe and political adviser Dr. Chuba Okadigbo, and other Yorubas, such as Ogun State party Chairman (and Chairman of ITT Nigeria) Chief M. K. O. Abiola and Attorney General Chief Richard Akinjide, are also highly placed in the party and the government.

These men are not stooges of some hidden Fulani oligarchy. Their placement in the inner circles of party and state power reflects a pattern of transethnic bargaining and accommodation very different even from the conservative National Alliance of the First Republic, to which the NPN more shrewdly might be compared.[8] Among their business and professional associates they have raised fantastic sums of money for the party. They reflect the increasing national integration and cohesion of the Nigerian bourgeoisie of whom, increasingly, the NPN is the political expression. Although men of substantial means support each of the five parties, no other party comes close to matching the NPN's capacity to draw support from all ethnic and regional sections of the Nigerian bourgeoisie. Contemporary Nigerian politics simply cannot be understood unless this national and class character of the NPN is appreciated.[9]

That the NPN is the most national of Nigeria's parties is demonstrated not only in its spread of unofficial power (and strikingly in the election results, below) but also in its official party leadership. Its national officers hail from 17 of the 19 states and at one time or another have come from all 19. Its closest competitors in this regard, the UPN and NPP, draw from only 13 states and are spread less evenly across the major ethnic groups (Diamond 1982b, n11). Many view these official structures as a facade, however. The belief has persisted through the 1979 election campaign and beyond that the parties of the Second Republic are only thinly disguised reconstructions of their ethnic and regional predecessors from the preceding civilian era. By this view, not only is the NPN a reincarnation of the Northern-based NPC, but the Unity Party of Nigeria (UPN) reproduces the old Yoruba-based Action Group, the Nigerian Peoples Party (NPP) the Igbo-based NCNC, and the Peoples Redemption Party (PRP) the old Northern Elements Progressive Union of the radical Hausa. (Even the party with no clear lineal antecedent, the Great Nigerian People's Party (GNPP) has been traced to the Bornu Youth Movement because of its strength in party leader Waziri Ibrahim's home state of Bornu.) The plausibility and popularity of this interpretation were heightened by the fact that the national leaders and 1979 presidential candidates of the UPN, NPP and PRP – Chief Obafemi Awolowo, Dr. Nnamdi Azikiwe, and Mallam Aminu Kano respectively – each led the party of the First Republic to which his current party is now compared (while Shehu Shagari and Waziri Ibrahim were both rising national figures in the NPC).

But this game of lineal descent yields a shallow and misleading view of party politics in the Second Republic. Not only has it been overtaken by subsequent party fissions and fusions, but it never fully squared with the origins and leadership bases of the parties (in particular the NPN's) or with the significant differences in their political platforms and philosophies.

To begin with, the Nigerian Peoples Party, before it divided into NPP and GNPP, clearly rivaled the NPN in ethnic breadth and national political strength. It had come together shortly before the lifting of the ban on political parties as an amalgam of three powerful political associations: Club 19 which, based in the Constituent Assembly among ethnic minority members and opponents of the Sharia Court, sought to express the interests of ethnic or subethnic minorities from all 19 states; the Lagos Progressives, led by veteran Lagos politician (and former NCNC Minister) Chief Adeniran Ogunsanya; and the National Union Council, organized from outside the Constituent Assembly by Alhaji Waziri Ibrahim, who had built a vast and hugely successful business empire during military rule (Ojigbo 1980, pp. 99-100; Kirk-Greene 1981, p. 35). Projecting vigorous concern for ethnic minorities and staunch opposition to the conservative dominance of the northern aristocracy and uniting the vitality and breadth of Club 19, the connections and savvy of Chief Ogunsanya, and the Northern Muslim base and considerable financial assets of Alhaji Waziri, the NPP had the look of a leading national contender between its formal launching in late September 1978 and its disastrous November convention. There, key elements of the other two factions walked out in protest over Waziri's insistence on contending for both the presidential nomination and the party chairmanship.[10]

With strength across the North and a solid political base up and down the eastern portion of the country – from Bornu to Plateau and Gongola down to Cross River and the Igbo heartland – the original NPP cut impressively across traditional ethnic and regional divisions. Neither the NPP formed by the November dissidents nor the GNPP that Alhaji Waziri's faction became was able to recover this breadth. Remaining virtually identical in substantive program, the two parties split between them their former strength (later losing to the NPN many races they might have carried as one party). The GNPP fell back upon Waziri's base in the Northeast while the new NPP – turning at a late and desperate moment to the reluctant

Dr. Azikiwe – rallied support from most Igbo political leaders but at the cost of being perceived elsewhere as a reincarnation of the NCNC. It is perhaps a telling irony that such a significant development in the structural basis of party politics was lost over what leaders on both sides concede was essentially a personality conflict. Yet even after the trauma, each party still crossed sectional lines, with the supposedly "Igbo" NPP drawing critical support from Christian areas of the Middle Belt that had never been associated with the NCNC,[11] and the GNPP still showing strength through much of the upper North and in the Southeast.

The UPN, by contrast, emerged not from bargaining and multiple associations but from the typically assiduous and exhaustive organizing efforts of its founder and dominating force, Chief Obafemi Awolowo. Certain of his political principles and national goals after more than three decades of political pursuit, Chief Awolowo constructed a party organization and program while potential competitors were busy drafting a constitution and exploring coalitions in the Constituent Assembly. As a result, the UPN was not only the first party to declare its existence but by far the most developed, emerging with virtually a full-blown platform and campaign machinery. But this highly personal and centralized process took its toll: the UPN generally failed to attract important politicians outside the area of the Western Region that Chief Awolowo had governed as Premier in the 1950s. Even Awolowo's old alliances in the Middle Belt could not be resurrected.

The PRP's lack of breadth stemmed from the hurried timetable of the transition. As a truly new party and the most ideologically explicit of any of those that were finally registered, the PRP needed more time to develop and to build a national base than the other parties. In fact, the PRP was not simply a revived NEPU. Although former NEPU politicians participated in its formation, the crucial founders appear to have been a new generation of radical and progressive intellectuals and civil servants, many of whom were too young to vote during the First Republic. Seeking a true, ideological alternative to the parties that appeared likely to emerge, they gathered in Kano and Zaria to flesh out the image, structure and program of a new radical party. They were critically handicapped, however, by their lack of national breadth and an experienced political leader with a recognized name.

What seemed the perfect answer to at least the latter need emerged when Mallam Aminu Kano was rebuffed in his pursuit of a major leadership position in the NPN. After leading the NEPU through a decade and a half of struggle against social injustice and political repression in the North, and then serving as Federal Commissioner of Health under military rule, Mallam Aminu was a logical and willing choice to lead the PRP. He brought with him to the party a broader national network of left-wing political activists including (from the Southeast) veteran maverick politician S. G. Ikoku, who became the PRP National Secretary and its Vice-Presidential nominee, and the widely known veteran labor leader Chief Michael Imoudu, who became PRP Deputy National President. But it was probably too late to build a truly broad national base – by the time Mallam Aminu set about to do so as PRP President, many potential supporters and candidates had already committed elsewhere.[12] And it was a costly concession to political reality for the young radicals. To have any chance of success, they had already been forced to seek and accept support from business and political elements who did not share their ideological objectives. With the nomination of Aminu Kano as the PRP presidential candidate, many more established forces rushed aboard the bandwagon of the party that seemed likely to ride the Mallam's enormous personal popularity in Kano State to victory. Both the absorption of wealthy businessmen and landowners and the personal identification with Aminu blurred the party's ideological distinctiveness and probably seriously blunted its capacity to build a transethnic ideological constituency.

Nonetheless, if the UPN and PRP were distinctly less national in their origins and leaderships than the other three parties, they cut a sharp national political profile in their party programs. These are not the vague manifestos of sectional parties offering amenities in place of ideology. They represent the most fully and clearly articulated of the five party programs, boldly seeking to build national constituencies around social democratic and socialist ideologies respectively. No other party proposes a Western-style social security system or so urgently and unequivocally commits itself to the provision of free education at all levels (and also free medical care and full employment) as does the UPN (UPN 1979a and b). Only the PRP explicitly calls for public ownership of key economic sectors – specifically, finance and banking, insurance, oil exporting, and capital goods – the closing of most economic sectors to foreign investment and participation, and federally administered rent control (PRP 1979). Unambiguously does the NPN stand apart from these positions: cautious and limited in its approach to the expansion of social services, bold and enthusiastic in its attitude toward foreign capital and technology, which it vows "to encourage, protect and induce" into Nigeria "as a fundamental policy" (NPN 1979, pp. 115, 117-21). Even in agricultural policy, where the parties are agreed on the urgent need to invest more heavily and raise production, the UPN and PRP emphasize collective farming, whereas the other three parties articulate a capitalist strategy of agricultural development featuring large scale and advanced technology (UPN 1979b, p. 12; PRP 1979, p. 16; WPN 1979, pp. 111-12; NPP 1979, p. 7).[13]

While it may have appeared in the heat of the election campaign that the five parties were "wooing the voters with promises of basically the same goodies" (*Africa*, no. 92, April 1979, p. 12), they are not the same in their political substance. They sharply diverge in the nature and scope of social services they would deliver through the state; in their visions of the respective roles of the state, private Nigerian capital, and foreign capital in the nation's economic development; in their priorities for economic development; and in the way they would relate the economic and political power of the state to distinct social classes. These divergences cumulate in a substantially consistent pattern that permits the approximate location of each party along an ideological continuum. To the left of the UPN and considerably to the left of the other three parties is the PRP. Its "democratic socialist" program seeks to use the state to redeem the "commanding heights" of the economy from foreign and elite control, to redistribute wealth more equally, and to generate autonomous development. Favoring an economically interventionist welfare state within the context of mixed but still substantially capitalist ownership, the UPN occupies a left position on the ideological spectrum like that of the "social democratic" parties of Europe. More to the center of the Nigerian spectrum, but more nearly "liberal" in contemporary terms, are the NPP and GNPP, envisioning capitalism tempered by state intervention to effect a more egalitarian distribution of wealth and social services (through intervention of a less sweeping scope and ambitious pace than favored by the UPN). Similarly liberal in its professed (though still more cautious) disposition to redistribute resources through state activity is the NPN, the most boldly capitalist of the five parties – classically liberal, and hence in contemporary terms "conservative" in its emphasis on the unfettered movement of private capital as the driving force of development.[14]

This rough ideological typology is consistent as well with the parties' statements of their social and political goals. The PRP advances a Marxist-Leninist analysis of Nigerian society, predicating as "the prime moving force" of contemporary Nigerian life a "constant and ever deepening struggle" between "the forces of privilege, . . . resolved to protect their interests at all costs under the existing order, and the forces of the people," determined "to replace a system of oppression and exploitation with a new society" (PRP 1979, pp. 4-5). The UPN, the NPP and the GNPP feature prominently the rhetoric of social justice and social change, and with the PRP, denounce exploitation and feudalism (long a code word in Nigerian politics for the dominance of the traditional aristocracy of the Northern emirates). The NPN manifesto, on the other hand, promises to preserve the role of traditional rulers "as instruments of stability in the maintenance of law and order" (NPN 1979, p. 125) and eschews entirely the rhetoric of social conflict and inequality, depicting the national challenge in terms of technical competence and national unity. Its national vision is distinguished for what it omits: a recognition that the interests of social groups may conflict in the building of a "prosperous and self-reliant Nigeria."

These differences in program and philosophy are substantial. Coupled with the differences in the social bases of the parties – which reflect important distinctions in how the parties articulate with the class structure and some notable crosscutting of ethnic and regional cleavages – they suggest that the political parties of the Second Republic represent, at least in their program and internal structure, a line of cleavage significantly independent of ethnicity and region and increasingly shaped by class alignments and broad ideological orientations.

THE REBIRTH OF COMPETITION: THE 1979 ELECTIONS

In the end it is not platforms or pledges but behavior that matters. The parties of the First Republic also differed in ideology and program (though not so sharply, and they were ethnically less diverse in composition). But those substantive differences did not keep the old parties from behaving and being perceived as ethnic parties. What is important is the way the parties actually project themselves to the voters, the way the voters perceive and respond to them, and the lines of cleavage that are actually mobilized in political conflict.

The five rounds of elections during July and August of 1979 provided the first real answer to these questions about the nature of politics in the Second Republic. At first glance, the answer was not reassuring to those who had wished for some transcendence of ethnicity. One is inclined to agree that "there was a sad level of regional and tribal correlation in voting behavior" (Dent 1979, p. 1406). The 89 percent of the presidential vote captured by Chief Awolowo in the four Yoruba states, the 96 percent of the seats in these four state legislatures captured by his party, the 85 percent of the Anambra and Imo vote captured by Dr. Azikiwe (Table 2.1), indeed the general tendency for most of the states to give rather solid backing to the party associated with its ethnic interest[15] are only some of the many facts about the election results one could cite in concluding that they show the "impossibility of eliminating tribalism or ethnic hegemonism from our body politic by legislative fiat" (Ofonagoro 1981, p. 2334).

At any level of analysis, communal attachments appear to be the most important and pervasive influence on voting behavior. This pattern will likely persist for some time to come. Yet for at least four reasons, the election results counsel neither depression nor despair in this regard. First, it may be argued that where ethnic voting appeared most powerful, the personality and political track record of the national party leader was at least as compelling a factor in the electoral landslide. This was most probable in the Yoruba States, particularly the three states of the former Western Region (Ogun, Ondo, and Oyo) where "there was some kind of unanimous agreement that the UPN leader did more for the West in terms of the development of roads, hospitals, pipe-borne water, and other social and welfare amenities in the short period he was Premier of the Western Region [1954-59] than all the governments since then" (Ollawa 1981, p. 305). Certainly the UPN emphasis on its four cardinal programs – especially free education, which Chief Awolowo had pioneered at the primary level in 1955, and from which a whole generation of Western voters had since benefited (Ojo 1981, p. 54) –

TABLE 2.1
1979 Election Results

	National Total	Four Yoruba States*	Four Hausa States**	Two Igbo States***
Presidential vote				
NPN	33.8%	7.8%	47.7%	11.2%
UPN	29.2	88.7	3.5	0.7
NPP	16.8	2.3	2.7	84.7
GNPP	10.0	0.4	14.6	2.3
PRP	10.3	0.3	31.7	1.1
Senatorial vote				
NPN	33.1%	13.3%	41.5%	14.1%
UPN	24.4	83.4	4.2	1.2
NPP	17.3	1.8	2.5	76.7
GNPP	14.9	1.3	21.2	6.5
PRP	10.3	0.1	30.6	1.4
House of Representatives Seats Won				
NPN	37.4%	4.5%	55.1%	8.5%
UPN	24.7	95.5	0.7	–
NPP	17.4	–	2.2	91.5
GNPP	9.6	–	5.9	–
PRP	10.9	–	36.0	–
State Legislative Seats Won				
NPN	36.2%	3.8%	52.0%	12.4%
UPN	24.7	96.2	1.0	–
NPP	16.8	–	2.5	85.9
GNPP	11.7	–	10.0	1.7
PRP	10.7	–	34.5	–

*Lagos, Ogun, Ondo, Oyo
**Bauchi, Kaduna, Kano, Sokoto
***Anambra and Imo

Source: Computed from "Nigeria Verdict – '79," prepared by Chief (Mayor) H. E. Oboh (in Okadigbo 1981, pp. 129-138).

played heavily and consciously upon this track record.[16] Furthermore, the UPN's stunning landslides in the Yoruba States were not simply the continuation of a previous pattern; they went far beyond anything the Action Group achieved in the 1950s and 1960s (Ojo 1981, p. 52; Sklar 1963). Moreover, Chief Awolowo also won a landslide victory in Lagos State, which has a large (perhaps one-third) non-Yoruba population, and which, as by far the most heavily urbanized and industrialized state in Nigeria, no doubt found particular appeal in the UPN pledges of free education, free health care, social security, higher minimum wage, support for organized labor, and so on (Ojo 1981, p. 54; Ollawa 1981, pp. 305-6; UPN 1979a and b).

Personality no doubt also played a role in the landslide triumphs of Nnamdi Azikiwe in Anambra and Imo States and Aminu Kano in Kano State. Dr. Azikiwe served the Eastern Region as Premier concurrently with Awolowo in the West, and there still burned in Igboland bitter memories of Awolowo's role in suppressing the Biafran secession. Aminu Kano had been firmly identified, especially in his native Kano, with the cause of the Hausa *talakawa* (commoners) since the days of the NEPU. As personality and ethnicity are difficult to separate – each of these three men were political giants in their homelands in part because they were seen as communal champions – it is also true that none of these "domineering and charismatic personalities" (Ollawa 1981, p. 307) has any obvious replacement and that their inevitable departure from active politics (Awolowo and Azikiwe are both past 70) will almost certainly mean significant erosion of the ethnic solidarity displayed in the 1979 voting.

Second, even if ethnicity shaped the voting choice, it often was not determinative. Three parties – the NPN, the PRP, and the GNPP – competed vigorously for the Hausa vote, and the four predominantly Hausa states (Bauchi, Kaduna, Kano, and Sokoto) evenly divided between the PRP and the NPN in their choice of governors. Although sometimes incorporating subtle and complicated layers of communal attachment, opposition to NPN candidates in these four states reflected predominantly class-based opposition to the social dominance of the traditional aristocracy with which the NPN was associated in many voters' minds. To this, and the long-standing populist appeal of Aminu Kano personally, were added a number of popular social and economic grievances (especially in Kano) – "inflation, unemployment, the high cost of living, the increase in social and income inequalities, relative deprivation, and long-standing policy dissatisfaction" (Ollawa 1981, p. 307). Hence, the NPN, which was thought to command the Hausa North (as the NPC had in the First Republic), won less than half of the presidential vote in these states and considerably less than half of the total Senate vote (Table 2.1). Indeed, President Shagari's highest percentages came not in the Hausa-Fulani states – not even in his home state of Sokoto – but in ethnic minority states in the North and South.

This suggests a third caveat to the theory of "tribal voting." If ethnicity remains the basic line of cleavage along which voters are acting in their electoral choices, the choices themselves are not as predictable as they once were. The NPN won resounding victories in the minority states of the Southeast and in a Middle Belt state (Benue) that had been a center of stiff resistance to the old NPC. Another Middle Belt state, Plateau, went with the NPP. It was the Action Group that had been the rising national party in the Middle Belt during the First Republic. The UPN did poorly there in 1979 but scored well in Gongola and carried Bendel State.[17] Some of these trends were at least latent in the electoral returns of the First Republic. But some were not. In either case, this is ethnic voting with a difference. If minority groups are opting en bloc "for new or old axes of opportunity and survival" (Ofonagoro 1981, p. 2334), their options have autonomy and consequences they did not have before. They cannot be repressed by regional centers of power. They deliver not just federal parliamentarians, but state governments. They are not locked into a single party, but free to search for the best axis of opportunity, and to realign if it disappoints. All of this follows from the new federal structure. If it is still ethnic politics, it offers plurality and flexibility unknown in the First Republic and is unlikely to reproduce the rigid polarization of ethnic alignments, which doomed that experience.

A fourth difference reflects, if only in a tentative, incipient fashion, the new party structure. Although in most cases the showings were modest, four of the five parties did demonstrate at least some transethnic electoral base, winning seats in the Federal House of Representatives in at least five states outside their supposed ethnic bases and showing even slightly better in the State House of Assembly elections (Table 2.2). The latter results in particular suggest the broad ethnic base the original NPP might have enjoyed had its strength not been dissipated by the split into two parties.

TABLE 2.2
Number of States Outside "Ethnic Bases" in Which Parties Won Seats*

Party	*House of Representatives*	*State House of Assembly*
NPN	11	12
UPN	5	6
NPP	5	7
GNPP	6	12
PRP	0	2

*The ethnic bases of the five parties are here defined as the states whose predominant ethnicity matches that of the Party's presidential candidate: Hausa-Fulani (Bauchi, Kaduna, Kano, Sokoto) for the NPN's Shehu Shagari (Fulani) and the PRP's Aminu Kano (Hausa); Yoruba (Lagos, Ogun, Ondo, Oyo) for the UPN's Obafemi Awolowo; Igbo (Anambra, Imo) for the NPP's Nnamdi Azikiwe; and Kanuri (Borno) for the GNPP's Waziri Ibrahim. In addition, to provide a more conservative standard for "transethnic base," Rivers State, with a large Igbo population, was counted as part of the NPP base, Kwara, with a large Yoruba population, was counted as part of the UPN base and Niger, which has had close ethnic and historic ties to the Fulani empire in the North, was counted as part of the NPN base. The NPP seats won in Rivers and UPN seats in Kwara were essentially Igbo and Yoruba constituencies respectively.

Together the NPP and GNPP won House of Representatives seats in 12 states (of the 19) and State House of Assembly seats in 15, not far behind the pace-setting standard of NPN victories in 16 and 17 states respectively. And this probably underestimates the potential strength of the original party.[18]

Moreover, one of the parties did leave some electoral mark in nearly every state and region of the country. This was the NPN, which won Federal House seats in all but three states (all Yoruba), and Senate seats in 12 of the 19. It won at least 10 percent of the presidential vote in 15 states, and of the Senate vote in 17 states. In every state but Lagos, it finished second in all five rounds of balloting if it did not finish first. While "retaining many of the former strongholds of the old NPC (Sokoto, Bauchi, Niger, Kwara)," it also made "significant inroads in the peripheral areas of support of both the Action Group (Plateau, Benue, Cross River) and the NCNC (Oyo, Bendel, Rivers)" (Joseph 1981a, p. 20). These are the seeds of a truly national political base. While no other party came close to matching this breadth of performance, its development would seem to press toward broadening realignments in response. In fact, this is what Nigerian politics has been in motion toward during the first three years of the Second Republic.

THE PATTERN OF POSTELECTION CONFLICT

As early as the 1979 elections – shortly before the fourth of the five rounds of voting – an alliance began to take shape between the UPN and the GNPP, with each party leader endorsing the other's gubernatorial candidates in states where the other party was clearly stronger (*West Africa* August 6, 1979, p. 1409). This attenuated for a time. During the final week of voting for the presidency, it was every party for itself, and it was the runner-up UPN that challenged, through several rounds of unsuccessful legal battles, FEDECO's declaration that Shehu Shagari had obtained the constitutionally required breadth of votes to be elected President directly. This heated controversy over just what was meant by "one quarter of the vote in each of at least two-thirds of all the [19] states" – official bodies from FEDECO to the Supreme Court ruling it meant "twelve and two-thirds" states, or a quarter of the vote in twelve states, plus two-thirds of a quarter, or one-sixth in the thirteenth state (just barely giving the NPN a first ballot victory) – set the stage for bitter and unrelenting political enmity between the UPN opposition and the NPN government (Joseph 1981b, pp. 80-88).

In the wake of the heated election campaign and the "twelve and two-thirds controversy," the incipient alliance blossomed and another formed as well. Building upon patterns of electoral cooperation (most notably in Kaduna), the nine UPN, GNPP and PRP governors began meeting late in 1979 and have continued meeting almost every month thereafter in regular sessions around the country. These meetings were billed as exchanges between heads of state governments with similar policy orientations and concerns. Repeatedly, the governors rejected suggestions that their association represented a political alliance of their three parties. Yet in the first two years of the Second Republic, the "Nine Progressive Governors" became the national rallying point for political opposition to the NPN. Substantively, this opposition focused on the balance of power between the center and the states and what the governors allege has been flagrant, repeated abuse of constitutional authority by the NPN. The communiqué from their March 1981 meeting in Kano contained a 14-point indictment of such abuses, including the appointment in each state of Presidential Liaison Officers, who have to some extent obviated the need for the federal government to work through elected state officials; the deportation of the Borno State House of Assembly majority leader, Shugaba Darman, which was overturned by the State High Court; and the misuse of the substantial federal power over the mass media, including the alleged jamming of the recently established Lagos State Television by the Nigerian Television Authority (*West Africa* April 6, 1981, pp. 727-769).

As these various issues peaked in the political tides, the political character of the nine governors' opposition was underscored by the prominence of the UPN and GNPP party leaders in the assault on the NPN. Chief Awolowo, in particular, continued his role from the election as the most outspoken and impassioned critic of the NPN, and if Alhaji Waziri Ibrahim's opposition was less frequent and strident, its overlap with Chief Awolowo's nevertheless encouraged the perception of a working alliance between the two parties.

Through the first 20 months of the Second Republic, the strength of opposition forces was tempered by a pair of working alliances the NPN had forged. One, a formal accord negotiated after the elections, gave the NPP a share of executive and legislative offices in exchange for its cooperation with the NPN in the National Assembly. The other, a *de facto* alignment, drew into the political orbit of the NPN a growing number of NPP, GNPP and PRP National Assembly members (mostly Senators), who were by law prohibited from crossing the carpet to the NPN, but who gave it reliable and pivotal support in major legislative confrontations, while also publicly appealing for national unity and decrying the attacks of their party colleagues on the NPN government.

Beyond the initial sharing out of Ministers and Assembly leadership positions, the NPP-NPN accord never worked as intended. The regular interparty consultations, through which the NPP expected to be integrally involved in the shaping of national policies, were not forthcoming. Denied this participation, the NPP withheld legislative support on critical issues such as revenue allocation. As both a result and further reinforcement of this noncooperation, the NPP's promised share of government appointments dwindled after the inauguration. On July 6, 1981, the party's leaders gave notice of its intention to terminate the accord, and the NPN then swiftly called on it to do so with immediate effect.

As the formal accord weakened and disintegrated over the two years, the informal alliance assumed greater importance for the NPN federal government and for national politics. Both developments presaged a basic party realignment. What was notable about the NPP's dramatic termination announcement of July 6, 1981 was not simply that the party finally crossed this Rubicon, but that its justification echoed, virtually point for point, the impassioned indictment of NPN abuses of power issued by the nine governors three months previously. Just as significantly, the NPP also echoed the tone of the nine governors' opposition, condemning the NPN abuses variously as "fascist tendencies," "crimes," and "hideous atrocities" (*Nigerian Statesman* July 7, 1981).

If this was in part the accumulated bitterness of a partner belittled and scorned throughout the now shattered marriage, so it was also the sudden and liberating relief of elements within the party – including two state governors – who had never been comfortable with the accord and had long wished to join with the nine progressive governors. Two political conflicts in particular had drawn the NPP closer to the opposition alliance in the previous 12 months. Both were cited prominently in the party statement terminating the accord. One dramatically widened the breach between the two parties. The other seems to have been the last straw.

The Conflict over Revenue Allocation

For a number of weeks at the end of 1980 and beginning of 1981, revenue allocation dominated national political debate. The issue of how to allocate national revenue between levels of government and between the component units at the subfederal level has historically been one of the most intractable in Nigerian politics. The Okigbo Commission was the eighth in 35 years to try to devise a fair and rational system. Testimony and submissions before it highlighted two lines of cleavage in the issue (wrapped within many layers of complexity). To simplify, there was the issue of how revenue was to be allocated between the states. Heavily populated, resource poor states favored heavy emphasis on population. Oil producing states favored heavy emphasis on the principle of derivation and special provisions to compensate them for the ecological risks of oil production. This was a classic instance of the federal system imposing truly fresh sources of cleavage, as the governors of the five oil states – two UPN, two NPN, and one NPP – bridged the bitter political divisions between their parties to unite on a common position (Governors 1980; *West Africa* September 1, 1980, p. 1641).

There was also the issue of dividing the revenue between the federal government, the states collectively, and the local governments. Here party alignments heavily shaped positions. UPN and GNPP governors favored the largest share: 40 to 50 percent for the states, 10 percent for the local governments, and (some of them) 10 percent for a special development and distribution fund. Two NPP governors proposed 50 percent for the center, 40 percent for the states, and 10 percent for local governments. NPN governors favored still larger proportions – over 50 percent – for the center. The Okigbo Commission proposal resembled most closely the NPN approach: 53 percent for the center, only 30 percent for the states, 10 percent for the local government councils and 7 percent for the special fund. In the bill it sent to the National Assembly, the Shagari Administration amended this slightly, proposing allocations of 55 percent, 34.5 percent, 8 percent and 2.5 percent respectively (*West Africa* February 9, 1981, pp. 259-62).

It was these figures in the Revenue Allocation Bill that became the object of heated political conflict in January 1981. The House of Representatives, where the NPN has enjoyed less success in embellishing its voting power through working alliances, settled essentially on the NPP's 50-40-10 plan. The Senate adopted the 55 percent federal government allocation President Shagari had asked for and reduced the states' share to 31.5 percent, leaving 10 percent for local governments and 3.5 percent for special funds. In one of the moments of highest political tension and drama in the Second Republic, a Joint Committee of the Assembly endorsed the Senate bill by a margin of 13 to 11 and forwarded it directly to the President, who quickly signed it into law.

This bypassing of the normal legislative path was strenuously condemned by prominent leaders of the UPN, NPP, GNPP, and PRP as unconstitutional. For a brief but blistering moment in February 1981, it united the nine progressive governors with their three NPP colleagues in a joint statement denouncing not only the whole legislative procedure (and the bill itself) but also the federal government's alleged obstruction of independent state TV stations, and warning ominously that the stage was "set for a repeat performance" of the tragedy of the First Republic (*West Africa* February 23, 1981, pp. 357-58). As much as the outcome of the bill, the manner in which it was passed sharply deepened and embittered the cleavage between the ruling party and the other four. Although the opposition scored a major victory when the Supreme Court ruled, on October 2, 1981, that its passage was indeed unconstitutional and that the bill was null and void, the bitter legacy of the conflict remained.[19]

The revenue allocation conflict also exposed and deepened serious cleavages within two of the four opposing parties. In the face of vigorous opposition from its partner in the faltering accord, the NPN could not have prevailed in the Joint Committee, as it could not have prevailed in the Senate without the votes of PRP and GNPP members. For voting with the NPN on the Revenue Allocation Bill and other "anti-party" activities, three GNPP senators, including the GNPP Senate Leader, Senator Jaafar Mangga, and the Deputy National Chairman, Senator Mahmud Waziri, were expelled from the party in February 1981. Subsequently, the rift within the party widened considerably, with seven of the eight GNPP Senators eventually being expelled from the party. Along with other dissident elements, the Senators have repudiated the authority of National Chairman Waziri Ibrahim and organized an alternative and competing party structure. Dissidents have also been a serious, if less devastating, problem in the NPP, which expelled or suspended a number of its senators who had been voting regularly with the NPN in defiance of party discipline.

The PRP Split

In the Peoples Redemption Party the roles were reversed. It was the party's most powerful national officers – its President, Mallam Aminu Kano, and National Secretary, S. G. Ikoku – who emphasized cooperation with the NPN, and the dissidents who denounced NPN policies and joined with the nine progressive governors. Indeed, the continued insistence of the two PRP governors – Mohammed Abubakar Rimi of Kano and Abdulkadir Balarabe Musa of Kaduna – on attending the meetings of the nine governors, in defiance of the party President and National Directorate, was a leading issue in the intraparty conflict. Beneath it stirred deepening cleavages of personality and political orientation. From the hurried coalescence into the PRP of so many strange political bedfellows in 1979, it was perhaps inevitable that these cleavages would eventually fracture the party.

In part, the PRP conflict embraced a struggle for operational control and future leadership between National Secretary Ikoku and other party officials, on the one hand, and the two governors and numerous other public officeholders on the other. This conflict over power and personality coincided with fundamental differences in political orientation. The governors represent a faction of the party more or less deeply committed to radical change and socialist principles. This orientation seeks a direct confrontation of the contradictions between social classes, and it viewed the nine progressive governors as "essentially a united front . . . an accepted strategy against any primary contradiction at both national and international levels" (Yahaya 1981, pp. 1349-53). This faction contains most of the founding elements of the PRP – including its prominent intellectuals and most of its members in the federal and state legislatures. National Secretary Ikoku, along with other party officials and office holders, represent a more moderate and varied group ideologically – some, like Ikoku, longtime prominent leftists, others mainly distinguished for their business or professional success or personal loyalty to Mallam Aminu – but all believing that short-term imperatives such as preserving national unity and building up the party's organizational and financial strength demand, at least for now, a strategy of gradualism and accommodation with the NPN (*West Africa* January 18, 1982, pp. 158-59). Thus, Aminu Kano rejected Chief Awolowo's appeal for a united progressive front in the election, and S. G. Ikoku negotiated a PRP agreement of cooperation with the NPN in Kaduna State (in December 1979) which was condemned and repudiated by the radical faction, in particular the Kaduna Governor and his administration (Chukumerije 1980).

These multiple cleavages ripped open in the spring of 1980 when, with Mallam Aminu abroad for medical treatment, the party establishment pushed a resolution through the National Directorate forbidding Governors Rimi and Balarabe Musa from further attendance at the nine governors' meetings. Unsuccessful in attempts to mediate the crippling conflict after his return to Nigeria, Mallam

Aminu threw his weight fully on the side of his own moderate instincts and closest personal ties, firmly endorsing the actions of the party establishment. Flatly refusing to surrender their autonomy as state chief executives, the two governors were first suspended and then expelled from the party, along with a number of their allies in the National Assembly.

Out of the bewildering tangle of lawsuits, counterlawsuits, and rival claims of legitimacy that followed, competing party structures emerged. Claiming to represent the authentic grassroots base of the PRP, the two governors summoned a party convention in December 1980, which expelled Aminu Kano and Ikoku and elected Chief Michael Imoudu and Governor Rimi as National President and National Secretary, respectively. Approximately three-quarters of the PRP members of the Senate and House of Representatives and a commanding majority of PRP state legislators in Kano and Kaduna lined up with the Imoudu PRP (*Africa* 118, June 1981, p. 15; *West Africa* January 18, 1982, p. 158). But the question remained: which was the real Peoples Redemption Party?

The answer would have important national political implications, not only for the next election but, more immediately, for the internal politics of the National Assembly where committee assignments are distributed by party. In the brief period that December between the dissident PRP convention and the appointment of the Joint Committee on Revenue Allocation, the Federal Electoral Commission officially recognized the Aminu Kano faction as the legitimate PRP. Despite the predominance of the Imoudu faction among PRP members in the House of Representatives, an Aminu Kano loyalist was given the PRP House seat on the Joint Committee. Seeking to install their own representative, outraged House members from the Imoudu faction forcibly prevented him from taking his seat when the Joint Committee convened in January. The following day, as Nigerian police stood guard in the committe chamber and surrounded the National Assembly building, the member from the Aminu faction took his seat on the Joint Committee and provided the margin of victory for the NPN's bill (*West Africa* February 9, 1981, pp. 259-62).

The decision of the Federal Electoral Commission to recognize the pro-NPN faction of the PRP was another blow to FEDECO's legitimacy. If not as controversial as its "twelve and two-thirds" decision, it nevertheless combined with that controversial ruling to leave "the losers deeply aggrieved and unsatisfied as to the integrity of the institution that had been charged with bearing the brunt of the constitutional effort to prevent escalation of competition into enmity" (Whitaker 1981, p. 12).

The Kaduna Impeachment

If the conflict over the Revenue Allocation Bill was a decisive tear in the already frayed fabric of the NPN-NPP accord, the impeachment of Kaduna Governor Balarabe Musa was the final rupture. The impeachment struggle embodied simultaneously several lines of political and ideological cleavage. On the surface, it culminated 20 months of confrontation between the radical PRP Governor and the conservative, NPN-dominated House of Assembly, ending in a stalemate in which the Assembly four times rejected all of the Governor's cabinet nominees, the Governor signed virtually none of the Assembly's bills, and court cases mounted right and left. More broadly, it was a confrontation between the NPN and the four-party alliance that had brought Balarabe Musa into office, but which, lacking even one-third of the seats in the Assembly, could not rescue him from the ensuing stalemate. Still more broadly, it marked a new chapter in the steadily polarizing conflict between the "progressive" parties and the NPN, drawing the NPP into the fold of the former for the second time in six months.

More deeply, it expressed the escalating confrontation of class forces in the North, which finds the radical young intellectuals and professionals of the PRP seeking to mobilize the peasantry against what they view as an oppressive and exploitative traditional aristocracy that has of late been merging with and transforming into a modern bourgeoisie in the North. Across these social and political cleavages, the impeachment also reflected and heightened the contradiction within the PRP between the moderate faction – which so abhors confrontation with the NPN that it endorsed the impeachment of its own governor – and the radical faction – which takes seriously the orienting observation of the PRP manifesto that "the forces of privilege" and "the forces of the people" in Nigeria are now "locked in a grim struggle for survival and ascendancy" (PRP 1979, p. 4).

As with the revenue allocation battle, layers of technical detail in the impeachment conflict must be scraped away if the raw features of the underlying cleavage are to be exposed. Fundamentally, the conflict did not turn on the specifics of the ten articles of "gross misconduct" filed by the House of Assembly against the Governor or the Governor's futile legal challenges to the hurried and partisan procedures by which he was impeached (*West Africa* July 6, 1981, pp. 1518-25). Because the Constitution (art. 56, sec. 170) defined gross misconduct as whatever two-thirds of the House said it was and barred judicial appeal of the House's substantive determination, the impeachment process could become what it became in Kaduna: a weapon of political conflict. Even sophisticated supporters of impeachment recognized that "impeachment is mainly a political step" (*New Nigerian* July 8, 1981).

The fundamental issue in Kaduna was the admitted refusal of the Governor to compromise on any issue involving his basic political principles and goals. Hence, he plunged forward with his program for a "social transformation" – abolishing taxes that had been instruments of exploitation by local elites, reorganizing local government and trade, investigating land transactions, inaugurating a mass literacy campaign, setting up new state-owned industries, and establishing a new state agency to coordinate his ambitious program of integrated rural development (Kaduna State Government 1980; Balarabe Musa 1981). When the NPN majority in the House blocked these initiatives, he proceeded unilaterally. These unilateral actions and appointments figured prominently in the ten articles of impeachment, but it was their substantive import much more than their procedural irregularity that motivated the impeachment. As an unsympathetic commentary observed in retrospect, "It is . . . not logical to expect the NPN to fold its arms and just watch on while Balarabe rams away at the very pillars of its power, namely land and the emirate system" (Haruna 1981). The PRP-NPN agreement of cooperation would have avoided the stalemate and impeachment. But so also would it have prevented Balarabe Musa and his allies from effecting their envisioned social transformation and so it was rejected by them.

The Kaduna impeachment was a national political conflict of high emotion. Among its revealing aspects was the swift and emphatic way in which not only the UPN and GNPP but the NPP as well rallied behind the embattled Kaduna Governor. All three parties sent teams of lawyers to aid Governor Balarabe in his legal challenges. All of their newspapers and publicity organs condemned the impeachment process from the very start as undemocratic and unconstitutional, their moral indignation rising as the process sped toward a climax. NPN newspapers, on the other hand, consistently applauded the exercise as a demonstration that the democratic process worked.

When the Kaduna House voted on June 22 to remove the Governor from office, these alignments were revealed in their sharpest relief. NPN newspapers bid "Good riddance to bad rubbish" (*New Nigerian* July 8, 1981) while the UPN *Sketch* printed its front and back pages on black background for a week to emphasize the darkness than had fallen over the land. NPP leader Dr. Azikiwe hailed Balarabe Musa as "the hero of our Second Republic" while GNPP leader Waziri Ibrahim warned that the impeachment "debased our constitution and our national integrity" and was "a continuation of the class struggle between the progressives and the reactionary elements" (*Sunday Sketch* June 28, 1981). *Sketch* Features Editor Oluwole Odetola was one of the many commentators and politicians to call for "a united front of the four parties to wrest power in 1983" (*Daily Sketch* July 8, 1981).

The Kano Riot

The prospects of such a realignment were undoubtedly advanced by the Kaduna impeachment, as they were by the revenue allocation conflict that preceded it and the termination of the NPP-NPN accord that followed it two weeks later. One further event during those turbulent few months also heavily affected the national political climate, despite its seemingly local character. This was the devastating riot in Kano which burned down much of the physical infra-structure of the state government on July 10, 1981.

Hardly had the dramatic news of the NPP-NPN accord's demise been absorbed when Governor Rimi refocused attention on the troubled North with a pointedly terse query to the Emir of Kano charging nine acts of deliberate disrespect to the state government and giving the Emir 48 hours to show cause why he should not be disciplined. The letter of July 7, which has been described as "most disrespectful . . . suitable for admonishing a clerk but . . . most unsuitable for addressing a [venerated] traditional and religious leader" (*West Africa* July 20, 1981, p. 1627), caused an immediate storm. When it became public on July 9, the Kano State NPN warned that the Emir was about to be removed from office and, as reported by the *New Nigerian* (July 10, 1981), "called on people of goodwill in the state to take every constitutional measure to defend their traditional institutions." A spokesman from the Aminu Kano PRP and conservative intellectual and religious leaders also condemned the query.

The following day violence erupted on a massive scale. Demonstrators burned down the state Secretariat (housing five critical ministries including Finance), Radio Kano, the State House of Assembly, the Ministries of Works and of Lands and Survey, the headquarters of the Imoudu PRP, the construction site of the state's new newspaper publishing company, and the residences of a number of key officials and advisers in Governor Rimi's Administration. In one of those residences the Governor's chief political adviser, Dr. Bala Mohammed, was trapped in the blaze and killed. In all, 11 people were killed, about 100 vehicles were burned, and damage was estimated at ₦ 100 million (*New Nigerian* July 11, 1981; *West Africa* July 20, 1981, p. 1635, January 4, 1982, p. 5).

The identity and motives of the rioters will probably forever remain a subject of intense debate and speculation, especially since the police made no arrests for almost 72 hours. Supporters of Governor Rimi alleged that the police also made no attempt to stop the violence and arson, which they maintain was orchestrated by the NPN and/or the Aminu Kano faction of the PRP with passive police cooperation. PRP members in the Federal House of Representatives charged that the violence had "nothing to do whatsoever with the query" but was engineered by the NPN and Aminu Kano to preserve their political power (*Daily Sketch* July 17, 1981). From this perspective, the riot is seen as a calculated attempt to accomplish through violence what could not be done in Kano through impeachment. The charge of an NPN conspiracy behind the riot was also leveled by the nine progressive governors, who were meeting (with Governor Rimi) in Maiduguri at the time of the riot. Conservatives in the North and newspapers sympathetic to the NPN have interpreted the riot as a spontaneous outpouring of popular anger at the Governor's attempted humiliation of the revered Emir (*New Nigerian* July 13, 1981; *West Africa* July 20, 1981, p. 1635). For the NPN and Aminu's PRP, the Kano riot signals that the radicals have misjudged the masses and overreached themselves in attacking traditional institutions. By this logic, their political decimation in the next election can only follow.[20]

The care and thoroughness with which the rioters chose their targets and the high degree of organization with which they seemed to move against them suggest that the riot was not wholly spontaneous. Whoever was responsible, it has become a fact of great political significance that the constituent elements of the progressive alliance responded to the violence from the assumption that the NPN was responsible, and that the riot signaled a new and most dangerous phase in the struggle against the "feudal" aristocracy of the North and the NPN's allegedly reactionary and antidemocratic rule.

Nowhere was this conviction more deeply felt than among the leaders of the radical PRP themselves, who were badly shaken by the murder of one of their most important intellectual leaders, no less than by the proximity and sheer enormity of the physical destruction. As one commented at the public memorial for Bala Mohammed soon after the riot: "The choice before us now is to give up the struggle – to surrender – or to continue the struggle and face possible death. For any intelligent and responsible person, there is no choice but the latter." On the same occasion, Governor Rimi revealed that his own life had been repeatedly threatened and warned: "Nobody will cause the kind of destruction of July 10 and think he can sleep in his house safely and quietly. . . . If they don't stop then we will hit in such a way that they will not hit again."

Such tones of militant outrage were apparent in the statements of support not only from the parties and newspapers of the progressive governors but, once again, from the NPP as well. While the (NPP) Plateau State Government charged the rampage was carried out "by a group of heartless, opportunist politicians in the name of tradition" (*New Nigerian* July 24, 1981), its newspaper went much further. In an unprecedented two-part editorial taking virtually the whole of the front page on consecutive days, it bluntly accused the NPN, in alliance with Aminu Kano's PRP, of organizing the riot, charged the police as "accomplices in the conspiracy," and appealed for sustained constitutional struggle against a "neo-fascist" NPN regime that was running "to all intents and purposes . . . a police state" (*Nigeria Standard* July 22, 1981).

In the month following the Kano Riot, editors from the *Standard* and two outspoken UPN newspapers, the *Nigerian Tribune* and the *Daily Sketch*, were arrested and charged with publishing false information (*West Africa* August 24, 1981, p. 1957). Soon thereafter, the Federal Inspector General of Police warned the country's newspaper proprietors' association that the police would no longer tolerate publications causing a breakdown of law and order, while the UPN Governor of Oyo State countered "that his administration would copy the Federal Government and prosecute newspapers which publish seditious and false information about his government." At the same time, two senior PRP officials in Kaduna were arrested in connection with the appearance of posters showing "a policeman trampling upon a man while a watching judge laughed" and bearing the caption, "Fascism" (*West Africa* September 7, 1981, p. 2073).

Whatever the immediate, precipitating cause of the Kano riot, there can be no doubt that the basic cleavage from which it sprang mirrors that in Kaduna – the struggle between competing class forces for control of the North. Conservatives seek to preserve the existing socioeconomic structure, and the institutions of traditional authority which remain, to a significant degree, the pillar of that structure. Radicals seek a rapid transformation of the socioeconomic order and hence a deliberate heightening of the contradiction between the structure of privilege and the demands for change. Toward this end, the Rimi administration has been implementing in Kano an array of policy initiatives similar to those of Balarabe Musa in Kaduna: ending exploitative local taxes, suspending the processing of land certificates in an effort to halt the expropriation of peasant lands, reforming chieftaincy institutions, reorganizing and reforming the judicial system, and launching an ambitious mass literacy campaign. The moderate faction of the PRP sees all this as a faster pace of change than the society can absorb, hence, its cautious and gradualist approach, which has pressed it toward a working alliance with the NPN.

Political conflict in Kano, as in Kaduna, thus pivots around the radicals' quest for a "social transformation." As one shrewd analysis has observed, "It is these revolutionary changes, and more so, the speed with which they are being introduced, that has made Kano the boiling cauldron of Nigerian politics" (*West Africa* January 4, 1982, p. 6).

Intrastate, Intraparty Conflict

Although national political conflict has been reducing gradually to a bipolar struggle between two broad political alliances, political conflict in the Second Republic has by no means been limited to these major realigning confrontations. Running throughout these successive national dramas, and encompassing virtually every one of the 19 states, has been a complex array of vigorous, local political conflicts within the states and within state party branches. These have generally escaped much national attention, but their independence from the major national lines of political cleavage has only modestly limited their intensity. Though most of the actual political violence has attended the confrontations between opposing parties in the states, intra-state, intraparty conflict has been free of neither vehemence nor violence. It too has gathered the intensity that seems inevitably to follow from a system in which class position and access to resources is so heavily determined by state control. Consequently, it has torn deeply into the cohesion of numerous state parties, in many cases damaging their reelection prospects.[21]

Intraparty conflict in the states has most commonly affected ruling parties – a logical consequence of the tendency for most states to be dominated by a single party. Since ruling parties exercise fairly monolithic control over power and resources in all but two states, it is natural that the competition for position and resources should revolve in and around them. (Some states where the NPN comprises the opposition provide a caveat to this, but conflicts in these NPN branches can be traced at least in part to the NPN's control of resources at the Center.)

Within state ruling parties, no cleavage has been more aggravated than that between the governor and the legislature. While so far only one governor has been impeached, threats of impeachment have been levied by angry legislators against the governors of Bendel, Ondo, and Cross River – all of which are one party-dominant – and Gongola, where (as in Kaduna) a "progressive" governor has been opposed by a more conservative legislature, even though his own party holds a plurality of seats. Tension has strained executive-legislative relations in several other states as well. To a significant extent, this tension stems from a constitutional structure that "has made the heads of . . . legislatures and the legislatures themselves very powerful. It only needs political will for a determined legislature to boot a governor out of office" (Ekpu 1981). With their power to obstruct the executive's budget and program as well, legislatures have the upper hand; but the governors, as executives, naturally wish to execute and grow impatient with resistance. Such mutual suspicion and jealousy are perhaps inevitable in a new and complicated constitutional system, and it will probably be several terms of office before the two branches of government adapt to some shared understanding of their proper balance.

The structural tensions have only exacerbated other sources of conflict. While allegations of incompetence, maladministration, favoritism, and corruption have been leveled against some governors, all of the conflicts have heavily involved the struggle for resources, in which ethnic and subethnic rivalries commonly come into play. Thus the award of defense contracts has become an issue in the bitter rivalry between the Senate Majority Leader and the Defense Minister (allied with the governor) for control of the NPN in Kwara; the governors of Bendel, Imo and Ondo have angered many legislators by siting new state universities in their home towns; factions in many states have tugged over the distribution of amenities; and politics in the Yoruba and Igbo states have been rife with historic communal rivalries: between the Ibadans and the Oshuns in Oyo State, the Ekitis and several Yoruba minority groups in Ondo, the Egbas and the Ijebus in Ogun, and the Waawa and Ijekbe in Anambra. In ethnic minority states, such as Cross River and Bendel, different ethnic groups that once collaborated to gain new states now divide in the struggle for resources, frequently pushing competing plans for new states. The latter tension has bitterly divided the NPN in Cross River State and led to the suspension from the party's state branch of one of the NPN's most powerful national barons – Senate President Joseph Wayas. In fact, agitation for new states has fueled intraparty conflict throughout the country, including the Yoruba and Igbo states. Not only are many communal groups advancing competing, mutually inconsistent demands, but few governors are eager to see the scope of their power drastically fragmented.

The factional maneuvering has frequently divided ruling party legislators against one another and against their elected leaderships. The news of a prominent officeholder being suspended or expelled from his party for "anti-party activities" is by now commonplace, and in the PRP and GNPP the competing factions have each expelled the other en masse. But a number of high legislative officers have also been removed or forced out in such intraparty battles: the House Speaker in Sokoto State, the Deputy Speaker in Bauchi State, and the entire party leadership (seven officers in all) in Ondo, to name a few. In Lagos State, the Speaker and six other legislators were suspended by the UPN for breaching that party's rigid code of discipline, and a federal Senator was expelled from the party after publicly criticizing the Lagos State Government and then announcing his intention to run against the incumbent Governor. In Ogun, recriminations between the Deputy Governor and House Speaker generated a furor so intense that the House had to be adjourned in February 1982 when legislators seemed on the edge of exchanging blows. In Plateau State, NPP legislators introduced impeachment charges against their Deputy Governor during 1981 because of his open advocacy of a breakaway Middle Belt State, and at the end of the year Kano Deputy Governor Bibi Farouk became the Second Republic's second victim of impeachment for backing the wrong side in the PRP struggle, or, as Governor Rimi's faction put it, for being "a highly irresponsible deputy and for selling out to the NPN" (*West Africa* January 4, 1982, p. 7).

This unfolding pattern of intrastate conflict has raised both hopeful and disturbing implications for democracy in Nigeria. In an important sense, the multistate system is working as intended. Although intraparty disputes have on occasion converged with national political cleavage, as in Kano and Kaduna, these state disputes have been mostly localized and cross-cutting. Frequently, even when they have reverberated nationally they have done so in fresh ways, pressing divisions (such as those within the NPN and UPN) that cut across the major lines of political and ethnic cleavage. Thus, intense struggles for power and resources within individual states generally do not infect the national political arena and exhaust its limited capacity for conflict mediation as they did under the regional system of the First Republic. A much more complicated and decentralized pattern of conflict now prevails.

On the other hand, the conflicts within states and parties, though localized, have nevertheless manifested more than a trace of the fanaticism that destroyed the first attempt at democracy in Nigeria. Everywhere that it has been employed or threatened, impeachment has been a more or less nakedly political weapon.[22] The "anti-party activities" that have become the routine justification for party suspensions and expulsions frequently amount, when the rhetoric is stripped away, to nothing more than independence from the party line and leadership on critical issues. Since strong parties by Huntington's (1968) criteria of institutionalization are crucial to the vitality of developing democracies, and while the politicians are still only getting the feel of the new institutional arrangements, dissident views have been quashed and punishments rendered in a style that suggests not so much party development as political intolerance. This same political intolerance and inflexibility has become perhaps the dominant feature of the interaction between the parties. Institutions, parties and even to some extent personalities have changed, but this cancer on the body politic remains.

PREPARING THE 1983 ELECTIONS

Since the 1979 elections, the Nigerian party system has been in constant motion toward a fundamental realignment. This movement began in the election itself with the electoral cooperation between the UPN and GNPP in a number of states; but its most striking first instance was in the gubernatorial election in Kaduna, where the UPN, GNPP and NPP all rallied behind the PRP candidacy of Abdulkadir Balarabe Musa, providing his narrow margin of victory over the NPN candidate after the NPN had swept the House of Assembly election. This four-party alliance crumbled after that one feat but since has been gradually reforming.

During the first two years of the Second Republic, several major political events advanced the process of party realignment: the formation of the "Nine Progressive Governors," and their development into a cohesive and articulate opposition force, the conflict over revenue allocation, the split in the PRP, the impeachment of Balarabe Musa, the breakdown of the NPN-NPP accord, and the Kano riot. With each new conflict pitting the ruling NPN against the four parties or party factions, the cleavage between the two sides deepened, and the talk of a merger or coalition among the latter escalated. By late 1981, negotiations toward such a union were clearly underway, and the nation was abuzz with rumors of an historic rapprochement between Dr. Azikiwe and Chief Awolowo that would bridge more than thirty years of political competition and conflict.

The road to union has not been an easy one. Suspicions and distrust remain, causing the UPN to boycott the first four-party meeting in Jos, in early December 1981. A fully attended meeting in Benin the following month, however, produced broad agreement on an electoral alliance to challenge the NPN in 1983. This alliance was formally realized in Maiduguiri in March 1982 at the conclusion of three days of meetings. There, the leaders of the four parties – Awolowo, Azikiwe, Waziri Ibrahim and Governor Rimi for the PRP – announced formation of the Progressive Parties' Alliance, with a governing council of the four party leaders and the governors of the 12 states, who had already become the "Twelve Progressive Governors."

As of mid-1982, the most difficult questions facing the alliance remained to be resolved. Most volatile of all is the question of a common presidential candidate, without which the rationale of the union largely disintegrates. In the wake of the Benin meeting it was reported that the parties had agreed on Chief Awolowo as the candidate; subsequently, there surfaced in the press an extraordinary exchange of letters between "Awo" and "Zik" in which the two giants of Nigerian political history appeared to agree, as Azikiwe put it, "to forget the vagaries of the past. . . . and forgive ourselves for whatever had happened . . . ," and to "go into a partnership in which," as Chief Awolowo described it, "you will be the nation's Guide, Philosopher, and Friend, and I its Chief Servant" (*West Africa* March 22, 1982, p. 821). The struggle for power within the alliance is unlikely to end there, however. No sooner had the letters surfaced when the NPP Governor of Imo State warned that his party would withdraw if the leadership of the alliance did not go to Dr. Azikiwe. It is entirely likely that the NPP leader, who will be 79 in 1983, wishes to step into the background as elder statesman. And certainly Chief Awolowo aspires for the nomination himself. But this is the essential problem: though widely respected as perhaps the country's most articulate public figure and able administrator, and though admired and even revered within his ethnic homeland, Chief Awolowo is also widely resented and distrusted in many other parts of the country as a paramount "tribalist." He has twice failed spectacularly (in 1959 and 1979) to win Hausa and Igbo votes in vigorous national campaigns, and many doubt that he can do so in 1983, even with the backing of the alliance.

It is partly for this reason that the radical PRP faction – which, after FEDECO's decision to recognize its rival, must merge with someone in 1983 to survive – has chosen not the party with whom it shares the most in common ideologically, the UPN, but rather the NPP and GNPP. This reflects not only the NPP's shrewd and determined courtship of Governor Rimi and his faction and the close relations between the radical PRP and the Plateau State NPP – who share a fierce common resistance to what they term the "feudal oligarchy" of the Fulani aristocracy – but also the pragmatic judgment of the PRP leaders that Chief Awolowo simply cannot carry the Hausa *talakawa*. For the UPN, which nursed dreams of an Awolowo-Rimi ticket that would finally take the North by storm, it has been another serious miscalculation.

Has the politics of the "progressives" then been reduced merely to the old-fashioned calculus of tribalism and opportunism? I think not. Whatever becomes of the four-party alliance, the union of the NPP, the Waziri Ibrahim GNPP, and the Imoudu PRP, which filed for registration with FEDECO as the Progressive Peoples' Party (PPP), is likely to endure through the 1983 elections. This owes not only to the need of the GNPP and PRP factions for some kind of merger to survive, but also to the convergence of ideological and substantive political interests between the three groups. Although the NPP and GNPP are undeniably capitalist – to the point where the NPP national secretary has flatly stated that any talk of the new alignment being socialist would be a waste of time (*West Africa* December 14, 1982, p. 2962) – their liberal-bourgeois vision of Nigerian development is closer to the PRP's than is the NPN's. They represent the ideological middle in national politics, and the PRP no doubt sees in the new Progressive People's Party and in the Progressive Alliance, just what it saw in the "Nine Progressive Governors" – "a united front . . . an accepted strategy against any primary contradiction . . ." (Yahaya 1981, p. 1353).

More significantly, what all four parties share most deeply in common is the belief that the tradition-based inequalities of wealth and power in the North constitute the primary and most pressing contradiction in Nigerian society and the conviction that the socio-economic domination of the hereditary elite in the North must be broken. For both Southern and Middle Belt progressives and Northern radicals, this is a view that has held essentially constant for thirty years. It brought them together during the fateful 1964 election in a United Progressive Grand Alliance strikingly similar in composition and tone to the one announced in Maiduguri in early 1982. It rallied them together in mid-1981 during the Kaduna and Kano crises. More than anything else, save perhaps their common desire for power, it is what motivates their common opposition to the NPN, which they perceive as the instrument of the hereditary aristocracy of the North, and which they believe is abusing the federal powers of incumbency at their common political expense.

The struggle over nominations may derail the Progressive Parties' Alliance, and the merging of liberal capitalist and democratic socialist platforms will surely strain the PPP. Indeed, should the PPP or the four-party alliance win in 1983, the united front will almost surely collapse when the radicals judge that it has outlived its usefulness and perhaps well before then. As much as their common electoral interest, it is their common substantive interest – their common, if loose, relationship to the Nigerian class structure at a decisive moment in its historical evolution – that brings them together and will likely bind them together at least through 1983.

Election Prospects

At first glance, this might appear to portend a Progressive Alliance victory in 1983 since it controls 12 of the 19 statehouses and would figure to register new gains by pooling its electoral strength. In four of the twelve states, however, the PRP and GNPP splits throw the electoral outcome into doubt, and in others as well, the NPN has been consolidating its own network of alliances. The dissident faction of the GNPP, now chaired by Senator Mahmud Waziri, a Fulani from Borno, will almost certainly formally join the NPN in 1983 (it, too, has nowhere else to go), and while Aminu Kano's PRP may remain an independent party if it can obtain registration, it is likely to cooperate with the NPN in a common electoral strategy (dividing up constituencies to contest). Hence, the NPN will have a potent alliance of moderates and conservatives in Borno, Gongola, Kano and Kaduna and could capture one or more of these states. Added to this are the defections it has won over from the NPP, particularly in the two Igbo States, where a number of prominent NPP Senators (now expelled) have all but joined the NPN and will almost certainly campaign under its banner in 1983; and also the intraparty tensions in several of the UPN states. These factors could produce significant NPN inroads in the Yoruba and Igbo heartlands, and possibly NPN governors (though not legislative control) in Ondo, Bendel and Imo if ruling party divisions are not resolved. But these same divisions could also cost the NPN control of Kwara, and perhaps Benue, in 1983.

All this adds up to the likelihood that if the process of realignment indeed reduces Nigerian politics to an essentially two-party system in 1983, it will probably produce the most evenly balanced and unpredictable national election in Nigerian history. Cross-cutting cleavage will almost certainly abound, and substantive appeals that cross cut ethnicity will have to become more prominent. For this reason, realignment into a more ideological, two-party system is the great promise of Nigerian politics. But it may also be the great peril.

Since the 1979 election and the subsequent conflict over the results, the temperature of the Nigerian body politic has been rising perceptibly. As politics has been gradually polarized into two broad alliances, bitterness, distrust and violence between their partisans and leaders have been steadily escalating. Mutual distrust reached the point in mid-1981 where Chief Awolowo vowed he would order his followers to smash any voting machines that were adopted for use in 1983, so certain was he that the NPN would rig the voting with them (*Nigerian Herald* June 15, 1981). NPN stalwarts are equally convinced that the voting machines are necessary to prevent massive ballot stuffing by the UPN. And in the North, political leaders of the progressive alliance are laying plans for a poll watching operation of unprecedented scope to prevent what they allege was massive NPN rigging in 1979.

Hauntingly, political violence has also been rising steadily. Apart from the mass destruction in Kano, there has been increasing violence between competing parties and party factions and between the bands of party thugs that disfigured the first Nigerian experience with electioneering. In clashes between UPN and NPN supporters in Ogun and Oyo, between GNPP and NPN partisans in Borno, and elsewhere, lives have been lost and substantial amounts of property destroyed. Well in advance of the 1983 elections, such clashes risked getting out of control. In a period of a week in June 1981, Oyo Governor Bola Ige declared the state a battleground between his party and the NPN, vowing "not to allow any NPN leader to campaign in Oyo State" (*New Nigerian* June 12, 1981), while the Anambra State Commissioner of Police warned of the "possible breakdown of law and order" in the state as a result of the introduction of thuggery and coercion and the importation of arms and ammunition (*Nigerian Chronicle* June 20, 1981). More recently, police officials have temporarily banned public meetings, processions and assemblies in Kwara, Oyo and Niger States out of fear of violent eruption of partisan passions (*West Africa* October 26, 1981, p. 2541; April 19, 1982, p. 1101; April 26, 1982, p. 1167).

The politicians themselves hardly have been a model of civility and decorum. At both the federal and state levels, legislators have come to blows (or been halted only by hasty adjournment) in the heat of confrontation. In April 1982, the House of Representatives, which had previously seen fisticuffs between rival PRP factions over seating on the Joint Committee on Revenue Allocation and a gun-waving incident by a PRP member, broke up in a tug-of-war between allies and opponents of the Speaker. When the Speaker abruptly adjourned the House for Easter recess (purportedly to forestall a no-confidence motion against him), more than a hundred angry members physically tried to prevent his departure, and in the ensuing scuffle the Mace, symbol of the House's authority, was smashed to pieces (*West Africa* April 19, 1982, p. 1050). Subsequently, the Speaker became the fourth major politician (along with three Governors) to allege the existence of a plot to assassinate him.

Political violence at the grass roots unquestionably has been stimulated by the behavior of the politicians, not only by their own confrontations, but by their rhetoric, which has been growing more inflamed, more inflammatory and more apocalyptic, with each side prophesying national catastrophe if the other wins. Note the following statements from UPN Chairman Chief Awolowo and NPN Chairman Chief Akinloye to their respective party conventions at the close of 1981:

> We must not misrate or under-rate the feudalist-reactionaries who are now using the NPN as their rear-guard platform. . . . They obsessionally believe . . . that is their destiny to rule Nigeria in perpetuity. . . . They would not hesitate to abuse and misuse the executive and judicial instruments at their disposal to harass and persecute the electorate as well as the candidates for election; they would try to resort to all kinds of rigging in areas where they feel comparatively weak or hopeless; and above all, they would strive to overwhelm the whole country with money, which they have acquired in almost unlimited quantity by hook and by crook, in a desperate effort to subvert the will and the choice of the voters (*West Africa* December 21-28, 1981, p. 3029).

> [The UPN is] in pursuit of its determination to destabilise the nation and to come to power even if it means the ruin of the nation. The UPN chief, as it is now too well known, is bent on mobilising all other parties to feather his own nest. . . . We must wage a relentless war against those enemies of the nation who want to destroy the Second Republic and destabilise the country (*West Africa* December 7, 1981, p. 2893).

Keen observers of Nigerian politics will recognize here the rhetorical excess that has been a familiar part of the political landscape for 30 years. But as any keen observer will know, such excess has played an important role in the country's past political traumas. It is just such fanaticism that the military leaders repeatedly sought to temper during the 1979 election campaign, during which they twice summoned the five presidential candidates to the barracks to upbraid them for their vitriolic exchanges and to warn each of them "to stop threatening that if he did not win 'there would be no Nigeria' " (Phillips 1980, p. 20).

As in 1959, when the British played a similar role, it took the steel frame of a neutral administrator to keep the electioneering from spinning out of control. This parallel invites a more chilling one, that already drawn with the Federal Election of 1964. Then, confrontation between two national political alliances not only consumed Nigerian democracy, in a wave of political violence, repression, boycott and fraud, but brought the nation to the brink of civil war (Post and Vickers 1973). It is a tragic feature of Nigerian political life that its politicians seem not to have learned the lesson of what happens when the waters of ethnic and political passion are obsessively and furiously stirred. A tidal wave drowns all boats.

The Future of Democracy in Nigeria

Unfortunately, the only thing that can be said with confidence in advance of the 1983 elections is that they are going to be an extremely tense and possibly extremely violent affair. This does not augur well for the future of democracy in Nigeria.

Few can seriously doubt that the Nigerian military will intervene if the 1983 campaign descends into the chaos and violence that destroyed the democratic process in 1964 and 1965. Indeed, it is unlikely that the military would wait even as long as it did then or strike as tentatively.

Economic misfortune further clouds the political future. The world oil glut badly deflated the performance of the Nigerian economy in 1981, reducing oil revenues (which account for 83 percent of government expenditures) by roughly 40 percent of what had been expected for the year in the Fourth National Development Plan, and forcing a series of painful austerity measures including a freeze on one-third of the expenditures in the plan and more recent sharp curbs on foreign imports (*Africa Report* November-December 1981, p. 28; *West Africa* April 26, 1982, pp. 1112-14). Although the glut appeared to be drying up by mid-1982, a shortfall of roughly 25 percent in oil revenue was nevertheless forecast for the year (*West Africa* April 26, 1982, p. 1113). It is a measure of the severity of the crisis that on April 20, 1920 the normally contentious National Assembly granted President Shagari the sweeping emergency economic powers he sought, but the positive effect of this statesmanlike display must be balanced against the economic pain that is being felt increasingly at all levels of society. Although temporary austerity seems no great political threat, prolonged crisis might seriously undermine popular support for the Second Republic. For new democratic regimes, unlike those that have been able to sink deep institutional roots over time, do not have a large reservoir of previous effective performance to draw upon in maintaining popular commitment. The newer the regime, the more likely a sustained failure of performance is to be perceived as institutional in nature.

To some extent, the future is beyond the politicians' control. But certainly their own comportment is not, and, from very early on in the Second Republic, there have been mounting signs that they are squandering some significant portion of that precious capital that is so difficult for a polity to accumulate: legitimacy. Doubt and cynicism about the politicians as a group is once again gathering in a fashion reminiscent of the final years of the First Republic. Now, like then, leaders of opinion are becoming disgusted with corruption, extravagance, selfishness, apathy, secretiveness, inefficiency, insensitivity, combativeness, tribalism and violence among the nation's politicians, particularly its legislators. In the newspaper columns of political commentators, the essays of intellectuals, the public statements of interest group leaders, the letters to editors by articulate observers, and the private discussions of ordinary citizens, the signs of eroding faith in the political system – the hallmark of political decay – are manifest.

Resentment over the high income and living of the nation's politicians has been a prominent theme, reflected in pungent and persistent criticism of the debate over legislative salaries and benefits that consumed so much of the National Assembly's attention at the outset of its deliberations.[23] The feeling was succinctly summarized by the title of a *Sunday Tribune* (June 14, 1981) column, "Our Legislators Are Greedy," which complained:

> Across the discussions of their salaries, accommodation, amenities, order of precedence and other privileges, you find their greed taking over right, left and centre. From the disco and booze loving law makers in Lagos to the chicken loving legislators in Calabar, they are a greedy lot.

Indeed, many Nigerians appear to share the view of *The Punch* labor columnist, Segun Obilana, that "politicians in this country . . . belong to the rich class" and portray "themselves as looters of the proverbial societal cake" (July 1, 1981). The feeling among many that the legislators "had gone into politics in order to look after themselves" has been further advanced by nagging problems of absenteeism and lateness in the National Assembly which "have been highlighted in the Nigerian press on several occasions" (*West Africa* April 19, 1982, pp. 1050-51).

The stock of the politicians fell further during the general strike of May 1981. In opposition newspapers, prominent play was given to a fundraiser held by the NPN at the height of the strike to dedicate its new headquarters. A handful of party "men of timber" raised a reported ₦ 5 million between them in a matter of minutes at the very time the NPN government was opposing the Nigerian Labour Congress' demand for a ₦ 300 per month minimum wage as inflationary. Dire warnings followed that such insensitivity would "lead to discontentment and uproar" and letters to editors like the following: "What causes inflation in any society is not the paltry sum which the worker is paid but the huge sum which the political class carts away from a nation's treasury" (*Daily Times* June 6, 1981). Sufficient have been such public outcries to move one representative to declare in House debate on the Minimum Wage Bill:

> I am haunted by fear of what may happen should things continue as they are now. Seeing these shameless displays of wealth and callous show of positions of power and privilege in the midst of miserableness and wretchedness, I am afraid, Mr. Chairman, I am afraid. And only a fool would not [be] (Fagbamigbe 1981).

Concern is also manifest over the general style of political intolerance – "impeachment, mud-slinging and intimidation by expulsion" (*West Africa* April 12, 1982, p. 990), and especially over the rising levels of interparty violence, "astonishing to observe," in the words of one letter writer, "after going through a gruelling civil war in the not so distant past" (*Daily Times* July 1, 1981). The widespread "tooth-and-claw" combat of politics and behind it "the apparent delight and proclivity of our politicians to politicize in a most outrageous manner every little difference of opinion" were prominent among the concerns raised by the respected *Daily Times* columnist Nelson Ottah (June 4, 1981). His cogent warning of impending danger, entitled "Herding the Swine Uphill," complained of nothing having been learned from the failure of the First Republic. Other global assessments have been even more certain and unforgiving in their judgments of political bankruptcy, as reflected in the commentary of a University of Ife academician:

> The last eighteen months . . . have left the average Nigerians baffled and disappointed. All hope in the ability of our politicians to learn and run the nation's affairs along acceptable and reasonable models has been dashed. . . . While our men in the National Asembly fiddle (presumably) pursuing their private business . . . [important government functions] are held up. Yet they insist on paying themselves in excess of what seems reasonable in comparison to other hard-working Nigerians and collect all forms of allowances under various pretexts. . . . Here are men unwilling to subject themselves to public scrutiny. Who are men such as these, to make laws for the conduct of lesser men? (*Sunday Sketch* June 7, 1981).

THE CHANGING BASIS OF NIGERIAN POLITICS

It is in these deepening currents of disaffection, and not the familiar bugaboo of "tribalism," that the danger to the Second Republic lies. The major political conflicts of the Second Republic have been generated not by ethnic cleavage but by party, ideological and class interests. These areas of conflict are distinct; they have overlapped in both stable and fleeting ways, but they do not wholly coincide. More important, they have been substantially independent of ethnicity.

This has been most apparent in the class conflict that has dominated the politics of the North and reshaped national political alignments, but is also reflected in the national cleavage between what may broadly be termed "the political class" – the incumbents of state power and the businessmen and professionals who benefit directly from its largess – and the popular classes. This conflict embraces not only dominant class action, in the use of politics to accumulate wealth and consolidate class position, but also increasingly frequent and intense lower class action, which varies from the gathering inchoate, popular revulsion over the corruption and self-absorption of the politicians to a number of more focused actions. These have included the May 1981 general strike, a strike by electric power workers ten months later that crippled the federal capital, numerous other industrial actions, and an uprising at the construction site of the Bakalori Dam in Sokoto in which peasant squatters protesting the expropriation of their land were evicted by the government in a bloody struggle.[24]

Ideological cleavage has been reflected in the commitment to alternative programs and policy directions that has played an important role in drawing together the progressives against the NPN. Crude calculations of political opportunity and threat have also heavily motivated this realignment process, and the positioning on such issues as revenue allocation, Presidential Liaison Officers, and other questions of the federal-state balance of power, on which the one party in control of the center and the four outside it have predictably taken opposite sides. But if these party-based cleavages have been opportunistic, even shallow, they have nevertheless been largely independent of ethnicity. Indeed, the two resulting alignments cross ethnicity, region and religion more impressively than any previous coalitions in Nigerian political history.

Of course, there are always caveats. Some would find in these alignments new evidence of the historic tension between the Yoruba and Igbo professional elite on the one hand and the Fulani aristocratic elite on the other. But careful examination of the substance of these conflicts and the alignment of political actors simply cannot assign ethnicity *per se* much significance. Ethnic and religious cleavage no doubt played some role in the discomfort that the Plateau State NPN felt with the NPN-NPP accord, but a more important ethnic factor in the accord's collapse was the bitter political competition between prominent personalities of the two parties *within* Igboland, and Anambra in particular. This has been intraethnic, crosscutting cleavage. So have been the internecine struggles within the PRP and the GNPP. All of these conflicts have tapped political interests – whether of parties or factions – as a cleavage independent of ethnicity. They simply do not fit the model of those who would argue that ethnic conflict is once again undoing democratic politics.

In fact, the politics of the first civilian regime do not well fit that model either. At that time, ethnic conflict was politicized and manipulated by political elites in pursuit of their party and class interests – the entrenchment of power and the accumulation of wealth (Diamond 1983). Within each region radical ideological challenges were advanced, most notably by the Northern Elements Progressive Union. Invariably, these challenges were coopted, ruthlessly repressed or overwhelmed in a floodtide of politically generated "tribalism." This strategy of calculated tribalism has not been abandoned in the Second Republic; locally, it remains commonplace, and nationally, it has been evidenced in crude attempts to revive the darkest moments of Yoruba-Igbo enmity from the Civil War as the UPN and NPP have drawn toward alliance.

What demands explanation, then, is not why Nigerian politics has shifted from the politics of ethnicity to the politics of class, but more precisely, why ethnicity has become more difficult to employ as "a mask for class privilege" (Sklar 1967, p. 6), and why class cleavage has surfaced more explicitly in politics and popular consciousness as the manifest basis of political division and conflict.

Certainly the changes in political structure play an important role. As a result of the creation of a multistate federal system, the substantial centralization of state power, and the legal prohibition of sectional parties, "it is no longer possible for power groups at subnational levels to prevent democratic changes" by the arbitrary exercise of state authority or the political mobilization of ethnic identity (Sklar 1981, pp. 15-16). Indeed, it was this very fact, foreseen so clearly two decades ago, that led progressives in the First Republic so vigorously to oppose the regional system and conservatives steadfastly to obstruct its transformation (Sklar, 1965).

Even deeper are the changes that have transformed the Nigerian economy and society in the past two decades – the dramatic increases in education, mass communications, urbanization, and industrialization, and the attendant erosion of traditional, hierarchical authority relations. This process is ineluctable and, where it proceeds, class-based conflict follows. Perhaps the most striking correlation in the election returns – although it cannot be more than suggested from the available data – is the degree to which the parties who now constitute "the progressives" swept most of the major cities in Nigeria, while the NPN scored strongest in those areas of the countryside least penetrated by modernization. This pattern is clearest in the North, where the PRP performed best in the two most urban and industrial states, Kaduna and especially Kano. As economic and social modernization spread to other states in the far North, the grip of the traditional elite will weaken, freeing peasants, workers and independent producers and traders to align politically on the basis of their class interests. Increasing levels of literacy and urban experience are likely to increase their class consciousness and their propensity to act on it politically (Lubeck 1979a and b). Moreover, in Kano, where this process has developed furthest, the result appears to be a broad and potent *talakawa* class consciousness, uniting various lower class groups "under a common populist ideology of equity and justice for the 'people' " (Lubeck 1978, p. 45).

None of this means that ethnicity and ethnic conflict are suddenly unimportant in political and social life. Ethnicity remains the most basic current of social differentiation and conflict. Ethnic cleavage clearly remains a prominent force in politics, not only in the election campaigns, but in the internal dynamics of the political parties. This has been especially so in the nation's most ethnically diverse party, the NPN, where jockeying for party positions and power has mobilized ethnicity to a significant degree, and where a caucus of elected officials from ethnic minority states has vigorously pressed demands in party councils for a larger share of federal development projects for their states.[25]

In the first two years of the Second Republic, ethnicity has found its most significant political expression in the proliferating movements for new states, which find " 'new' minorities now suddenly claiming cultural, historical and ethnic differentiation from groups of which they had hither to been part and parcel" (Ojo 1981, p. 49). Here ethnicity interacts with party and class cleavages in subtle, complex, and familiar ways. New states will mean not only cultural and political autonomy, and more federal resources for ethnic and subethnic groups, but new statehouses, new political offices, and enormous, new panoplies of patronage for ethnic elites. Here the class interests of elites and ethnic interests of their groups may converge. New states, depending on how their boundaries are drawn, will also mean that some parties are weakened and others strengthened. Here party and ethnic interests may converge. This is to concede only one of several possible ways in which ethnicity may vigorously rebound into national politics.[26] But it is also to underscore that the way it is least likely to happen is by the route most popularly imagined – the sudden political explosion of mass-based cultural conflict or socioeconomic competition.

The fundamental change in Nigerian politics is this: although ethnicity persists as a salient political and social cleavage, it no longer organizes, much less polarizes, national political conflict. It no longer can be manipulated to block change and suppress dissent. It no longer looms as an imminent threat to the democratic future.

And yet, observing the rising bitterness and violence of politics in the Second Republic, it is difficult to summon a sanguine view of its future. Political intolerance is poison in a democracy, and halfway through the first term of the Second Republic, it had reached alarming proportions. Popular legitimacy is the lifeblood of any political system that rests on the consent of the governed, and this is seriously eroding. If ethnic conflict is not the source of the problem, what is?

It is important to stress first something else that is not. The *source* of the problem is not an undemocratic political culture. There is an undemocratic pattern of political behavior in the country, but this in itself begs the question rather than answers it. Opposing partisans are not vilifying and killing one another because they do not intrinsically value reason, moderation and the democratic process. Although conciliation and compromise are, admittedly, styles that need to be developed in this young regime that has followed 13 years of military rule, the tragedy of the Second Republic – and of the First – involves the degree to which so many politicians who do value democracy nevertheless lose sight of and abuse its necessary limits. There is something much more fundamental at work here than attitudes and values.

The basic problem of democracy in Nigeria is that no form of political competition can be expected to determine so completely the position of entire classes in society and the class position of individuals without a fierce and desperate struggle. No democratic process can mediate the whole distribution of socioeconomic resources without intense strain. In a context of widespread poverty and scarcity, probably no democracy can bear such a load for long and survive.

There are, then, two basic causes of fanaticism and decay in the Second Republic. One is new, the other is not. What is new is the growing polarization of class forces, emanating from the North but gradually encompassing the national political economy. The important role of this class cleavage in motivating the realignment into a two-party, or two-alliance, system is deeply ironic. Here, finally, is the decisive transcendence of the politics of ethnicity, the classic cross-cutting cleavage. And yet, the tone of the political conflict flowing from this, especially in the North, suggests that this cleavage may, in one sense, be cutting *too* deeply. As the broad amalgams of class and ideological interests are pitted against each other regularly and furiously in successive political conflicts, their competition becomes ever more polarized and resistant to compromise. This is, of course, precisely what the radicals seek: a heightening of the social and political contradictions. And it may be, on balance, a salutary turn of history for the Nigerian people. That is for Nigerians themselves to decide. What can be proffered from the limited wisdom of social science is the strong likelihood that such polarization will increase political intolerance and violence and reduce the Second Republic's chances of surviving. Its effects in this direction through the first 30 months of the Second Republic are difficult to dispute.

What is not new is everything else that is at stake in politics – the salaries and perquisites of office that constitute automatic elite status; the government contracts and import licenses that constitute, for both the awarders and the recipients, a primary means for the accumulation of wealth; the jobs, the commissions, the development projects, and all the other components of a desperately expectant people's aspirations; and, of course, the coercive machinery to consolidate control over all of this. In Nigeria, state power is today – only much more so – what it was two decades ago: the overwhelmingly dominant route of access to the resources and opportunities of class formation. If the articulation of the private sector in the past 15 years has opened possibilities for upward mobility outside the state that did not exist in the First Republic, so the petroleum boom has opened possibilities for accumulation of wealth in office that could not even have been imagined two decades ago. Moreover, the remarkable growth in power of the Nigerian state, which has "had to spearhead economic development in the absence of a strong indigenous capitalist class" (Ake 1981a, p. 1163), has proceeded to the point where, as Professor Ake has already been quoted here, "the Nigerian state appears to intervene everywhere and to own everything including access to status and wealth." Pervasive state control over the economy makes private business success, in principle, heavily dependent on political favor and connections; the continuing failure of the Nigerian bourgeoisie to invest in economically productive activity makes private business, in reality, virtually a hostage of the state. All of this makes the prospect of state power in the wrong hands a horrifying one to an emergent dominant class.

The implication for political behavior of this type of social structure remains in the Second Republic what it was in the First. Those who aspire to position in the dominant class must aspire to political power, and the basis of class formation in political power results in an extraordinary premium on political power (Sklar 1979; Diamond 1983). This high premium motivates what Ake (1973) has termed a preference for "efficiency norms to legitimacy norms" – a willingness to violate whatever legitimate methods of contestation appear to stand in the way of achieving power. The breakdown of constitutional norms, in the context of a high premium on power, generates the high levels of mutual fear and distrust – what Ake terms "political anxiety" – that have been observed in the Second Republic. Hence, "politics becomes warfare, a matter of life or death."

It is this political intolerance – the unwillingness to hear out the opposing position and allow it a fair opportunity to prevail, the reluctance to risk defeat in elections, the refusal, as Nigerians so often put it, "to play by the rules" – that constitutes the fundamental danger to democracy in the Second Republic. Astute observers inside and outside Nigerian politics recognize this with striking frequency, and yet they seem powerless to eradicate it. For as a phenomenon more fundamentally of class than political structure, it does not easily yield to constitutional innovations.

Even the imaginative and far-reaching changes in political structure that preceded the birth of the Second Republic have not been able to buffer it sufficiently from the social and economic pressures bearing down upon it. It is unlikely that the feverish temperature of Nigerian politics can be substantially reduced unless ways are found to reduce these pressures. In the long run, the pressure on political competition of a swollen state figures to recede if Nigeria's oil wealth can finally be invested in broad-based development and vigorous generation of indigenous private enterprise. The more private economic opportunities proliferate and become attractive and the less the life positions and aspirations of ordinary Nigerians depend on what they get from the state, the less anxious and desperate political competition will be. To some extent, this is merely to reiterate the classic thesis of a strong association between moderate partisanship and broad prosperity, between democratic stability and a large middle class (Lipset 1960, p. 51).[27]

The problem, as other authors in this volume address, is getting from a present riddled with inequality, stagnation and waste to such a future of broadly based and self-sustaining growth. Along the way, the class contradictions that are inevitable in the phase of development Nigeria has entered somehow must be faced. If this is to be done democratically, it can probably only be done gradually, but it must also be done in a way that brings meaningful change. This will require the achievement of what now seems most elusive – some minimum of mutual confidence, understanding and restraint between the competing political forces. Conservatives must be able to trust that their class interests will not be wholly trampled and dismantled in the event of their electoral defeat; progressives and radicals must be able to trust that a conservative government will not sabotage social reforms and repress popular mobilization by labor and other lower class groups.

Democracy requires compromise and patience. This is its great strength and also its great weakness. It may be that the social cleavage – the competing visions of distribution and development – now dividing "progressives" and "conservatives" in the Second Republic is too deep and too diffuse to be contained within a democratic framework. Certainly there are those at both extremes who wish for a more decisive resolution of the cleavage and others who simply wish for it to be removed from the wretched nastiness of politics. But because it springs from an inexorable historical process, it will remain at the forefront of political conflict in Nigeria for quite some time, whether politics remains within the Second Republic or reverts back to the military arena.

With all its frustrations and tensions and turbulence, the democratic process still appears to offer the best hope for peaceful change – for gradually accommodating the existing class structure to emergent populist pressures without massive bloodshed. Should the democratic alternative once again fail in Nigeria, a unique historical opportunity for peaceful and constitutional reform may well be lost. In that event, the options for the resolution of widening class conflicts would be tragically narrowed.

NOTES

The majority of references in this chapter may be found in the section entitled, "Current Works on Nigeria – Politics & Society."

1. Although the middle and upper classes have clearly enjoyed disproportionate access to higher education, rapid university expansion appears to have drawn in large numbers of students from lower-class families as well. Hence one study estimates that while the most privileged four percent of the population accounted for more than a quarter of university students in 1977-78, the lowest income group (80 percent of the population) nevertheless accounted for a majority of the students (Sahota 1980: Table A7).

2. For more detailed analysis of these trends and related changes in economy and society during military rule, see Diamond (1982a).

3. A solemn political goal for many Muslim Assemblymen from the North, this proposal for a separate arena of litigation for Muslims alarmed many non-Muslims as an apparent contradiction of the constitutional separation of religion and state. With the Assemblymen from Yorubaland – the most religiously pluralistic and tolerant area of the country – playing the crucial mediating role, the controversy was resolved in compromise (Laitin 1981).

4. Specifically, the Constitution (art. 65) requires that the executive committees of the parties include representatives from at least two-thirds of the states; that party membership be open to all Nigerians; that the party name, emblem and motto bear no ethnic or religious connotation; that all parties situate their headquarters in the Federal Capital; and that only parties may campaign for votes (Joseph 1981a, p. 17).

5. General Obasanjo's dim view of politicians became known at several points during the final year of the transition, as when "he told an interviewer there were only two kinds of politicians: those who do not know what they are talking about, and those who do know but deliberately deceive the public" (Phillips 1980, p. 20).

6. The others ranged from 19 percent to 45 percent for the NPP. It was alleged that the Inland Revenue Department "failed to process the tax papers for candidates of certain parties on time" (Koehn 1981, pp. 30 or 44).

7. The most striking instance of continuity was in the person of Alhaji Aliyu, Makaman Bida, the former deputy to NPC President and Northern Premier Sir Ahmadu Bello, and the highest ranking survivor of the NPC leadership, who served as the first Protem National Chairman of the NPN and, until his death in March of 1980, as the party's Grand Patron (Okadigbo 1981, pp. 21-22).

8. The Nigerian National Alliance of the First Republic – the electoral coalition of the NPC and the conservative, regionalist party of western premier Samuel Akintola – represented the first political attempt to unite conservative dominant-class elements in the North and South. Indeed, many of the leading Yoruba politicians in the late Chief Akintola's party are now prominent in the NPN. But the NPN constitutes a much more truly national party. Not only does it draw significantly from Igbo and northern minority politicians who were absent from the NNA coalition, but it includes integrally within the framework

of a single party Yoruba and southern minority politicians who were joined with the NPC in 1964 only in a loose, hierarchical and northern-dominated alliance of distinct sectional parties.

9. The debate about the character of the NPN turns not only on whether it is really dominated by a "Fulani oligarchy," but also on the extent to which it is a *captive* of the dominant class in Nigeria. Opponents label the NPN the party *of* the wealthy in Nigeria; proponents claim it is a "mixed-breed" party that unites rich and poor, peasant and professional, around a pragmatic program symbolized by its emblem of maize and a house, for food and shelter (Okadigbo 1980, pp. 21, 40-41). During the campaign, Alhaji Shagari repeatedly rejected charges that the NPN "belongs to the wealthy class . . . and will . . . protect the interests of that small minority at the expense of the masses," stating at one point: "The majority of the people in the NPN are the ordinary peasants in the country – that is a fact. . . . The fact that we have a lot of wealthy people does not mean that we are dominated by wealth" (Ojigbo 1980, p. 177).

10. The NPP split is discussed in Joseph (1978, p. 82, 1981a, p. 18), Ojo (1981, p. 50-51), and Kirk-Greene (1981, p. 35). These accounts trace the schism to the dissidents' opposition to Waziri Ibrahim's bid for the presidential nomination, favoring Dr. Azikiwe instead. But Chief Ogunsanya and other leaders of the current NPP insist that their opposition was to Waziri having both the presidential nomination and the party chairmanship and that they drafted Azikiwe to run only after the split became irreparable. Exaggerated fears on both sides of losing party control may have aggravated the personal and factional tension. It is also likely that "concern for the place of the Ibos in the new dispensation" of the Second Republic played an important role in Dr. Azikiwe's decision to endorse the dissident NPP faction and then accept its presidential nomination, reversing his earlier vow to remain above partisan alignment in the election (Ojo 1981, p. 50).

11. Middle Belt politicians play an instrumental role in the NPP leadership. Its original and current National Secretaries are both Middle Belt Christians (from Benue and Plateau, respectively), and its Governor in Plateau State, Solomon Lar, figures prominently in speculation for the 1983 Presidential election. (In addition, the NPP Chairman, Chief Adeniran Ogunsanya, is a Yoruba from Lagos.)

12. Mallam Aminu also appears to have alienated much of his potential non-Muslim base in the Middle Belt and South by aligning in the Constituent Assembly with the adherents of a Sharia Court of Appeal (Ojigbo 1980, pp. 184-186).

13. The identification by the NPN of food and agricultural policy as its "topmost priority" may be seen to reflect not only the nation's economic realities but also a political strategy that looks to the peasantry (rather than the urban popular classes) for its mass political base. By contrast, the more openly sympathetic stance of the UPN and PRP toward organized labor – emphatically endorsing "the right to strike, including the right to call a general strike and to organize sympathy strikes" (PRP 1979, p. 23) – reflects the prominence in their political strategies of the urban popular classes.

14. This characterization is roughly in agreement with that of Joseph (1978), who classifies the PRP and UPN as "centre-left," with the former being more socialist and the latter "Nigerian Welfarist" or "New Deal," and the other three parties as "centre-right." This penetrating assessment explores the significant ideological tensions within these parties, for example, between the socialist principles in the PRP platform and the more moderate "democratic humanism" of the PRP leader Aminu Kano. Recognizing the PRP as the most "class-based party," he nevertheless notes that several more truly socialist parties failed to obtain registration. He further distinguishes the NPN as the most consistent with the longstanding strategy of Nigerian conservatives of an "equal division of the national cake" among ethnic groups (as opposed to individual equality). This strategy, which delivers the goods of development through elite "sons of the soil" preserves the "basic patron-client relations of Nigerian society."

15. As Koehn (1981, pp. 36-41) demonstrates, one party dominated the voting in 17 of the 19 states, winning a majority of the seats or popular vote, typically a huge majority, in each of the five rounds of voting. Only in Kaduna, where an NPN edge in the other elections was offset by a PRP gubernatorial victory, and in Gongola, where the GNPP won only pluralities in a tight three-way race, was the pattern broken.

16. This interpretation is reinforced by the considerable improvement (five percentage points) that chief Awolowo registered in the Presidential election over his Party's showing in the Senatorial voting – a feat that no other Presidential candidate achieved (Table 2.1). Dudley (1981, p. 286), however, dismisses the likelihood that those factors could have generated such an overwhelming vote, suggesting that "the most plausible explanation . . . would seem to lie in a fairly large-scale rigging of the vote."

17. See Ollawa (1981, pp. 300-304) for an explanation of the electoral alignments of the minority states.

18. As further evidence of movement toward a more cross-ethnic pattern of political identification, Whitaker (1981, p. 10) cites such other features of the election outcome as the following: that no party won all the elected posts within its cultural area, state or region; that no party failed to win a significant number of its votes outside its cultural area, state and region (a conclusion one might dispute for the PRP); that no party scored a majority or plurality nationally merely by virtue of victory in its home cultural area, state or region; and that of the parties associated with the three major ethnic groups, only the Yoruba party (UPN) could be said to have become more parochial.

19. Two months later a new bill passed identical to the old one save that the allocation to the states was increased 3.5 percentage points and that of the center reduced by a corresponding amount (*West Africa* December 14, 1981, p. 3012).

20. From the very beginning, Mallam Aminu has been far more keenly sensitive to the position of traditional rulers in society than the younger, more radical elements in the PRP. Soon after the Kano riot he traveled to Katsina to pay his respects to the new Emir, one of the North's most important traditional rulers.

21. The following details of intrastate political conflicts are drawn primarily from *West Africa* (various issues, 1981-82), in particular Olu Akinyeye's

series on politics in the States, "Towards '83," published during the first half of 1982.

22. Shortly after the impeachment of the Kano Deputy Governor this was evidenced anew when the Kaduna Legislature threatened to impeach *both* the new Governor and the new Deputy Governor over the former's refusal to sign a bill creating new local governments (*West Africa* January 25, 1982, p. 276).

23. "The fact that the matter was being pushed at the time when the government was appealing for wage restraint and refusing to end the wage freeze imposed by the military made the legislators all the more unpopular" (*West Africa* April 19, 1982, p. 1051).

24. The several thousand peasant families seized the site after appeals to numerous sources of both modern and traditional authority failed to bring what they considered fair compensation for their land (Katsina 1981). Though the government has officially acknowledged the deaths of no more than a dozen or so peasants, PRP leaders maintain that more than a thousand peasants were killed and buried in mass graves, and the incident has become a cause célèbre in the national political struggle between "the progressives" and the incumbent government.

25. The caucus began meeting in the first half of 1980 with prominent NPN politicians from Bendel, Benue, Cross River, and Rivers States. However, it was not until these politicians gathered later that year in Makurdi for the funeral of Senator Joseph Tarka – who had been a moving force in the effort and a long-time critic of majority group dominance in Nigeria – that they resolved to develop their consultations into a regular, ongoing caucus. Inadequate development of roads and insufficient siting of industries in their states were among their leading concerns at the outset. Instances of open conflict between ethnic minority and majority leaders within the NPN are documented in Elaigwu (1981, pp. 40-41). The ethnic competition and bargaining within the NPN is further reflected in its "zoning" distribution of major national offices and nominations. This in itself is a source of tension: while President Shagari is expected to be renominated in 1983, some NPN politicians from western states are jockeying for the NPN presidential nomination with the expectation that it is now their "turn," and a major test of the arrangement and of the coherence of the party, will almost surely come in 1987 (if not 1983) when there will be no incumbent candidate.

26. The intractable problem of the national census will likely be another, although for this very reason it will probably be postponed until after the election.

27. Lipset's (1960, pp. 27-63) rich articulation of this thesis more than two decades ago retains a stunning relevance for contemporary Nigerian society. The following propositions ring especially true in the current Nigerian context:

> A belief in secular reformist gradualism can be the ideology of only a relatively well-to-do lower class (p. 45).
>
> The poorer a country and the lower the absolute standard of living of the lower classes, the greater the pressure on the upper strata to treat the lower as vulgar, innately inferior, a lower caste beyond the pale

of human society. The sharp difference in the style of living between those at the top and those at the bottom makes this psychologically necessary. Consequently, the upper strata in such a situation tend to regard political rights for the lower strata, particularly the right to share power, as essentially absurd and immoral. The upper strata not only resist democracy themselves; their often arrogant political behavior serves to intensify extremist reactions on the part of the lower classes (p. 51).

The general income level of a nation also affects its receptivity to democratic norms. If there is enough wealth in the country so that it does not make too much difference whether some redistribution takes place, it is easier to accept the idea that it does not matter greatly which side is in power. But if loss of office means serious losses for major power groups, they will seek to retain or secure office by any means available (p. 51).

3

INCOME DISTRIBUTION AND POLITICS IN NIGERIA

Henry Bienen

It is rather daunting to try to analyze the political economy of income distribution in Nigeria. More so than in many developing countries, the availability of data collected in the past and the present availability of relevant data constitutes one of the most serious obstacles to analysis. The scope of income data being collected in Nigeria is hardly amenable to rigorous statistical analysis. We do not even have an accepted population census. Almost no national aggregate data exist for the rural sector that would allow us to make a confident judgment about intrasectoral income distribution. The Agricultural Census of 1975 still has not been made widely available. Thus we have to rely on work done by scholars from their studies of specific areas in Nigeria to give us some understanding of rural sector differentiations. There is, of course, some aggregate data collected by the national government and especially for the urban and industrial sectors. The Nigerian government has been carrying out surveys through the Household Survey Unit of the Federal Office of Statistics, and consumption and expenditure surveys exist for the 1970s.[1]

Beyond difficulties with the data (and there are no societies for which we have data that satisfy us for all measures and aspects of income distribution), our ability to stipulate causes and to isolate political and economic effects when we analyze equity issues is not convincing. There are no widely accepted theories of income distribution across time and place that we can apply to specific countries.

Furthermore, Nigeria is an extremely heterogeneous society. We cannot expect that culturally associated understandings of wealth and poverty and the ways that people are grouped will necessarily be the same throughout the country. Thus if we want to try to understand the import of interpersonal, interstate, and intersectoral income distinctions, this necessitates sensitivity to the variety of meanings attached to wealth and poverty and inequality in different parts of Nigeria. For some areas we do have extremely detailed empirical work on the relationships of social values to social structural variables such as patterns of landholding and stratification (Hill 1977), the relationship between fertility and attitudes (Caldwell 1976), and perceptions of inequality as related to occupational data (Imoagene 1976; Lloyd 1974). The more we look at specific studies, the more we learn to be careful about generalizing any discussion of the political variables that pertain to equity issues in Nigeria and the more we learn to take great care in our use of terms like class and ethnicity to discuss distinctions within Nigeria.

With these caveats, I do want to draw a rough picture of inequality in Nigeria and then try to briefly understand the political implications of inequality.

INEQUALITY IN NIGERIA

A number of tentative studies do give various measures of concentration of income for Nigeria or for parts of Nigeria and they show a high concentration of income. Teriba and Phillips (1971), using the data from the income tax returns of 1966/67 in the former Western State, put the concentration coefficient at .47.[2] Aboyade (1973) in a survey of 1,635 households conducted in 1967 in all states except three of the then Eastern Region found a concentration ratio of .58. Fajana (1979), using the tax returns of 1965/66 and 1970/71 of taxpayers who paid withholding taxes (Pay as You Earn) of the former Western State calculated coefficients of .51 and .53 respectively. Omorogiuwa (1982), using personal income tax data (which includes self-employed as well as P.A.Y.E. taxpayers), calculated before tax Gini coefficients for Bendel State of .39 in 1965/66, .515 in 1970/71 and .39 in 1971/72. For the Western State the corresponding figures were .37, .28 and .31.

A number of scholars doing cross-national studies have presented measures of income inequality for Nigeria at an earlier period too. Thus Adelman and Morris (1971) present data for Nigeria showing the richest 5 percent accounting for over 38 percent of income, and the poorest 20 percent accounting for 7 percent. Odufalu (1981) gives the poorest 34 percent of the taxpayers about 7 percent of the income and concludes that the degree of inequality in Nigeria has been widening. Etim and Erontini (1979), averaging the years 1969-72, get a figure for all Nigerians of the poorest 20 percent close to Adelman and Morris; the poorest 60 percent get about 4 percent more income than their figures and the richest 20 percent get less than Adelman and Morris showed. A problem in making comparisons is that taxpayers may be compared to income earners, or P.A.Y.E. taxpayers may be compared to all taxpayers, including the self-employed who understate their earnings significantly.

Diejomaoh and Anusionwu (1981a) review the literature and examine the different uses of sources by investigators and the variety of data bases employed. They conclude that past studies have very serious limitations. They argue that there is good reason to believe that the different states in Nigeria may not have similar distributions of personal income and thus we cannot generalize from studies done in southern Nigeria to the whole country. From their own analysis, Diejomaoh and Anusionwu suggest a widening of income inequalities in the modern wage employment sector from 1960-70. Contrary to expectations, the Udolji wage review produced a worsening of income distribution in the public sector. Around 1975-76, they found a trend to sharp inequality in the modern sector after a moderate degree of inequality in the 1960s. They see interpersonal income distribution nationwide moving from a Gini index of about .5 in 1960 to about .6 in 1969 and perhaps above .7 in 1975/76. They then see a decline in inequality after 1976 as a result of sluggish performance in the modern sector and especially the oil sector in 1978 and a rise in agricultural production of about 3 percent in 1976/77. With the renewed boom in oil prices in 1979/80, income inequality might be increasing again.

Oil emerges as a critical factor in producing income inequality through a sharp increase in the differentials of labor productivity and per capita income between rural and urban populations. Without oil, according to Diejomaoh and Anusionwu, the Kuznets ratios (labor productivity in the nonagricultural sector divided by labor productivity in agriculture) would have been about 3 in 1975 instead of above 5. Nigeria would have been toward the lower end of the range of inequality for developing countries without the oil factor, although inequality would have increased in any case even without the oil boom in the 1970s, since per capita urban incomes still would have increased much faster than per capita rural incomes. It has been the public expenditure pattern of the Nigerian government fueled by oil revenues that has led to maldistributive effects on the Nigerian economy.

There are, of course, many problems in analyzing interpersonal income distributions, even apart from the data and intertemporal comparison difficulties. For one thing, interregional and interstate inequality has been very marked. Indeed, interregional distribution was better documented than intersectoral or household shares of income throughout the 1950s and 1960s (Rimmer 1981). Estimates of regional GDP per capita in 1950/51 showed a higher figure for the West than for the North or East. Political actors in Nigeria were aware at that time that regional inequality in income per capita was low compared to other disparities measured such as enrollments in schools, telephone services, hospital beds provided, and so forth. The demonstrable disparities between concrete and visible services and projects were politically more significant than differences in regional income per capita. Political struggles in Nigeria centered on where the Federal Government would invest or distribute services and whether revenue allocation formulas would work to the detriment or benefit of various regions and then states. There would not be much dispute that political struggles over distribution in Nigeria for the first decade or so of independent rule were largely defined in regional and ethnic terms.

There has been a continuation of disparities between states. While the disparities have narrowed in some areas – for example, in per capita electricity consumption – they have remained or even widened in others. Inequality of access to financial markets is very pronounced, and as the Nigerian economy becomes more developed, this becomes an important future determinant of distribution (Teriba 1981, pp. 492-93). Similarly, Lagos continues to increase its share of national industrial output.

The massive Universal Primary Education program has increased enrollments in all states, but, despite large strides made in Benue-Plateau, the northern states remain far behind. The gap in certain states' enrollments as a ratio of national average has lessened in primary schooling, but the secondary school enrollment gaps remain huge. Thus in 1977-78 the Northwestern State's primary school enrollment was .46 of the national average and the corresponding figure for secondary school enrollment was .34. In the Northeastern State the figures were .70 and .16 respectively (Diejomaoh and Anusionwu 1981b).

Urbanization has been proceeding rapidly in Nigeria, and rates have been very high not only in Lagos and the larger cities but in new state capitals and medium sized cities like Ilorin, Jos, and Port Harcourt. For wage earners and the self-employed, however, wages were highest in the former states of Lagos, East Central, West, Mid-West, Southeast and Rivers (Ayeni 1981, p. 249).

It is not clear then that urbanization and industrialization are narrowing gaps between states or that deliberate policies of investment and educational development are bringing this about. Analysis of investments by the Nigerian Industrial Development Bank shows the heavy concentration of projects in Lagos and the former states of the West. This is also true for the mortgages of the Federal Mortgage Bank and the lending operations of the Nigerian Bank for Commerce and Industries (Teriba 1981).

The proportionate representation of particular ethnic groups in the top 20 percent and the bottom 30 percent of asset holders in Nigeria varies enormously. Wealth in Nigeria is concentrated in the southwest and in the oil producing areas; the poorest areas tend to be neither Moslem nor Christian. The Moslem North occupies an intermediate position. I will discuss the implications of this for the politics of ethnicity below. Before so doing, it is necessary to present a rough picture of sectoral and intrasectoral income differentiations so that we can also assess the ramifications of class politics in Nigeria.

Observers of Nigeria's economy have noted the rapid growth of the urban and industrial sectors, the relatively poor performance of agriculture, and the widening gap between rural and urban incomes. The absence of hard data on rural intrasectoral income distribution has made it difficult to quantify the impact of rural inequality on the total distribution of income in Nigeria. Policies aimed at income redistribution have focused on incomes within the urban sector rather than on urban to rural redistribution or within rural redistributions for a number of reasons. Politically, urban to rural redistributions would be difficult to implement. Moreover, the direction of the economy, even without the oil impact, has accentuated rural-urban differences in per capita income as a result of the development and expenditure policies of the Nigerian government. Government would have to revise fundamentally its policies to alter the trend of increasing rural-urban inequality.

Policymakers can hope to lessen urban inequality through wages and salaries, which are the most sensitive aspects of incomes policy. By contrast, with about 70 percent of the Nigerian population still living in rural areas, it is difficult to carry out income redistribution by urban to rural income flows. Thus while all observers have been conscious of lower average incomes in rural areas, of literacy rates in rural areas half those in urban areas, of relatively small amounts of investment, both public and private in the rural sector, political pressures, the availability of data, and a sense of what can be done have all worked to keep the focus of attention on intraurban questions pertaining to relative income shares.

The Third Five Year Plan, published in March 1975, emphasized not only an increase in income but a more even distribution. It stressed, however, that delivery of welfare through subsidized public services would be a primary mechanism for bringing about more even distributions. The Guidelines to the Third Plan, published in September 1973, argued that a community of 20,000 was the size above which basic amenities should be delivered. Although reduction in disparities between rural and urban areas was an aspect of balanced development, it was one not easily reconciled with the desire to use social services and public utilities for the relief of poverty when delivery of those services and utilities was to go to communities above 20,000. The Third Plan also called for provision of overhead capital to smaller communities and for measures to raise agricultural productivity, but there was to be no frontal assault on rural-urban imbalances.

The Second Plan (1970-74) had put over 80 percent of total planned investments in the urban areas. Nigerian Federal Government expenditures on agriculture went from a figure of 0.5 percent of current expenditures in 1971 to 1.4 percent in 1975. The Federal Government's capital expenditure on agriculture went from a 1971 figure of 4.8 percent to 6.0 percent in 1975. Government was not trying very hard to alter the rural-urban trend.

Many observers have assumed a rough equality within the rural sector so that less concern has been manifested with regard to rural inequalities. The view has been that Nigeria does not have a high concentration of land ownership. Significant numbers are landless or tenant farmers. Nigeria is overwhelmingly a country of smallholders on the land, but there are major distinctions between cashcrop farmers and largely subsistence farmers, and between farmers who produce for export and those who produce for internal markets. With the growth of the internal market, former exports like groundnuts and palm oil are being consumed domestically and cocoa remains the major crop that is produced largely for export.

This rough-and-ready view of the rural sector is confirmed by macro and micro studies. Diejomaoh and Anusionwu (1981a) conclude that in relative terms the best distribution is in the agricultural sector and the worst is in manufacturing and transport sectors. There has been relatively little commercialization of land in rural Nigeria except on the fringes of important urban centers. Nigeria has not had a large and visible rural "land problem."

Matlon (1981a) has provided us with a detailed and comprehensive picture of size distribution of income from an analysis of survey data from three villages. The picture he provides cannot be said to be representative for all of rural Nigeria, of course, but the study villages were generally representative of northern Nigeria. Compared to estimates obtained by rural surveys conducted elsewhere in Nigeria, a generally high degree of income inequality was found. The Gini coefficient calculated on income per capita was .28 and the ratio of mean per capita income between poorest and richest deciles was 1:5. From a national perspective, however, the average level of income was so low that even the richest households included in this survey would be considered among the relatively poor in Nigeria. In other words, Matlon shows us a relative degree of rural equality compared to the urban sector in Nigeria and a generalized poverty that prevails.

Urban inequalities, on the other hand, have struck all observers of Nigeria, including the ruling elites. One can see these inequalities in wage structures within the urban formal sector and between the urban formal and informal sectors. And one can see these inequalities in housing, access to services, and generalized life styles.

When we turn our view to the urban sector, we have a fairly good idea of the size, structure and operation of formal sector labor markets. The informal sector is much less well documented in Nigeria as in most developing countries. The public sector in Nigeria has accounted for more than half of modern sector employment. Within this modern sector, there is a small but important class of self-employed, relatively high income earning professionals. The informal sector covers a wide range of occupations. There are few barriers in the form of educational qualifications or capital requirements for entry. Most migrants who move from rural to urban areas enter the informal sector. They may move up in income within this sector through apprenticeships and through accumulation of some capital through savings. A few may even become large traders or transporters. Overwhelmingly, most remain in the informal sector and are not able to move into either modern sector ownership or employment.

Mobility within the modern sector is determined largely by intrasectoral differentials in earnings and employment opportunities. Movement from public to private sectors or between occupations has been shaped only in part by market forces. Institutional forces have been expressed through trade unions and especially through the pressures by public sector employees on wage commissions (Rimmer 1981; Fajana 1981). Demands by labor have not been for redistribution but for more wages in absolute terms and for better standards of living.

Between 1963-1974, labor's share in industrial value added never exceeded 26 percent. Labor did poorly in Nigeria during the initial period of military intervention and the subsequent Civil War. A freeze was imposed on wages and The Trade Disputes Decree of 1968 made some types of strike actions illegal. Nigeria continued to have strikes and work stoppages even under restrictive legislation during military rule, but it is clear that times of crises impaired labor's ability to increase its share of total value. Much of the ground lost by labor between 1965 and 1970 was regained in 1970-74 (Fajana 1981, p. 196).

It is important to note that total industrial wages rose more than five fold from 1963 to 1974. Labor was able to protect itself during a period of inflation by getting catch-up wage increases through wage commission recommendations. Neither the informal sector nor the rural sector was able to protect itself to the same degree. The intersectoral earnings gap widened between 1964 and 1972. The bottom layer of the formal sector is composed of those employed in small establishments, but for the urban sector as a whole, the bottom layer is from the self-employed in the informal sector. In 1975, in urban Nigeria, the low income self-employed had an average monthly income that amounted to 62 percent of average income of the *lowest* paid wage earners (Fajana 1981, p. 225).

Income differentials are extremely skewed within the self-employed group, but overwhelmingly, the self-employed comprise the lowest income group in the urban sector. The lowest level of the self-employed do get somewhat greater incomes from imputed rents and from their consumption of their own production, but the figures do not change significantly. The middle and upper levels of the self-employed do better than wage earners within upper and middle categories (Ayeni 1981, p. 247). There is a great deal of variation by state for the average income of the self-employed both as a share of average income of wage earners and in absolute terms, but in 1975 only in one state in Nigeria, the Rivers State, was the average urban income of the lowest self-employed higher than the lowest level of wage earners (Ayeni 1981, p. 251).

When we look at interindustry and occupational differentiations, no great surprises appear from the Nigerian data. From 1963 until 1970 there was a narrowing of interindustry earnings differentials and since then a reversing of that trend (Fajana 1981, pp. 200-201). There was stability of the industrial wage hierarchy beween industries. Differentials can be attributed to differences in productivity levels. Average earnings of workers with complete primary education is about 1.7 times that of illiterates; workers with secondary education had average earnings about 1.6 times the level of primary school graduates and 2.7 times that of illiterates, whereas university graduates had average earnings about 12 times that of illiterates and about 4.5 times the level of secondary school graduates. The lifetimes' stream of earnings of university graduates compared to illiterates is about 25:1. The relative gaps among Nigerians with disparate levels of education narrowed from the 1960s to the 1970s (Diejomaoh and Anusionwu 1981b, p. 385).

Nonmarket forces also have helped to account for productivity distinctions. Government protection of certain industries has been important. In the drive to industrialize, Nigeria encouraged foreign firms to establish industries through tariff concessions, tax advantages and an overvalued currency. Large scale establishments benefited more than small ones, accounting for their relatively high capital intensity and labor productivity. Protection has also allowed relatively high prices for certain goods.

Nigeria does show some compression of earnings between 1963-1974. During this period, average earnings of non-Nigerians as a percentage of all employees' average earnings fell. Also during this period, there was movement toward compressing earnings between professional/managerial and clerical employees. The higher the average earnings of a group, the lower the percentage increases in its earnings. The bulk of income share lost by professional and managerial personnel went to manual workers. Clerical personnel held their shares. Within the Nigerian civil service, wide differentials obtain between grades, but they are declining. Indeed, a federal government permanent secretary's wages were reduced from 36 to 17 times that of an unskilled laborer's between 1954 and 1975 (Fajana 1981, pp. 210 and 215). This is still more than five times the gap in Britain and if fringe benefits were included the Nigerian gap would look even larger. In 1977/78, incomes policy guidelines allowed for higher wage increases at lower salary levels.

Summing up, it is clear that so far people in the rural sector and the urban informal sector have done less well through Nigeria's industrialization than those in industrial employment. Not much progress has been made in reducing the level of urban unemployment or in achieving a more equitable distribution of income. The situation is not an unrelievedly negative one, however. Individuals migrate to cities in Nigeria overwhelmingly because of perceived economic opportunities (Sada 1981). Significant investments are made by urban migrants back in their rural areas. Of course, the wider exchange between rural and urban areas includes terms of trade between them and the ways that government revenues are used for investment and welfare benefits. The Federal Government is still investing overwhelmingly in urban compared to rural areas given population size in the two sectors, and most of its expenditures tend to accentuate gaps in income distribution.

Nigeria, then, follows a pattern common to many developing countries. There has been rapid growth in GNP and especially in the manufacturing sector. Urbanization has been proceeding at very high rates even compared to most developing countries. Employment in the modern sector, however, has not kept pace. Thus a huge informal sector has been created. The impressionistic view held by many Nigerians and non-Nigerians that the oil boom of the 1970s has led to a worsening of the equity picture does seem substantiated, but there are qualifications to this statement. High rates of inflation since 1975 probably affected the urban informal sector worst of all since formal sector employees were better able to protect themselves, and people in the rural sector were more insulated by being able to provide themselves with foodstuffs and housing than those who lived in urban areas. Nevertheless, we do find a compression of money wages within the formal sector. Migration from rural areas to the urban informal sector may be depressing incomes in that sector, but labor markets seem discontinuous enough in Nigeria and/or protected by institutional means to the extent that the labor pool in the informal sector does not depress formal sector wages.

With economic development, Nigeria's income distribution initially became increasingly unequal as educational development advanced. The 1970s as compared to the 1960s, however, witnessed a reduction in income disparities between individuals with different levels of education. Current Nigerian levels of income in relation to educational differentials are comparable to those in other developing countries. In general, Nigeria's situation does not appear to be one of a general and unequivocally rapid worsening of income distribution despite rapid growth in GNP, industrial output, and urbanization, and a weak agricultural sector, plus an oil boom, pumping large new revenues into the economy.

POLITICAL IMPLICATIONS

It has been argued that political competition in Nigeria would shift from its former ethnic or communal base to a more class-oriented competition once the Nigerian Federal Republic of three then four regions was turned into a Federation of twelve and then nineteen states. Indeed, the creation of more states in conjunction with a centralization of authority under military regimes who have controlled large new oil revenues shifted the focus of distributional debates away from the states and regions to some extent. After a civilian regime returned to power in late 1979, however, revenue allocation between the Federal government and the states and among the states continued to be a major issue. A clear shift to class and sectoral terms of reference is not now taking place and is not likely to take place in the future in Nigeria in any simple and straightforward fashion.

In "objective" terms Nigeria is forming classes, but most Nigerians do not perceive classes forming. Survey analysis shows a small but positive correlation between status and evaluations of how well a respondent has fared and his expectations for the future. But variations in perceptions of equity in society do not have any significant relation to the respondent's actual status. Survey analysis supports political and institutional analysis that Nigerians are not likely to be mobilized widely on the basis of class membership or status grounds.[3] Similarly, the elections of 1979 do not support the view that class-based parties have emerged in Nigeria.

It is true, of course, that parties that called themselves socialist such as the Nigerian Workers' and Peasants' Vanguard Movement either were not allowed to contest or never went through the final process before the Federal Elections Commission in order to register. Thus, no explicitly workers' party contended. Although elements within the Unity Party of Nigeria (UPN) and the Peoples Redemption Party (PRP) saw their parties as socialist, it would be more accurate to see these parties as populist. For while the UPN called its ideology socialist and argued that free education, free medical care, rural integrated development and full employment could only come about in a socialist system,[4] all parties declared for the provision of more services, especially health, education and housing. The emphasis was more on service delivery than on direct redistribution of personal incomes. Spokesmen for the UPN accused the National Party of Nigeria of being led by capitalists. Indeed, the NPN, led by Shehu Shagari, was clearly more conservation in tone. The UPN, however, also called for a lifting of a ban on import controls and for removing government restrictions on trade and commercial activities. It thus tried to appeal to businessmen, too. Indeed, at the very time that the UPN renewed its pledge to introduce a minimum income of 2,500 naira per annum for workers and farmers within its first term four year government if elected, it also announced its intention to let Nigerians invest and establish new businesses. During the campaign, the UPN seemed at times suspicious of state controls.[5]

The PRP did call for the state to take the commanding heights of the economy and its manifestos were more conventionally socialist than the other parties although many ideas remained highly general in its programs. It, like the other parties, avoided getting into details on the old vexing issue of revenue allocation between the states and between the Federal Government and the states. The PRP tried to paint the NPN as a party committed to restoration of the powers of traditional leaders (Panter-Brick 1981).

Though there were programmatic distinctions between the parties and though they campaigned all over Nigeria, their strengths were less that of programmatic appeal to economic strata than the appeals of personality and ethnic coalition building. Nonetheless, given the history of Nigeria's elections, it was no small task that parties tried to campaign nationally and that they were able to hold rallies and to operate outside their base areas.

The data on the Federal and state elections of 1979 leave much to be desired. Without having a better sense of the relationship between census districts and constituencies, and in the absence of voter surveys, it would be extremely risky to relate voting to income and occupational patterns. However, the ethnic patterns of the 1979 elections do emerge rather clearly. Even a cursory glance at the electoral data shows how heavily dependent each party was on its core constituency. The UPN won twenty out of its twenty-eight Senate seats in the four states of the old Western Region: Ondo, Oyo, Ogun and Lagos. These are all predominantly Yoruba areas. The UPN won four more seats in Bendel, parts of which have some Yoruba speakers, although non-Yoruba UPN candidates won in non-Yoruba areas in Bendel State. Old party alliances were more important than ethnicity in Bendel State. Yorubas won two seats in Kwara State which has a significant Yoruba population. The Great Nigerian Peoples Party (GNPP) won half of its eight Senate seats in its home area, Bornu, and two more in the contiguous Gongola State. Two GNPP Senate seats were won in Cross River, where there are no significant numbers of Kanuris but where the GNPP state chairman was strong. The same pattern holds for Nigerian Peoples Party (NPP) and PRP Senate seats. The latter won five seats in its home Kano State and two more in contiguous Kaduna State, both states where old hostilities against the Sokoto Emirate prevail and where the former NEPU was strong. Of the NPP's 16 Senate seats, ten were won in the two Igbo states, Imo and Anambra. The NPP victories in Plateau State were not Igbo-based but were won through electoral alliances with Plateau leaders. Only the NPN showed strong support throughout the country in legislative elections, winning State Assembly seats in seventeen out of nineteen states and coming in first or second in all but six of the ninety-five Senate races.

The presidential results tell the same tale. Awolowo's vote was overwhelming in the Yoruba speaking states. He also pulled heavily in Bendel and Kwara, states with Yoruba populations. The vote for Azikiwe and the NPP was heavily based in Igbo-speaking areas. Waziri Ibrahim's GNPP vote was widely spread but a majority was received in Bornu State where Kanuris dominate.

The NPN had the broadest base of support, winning heavy majorities outside of the old Northern Region in Rivers and Cross River States. Indeed, the NPN was able to do well outside of the "dry" North or "Holy North," that is, outside of dominant Hausa-Fulani areas, by getting more than a third of the vote in Gongola State and Bendel State and Plateau State. However, the latter has about one-third Hausa-Fulani population, and without knowing the constituency breakdown of the vote, I cannot correlate NPN voting with ethnicity. It is clear, however, that the NPN received more votes than Hausa-Fulani population share in Niger State and Kwara State and less than the Hausa-Fulani share in Kano and Kaduna States since the PRP took votes in those two states.

The NPN was able to draw its support both from Moslem and non-Moslem areas of the country. The NPN had to share Moslem votes in the North with the PRP and the GNPP who were also led by Moslems, Mallam Aminu Kano and Alhaji Waziri Ibrahim. In the South, the UPN did well with Moslem voters in Yorubaland.

There are very good reasons that Nigeria's contemporary politics have not been dominated by class based organizations. In the First Republic, political competition and economic strategies were not defined primarily in income strata, class or functional terms. The overt political struggles in Nigeria were largely defined in regional and ethnic terms. An examination of the literature on the organization, operation, and functioning of ruling political parties, their manifestos, and the ideologies of party leaders in the 1950s and 1960s fails to demonstrate any translation from general statements to policies in order to deal with inequality in programmatic terms. None of the major political parties that controlled national or regional governments in the 1950s and up to 1966 could be called socialist parties or parties strongly committed to equity issues. Even major opposition parties, some of whom had distinctive social compositions, were not organized on a class basis and did not structure their opposition primarily on a platform of redistribution.

It is a large generalization but perhaps not too inaccurate to say that ruling civilian elites, both former party politicians and civil servants, and military officers who have ruled Nigeria since 1966, have been committed to economic strategies which focused on overcoming underdevelopment and increasing Nigerian control of the economy. Distributional issues were raised during civilian rule prior to 1966 but they were raised in terms of revenue allocations between regions and then states. Until very recently, less attention has been paid to income distribution as a matter of rural-urban cleavage or as between groups defined in either income, occupational, or class terms. Although Nigeria has had periods in its history (such as during the First Republic) when welfare politics were salient, the primary meaning of distribution and welfare was in terms of the division of public resources among territorial units. Many factors have led to the ascendance of ethnic-territorial criteria for distribution: general poverty; the introduction of electoral politics; the attempt to mobilize support by appeals to communal blocs; the weakness of class groups given the relative lack of differentiation within the Nigerian economy of the 1950s and 1960s; and ideas of welfare that stressed raising absolute levels rather than interstrata comparisons (Rimmer 1981).

Arguments have also been made that elite commitment to communal politics – to competition structured in communal/ethnic terms – has been a mask for the maintenance of class privilege in Nigeria. That is, elites have deliberately fostered ethnic competition to obscure exploitation of one class by another. We would still have to account for the reasons that elites were successful in so doing even if we accept that explanation. We can start with the proposition that Nigerian elites were based in their separate regional entities. Even those who operated in national arenas had regional party bases for their national power. Their ability to operate at the center of power in Nigeria depended on maintaining regional power and building regional constituencies. One major shift that took place when the military took power in 1966 was that the armed forces personnel, although split by ethnic origin and having ties to ethnic groups, had a national institutional base of power. The segment of the armed forces that tried to create a regional base failed when Biafra collapsed.

Class issues did not dominate organized party politics before and after military rule because of the complexity of those politics, which in turn reflected the complexity of Nigerian society in ethnic/communal terms as well as in occupational/class terms. Populist parties could be conservative as when they upheld the importance of chieftaincy. Communal appeals were made as regionally based parties contended with each other, and they were also made to offset the potential appeal of radicalism to lower class elements. The fact is that conservative and communal appeals were frequently successful.

It should be no surprise that there has been no clear movement from ethnic to class identifications and that ethnicity has remained an important organizing tool for party politics in Nigeria. It is true that during the military period communal politics became less overt and the nineteen states became less significant bases of power than the old regions were. The social composition and occupational structure of society have changed since 1960. Occupational differentiation has proceeded; the industrial working class is growing in size although it is still a small part of the urban employed. The commercial and business sectors have expanded as the parastatal and public sector organizations have strengthened. That is, the growth of the private business sector and the middle class in private employment have gone on along with the growth of the state sector.

Different observers, examining the same "facts" have concluded that state capitalism is proceeding in Nigeria or that Nigeria is becoming a private capitalist dominated state; that Nigeria is becoming a socialist state rarely has been argued. Perhaps more significant than the debate over what label to put on Nigeria has been the disagreement over the kinds and intensities of pressures that are building from below for egalitarian change.

Studies of Nigeria give us a very complicated picture of the relationship between class and communal interests as expressed in behaviors during strikes, trade union organizing, demands for better work conditions, employment, job security, and wages. Microstudies of workers in Nigeria indicate that there is great variation in the relationship between ethnicity and class and in the development of class consciousness. The variables that appear explanatory include the specific issue of protest, the structures available through which people compete, the ethnic homogeneity or heterogeneity of the labor force, and place of residence. That is, the kind of city, pattern of migration, place where the industrial work force is recruited from and its relationship both to rural areas and to the informal sector are all significant factors. We cannot ignore the wider urban environment in which workers live. The content of traditional customs matters, too. Source of capital and technology, degree of product differentiation within the corporate structure, nature of the industry as domestic or foreign controlled, the relationship of wages to total costs, all shape the kinds of demands workers make, the response to demands, and the organizations which evolve.

Even with massive oil revenues, Nigeria remains a poor country in per capita and in infrastructural terms. Oil provides the opportunity to gain control over the economy and to try to establish new growth patterns. Politically, Nigeria's rulers undoubtedly know that people care more about raising standards of living than in making relative comparisons. This recognition, and the reality of the weakness of class based politics in Nigeria, gave and gives leaders a great deal of political latitude. Of course, job insecurity, gaps between union leaders and rank and file, and repression limit workers' organizations and demands in Nigeria as they do elsewhere. In addition, class conflict is limited in Nigeria by desired patterns of social mobility, by the ways that political factors operate, and by economic competition that is structured by ethnic factors. So far, the demands made in urban Nigeria have been for better standards of living, not for redistribution of income and assets. Many Nigerians who do make income comparisons do so in terms of spatial and/or ethnic distinctions. When a group, rather than individual, basis for perceiving inequality exists, the group in Nigeria frequently is an ethnic one.

Nigerian political elites have acted as if inequality were an ethnic rather than class question in Nigeria. These actions are related to mass attitudes. (We leave aside the question about how much elite actions have been responsible for forming mass attitudes or how much elites simply respond to a wider reality.) To play distributional politics would involve one in ethnic conflict.

This may partially account for the widely shared view among Nigerian elites that the only way to raise standards of living is through sustained growth of the Nigerian economy. This is a self-interested view but that does not make it incorrect. The criticism that can be made of Nigeria's policies under military rule is that a strategy of agricultural growth was not seriously undertaken so that both sustained growth and a rise in welfare of rural people, who still constitute two-thirds of Nigeria's population, did not come about. Arguing this is different from arguing that the Nigerian Government should have redistributed assets or nationalized private property or taxed away private wealth more vigorously.

CONCLUSIONS AND A LOOK TO THE FUTURE

Nigeria is undergoing rapid social and economic change. The composition of exports has altered vastly in the last decade. Urbanization is extremely rapid. Indigenization of the economy has been undertaken in the industrial and banking sectors. Authority was centralized under a new multistate system and through a civil-service-military coalition which has seen its own interests furthered by centralization.

Income distribution issues were not salient in the first civilian period of Nigeria's independence. During military rule, various plans and pronouncements mentioned equity concerns with increasing frequency, especially toward the end of the period of military rule. Income distribution was not, however, the main concern of public policy in the economic and political realms. There was no strong pressure from below to move the system to deal frontally with equity issues, either conceived as rural-urban distributions or in class terms. Insofar as Nigeria has seen its politics governed by distributional issues, these have been communally defined for the most part and they have centered on allocations from the center to regions and states in the Nigerian Federation.

There has been no clear development of a class based politics in Nigeria. Neither peasant organizations nor trade unions in the industrial sector have been strong organizations pushing for redistribution of income. People in the urban informal sector similarly have not constituted a force for effective radical change. The relationships between formal sector and informal sector workers are complicated and variable by city and region and ethnic community. So are the relations between laborers and owners of the means of production.

It is very difficult to speak generally about relationships between class and ethnicity in Nigeria. It would be misleading to generalize the importance of class and ethnic issues over time and place in Nigeria. The meanings of wealth and equity vary within and between communal and occupational groups. Too hard a fix on per capita income figures would not capture the reality of situationally defined gains and the roles of families and communal groups in definitions of wealth and equality.

Power and status in Nigeria do not rest principally on private economic resources. Control of the institutions of state is critical for elites. Communal stratifications are critical facts for elites who contend for power. Elites themselves are highly fragmented in Nigeria. This may provide a wedge for reformist politics and strategies since Nigeria does not have strong countrywide landed aristocracies or many large scale national capitalists. Thus, while there seems still much political space in Nigeria for rulers to avoid a politics of reform since demands from below are not well organized, there are policies that will be undertaken in the name of strengthening the state or increasing national authority which can be more egalitarian in their thrust. Nigeria is not a country where an elite is holding on for dear life against reform for more egalitarian distribution. Yet policies have aimed more at growth and control of the economy than at income redistribution. There does not appear to be sufficiently effective pressure from below to alter these directions in the short run. They might, however, be altered by reform-minded elites for their own purposes and goals. The pressures to come to grips with income differences may well rise as civilian politicians build new grass roots networks. Some politicians did campaign in 1979 using equity slogans and the outlines of programs for social change.

The history of civilian rule in Nigeria during the 1950s and 1960s was not one of radical party politics. We do not see class-based parties, strong political trade unions or populist rural organizations dominating Nigeria's politics in the short run. Nor was a populist military leadership committed to radical change in the past. Of course, social and political factors change as well as economic ones. Indeed, important alterations in the relationships between state and society and in centralization of power in Nigeria have occurred already. It is conceivable that a different leadership, civilian or military or some coalition thereof, could come to power in Nigeria with new commitments and different strategies. However, the constituency and organizational foundation for such a leadership would be weak. Such leadership would have to build its own base which is difficult to accomplish. Thus it makes sense to look at future possibilities for what can be called reformist or incremental policies in a political framework not radically different from what has been known so far in Nigeria.

NOTES

The majority of the references in this chapter may be found in the section entitled, "Current Works on Nigeria – Politics and Society."

1. There is also a large national survey conducted by the Department of Political Science of the University of Ibadan which is partially analyzed in Morrison (1981, pp. 173-92). For a discussion of data problems in Nigeria see Bienen (1981a, in Bienen and Diejomaoh, 1981, pp. 1-2). I have relied on this paper and on work presented in Bienen and Diejomaoh, and in forthcoming work I have done on the Nigerian elections of 1979.
2. The higher the Gini index the greater the inequality.
3. For analysis of survey data on Nigerian attitudes, see Morrison 1981. For political and institutional analysis on which the following is based, see Bienen (1981b, 1982).
4. See the statement by Chief Bola Ige, successful gubernatorial candidate of the UPN in Oyo State (*Daily Times*, Lagos, February 6, 1979).
5. Agence-France Press, No. 2587, May 25, 1979.

4

THE POPULAR CLASSES AND THE OIL BOOM: A POLITICAL ECONOMY OF RURAL AND URBAN POVERTY

Michael Watts and Paul Lubeck

> The blessing of oil [in Nigeria] is that it brings in lots of money. The curse is that it concentrates that money in few hands.
>
> *Economist* January 23, 1982

> The petro-naira has not blessed [Nigerian producers] with the essentials of existence, rather its abundance is part of the process of denying them the benefits of what they produce. They continue in their poverty.
>
> Yusufu Bala Usman, *For the Liberation of Nigeria*

For the uninitiated, a visit to Lagos, Kano or Kaduna can be deeply traumatic. Most visitors are baffled by what seems like massive chaos in the face of apparent material plenty. Nigeria is one of the world's ten most populous nations, of great strategic significance, petroleum rich and, for some at least, a "little Brazil" in a continent generally wracked by abject poverty. And yet, in spite of the huge surge of petroleum revenue in the 1970s, Nigeria seems to operate in a constant failure mode. As a highly critical *Economist* report (January 23, 1982) lamented, "How can so much money and such high hopes engender such chaos?" Indeed, the massive importation of consumer goods over the last decade and the rapid growth of the public sector can obscure both the anarchistic quality of social life in the oil-boom era and the extent to which the material benefits of petroleum have been inequitably distributed. A closer examination of contemporary Nigeria, however, quite clearly reveals the social strains imposed by an economy firmly placed on a laissez-faire roller coaster. In 1979 two million man-days were lost to industrial disputes; at least fifty peasants were reported killed in 1980 during a violent confrontation on a large, state-funded irrigation project near Sokoto; and a Basic Needs report by the International Labor Office indicated a significant deterioration of living conditions among the rural and urban poor since the oil bonanza. All this was concurrent with the release of the Annual Report of the Central Bank of Nigeria which, at the time of publication, had "no actual data on federal government and expenditure"!

What is to be made of all this? It is all too facile to leave an explanation of these conditions at the level of 'corruption,' of predatory statism or, as the *Economist* put it, of "Nigeria's chucking it away." We would like to discuss the last decade of Nigerian development in terms of the leading role of state expenditure in capitalist development and class formation. More specifically, we will examine both the impact and distributional effects of this oil-funded capitalist transformation on what we refer to as the rural and urban popular classes, and the specific forms of popular resistance and dissent that the oil boom has spawned.

At the time of Independence in October 1960, Nigeria had become self-sufficient in crude oil, producing rather less than 20,000 barrels per day. Petroleum self-sufficiency had not, however, been easily won. Exploration had begun in the late 1930s but, following its suspension during the Second World War, drilling operations were not undertaken until 1951. The first significant discovery was made at Oloibiri in the Niger Delta in 1956, and oil production on a commercial scale commenced in 1958. At Independence there were four fields in the Eastern Region and two in the West; by 1980 in the Niger Delta alone there were 150 producing fields connected to five export terminals by a network of pipelines. By virtue of its light gravity and low sulphur content, Nigerian crude was attractive to the oil companies and accordingly acquired a handsome premium. In 1961 production was 46,000 barrels per day (b/d). With the construction of the trans-Niger pipeline in 1965 and the exploitation of offshore fields, production leaped to 275,000 b/d and to 420,000 b/d prior to the civil war. Despite the total logistical and administrative breakdown caused by the civil war, the million barrel daily mark was passed in 1970 and by 1973 had doubled to 2.06 million b/d.

When Nigeria joined OPEC in 1971, a Nigerian National Oil Corporation (NNOC) – subsequently renamed the Nigerian National Petroleum Corporation in 1977 – was created as a vehicle for partnerships with foreign oil companies. The government's share in the companies was 35 percent after 1973, rose to 55 percent in 1977 and to 60 percent in July 1979. By late 1979, NNPC had title to 1.7 million b/d from its joint ventures making it one of the world's largest sellers. In fact, by 1972 oil had already constituted 83 percent of Nigerian exports, but after OPEC's 1973 initiative which raised the price of crude, Nigeria's terms of trade improved threefold – a windfall gain roughly equal to 15 percent of 1974 GDP (Table 4.1). Oil's share in federal government revenue rose from 17 percent in 1971 to 71 percent in 1973 to 86 percent in 1975. Total public spending rose from less than 20 percent of GDP in 1970-73 to 35 percent in 1974-77.

Prior to the civil war and the oil boom, the political and fiscal strength of the federal center was relatively weak in relation to the regions. The State apparatus was certainly open to foreign capital and charged with the support of private Nigerian enterprise but, in practical terms, state patronage favored the merchant capitalists, the buying agents, the contractors: those actively engaged in primitive accumulation. The number of federal economic institutions such as the Central Bank was limited and the federal plan was in reality the

TABLE 4.1
Petroleum Production and Revenue 1973-79

Year	*Crude Petroleum Production (1975 = 100)*	*Crude Petroleum Exports (millions)*	*Volume of Crude Petroleum Exports (1975 = 100)*	*Crude Petroleum Export Price (1975 = 100)*
1973	115	1,933	116	33
1974	126	5,665	128	94
1975	100	4,593	100	100
1976	116	5,894	116	108
1977	117	7,046	120	122
1978	106	6,033	108	118
1979	129	10,034	130	174

Source: International Financial Statistics, Vol. XXXIII #12(1980, p. 288).

conflation of individual regional plans. Federal activity was most important in the realms of infrastructure and public utilities.

Following the civil war, however, the state was expanded, centralized, and increased its direct involvement in production. The emergence of oil revenues not only permitted a measure of autonomy from foreign aid but allowed a consolidation of state ownership, the restructuring of the Nigerian economy, and the genesis of a powerful, centralized bureaucracy. The growth of the federal budget (Table 4.2) in conjunction with the creation of new states in 1967 and the transformation of revenue allocation made the state governments increasingly dependent on transfers from the vastly enlarged federal pool. The level of statutory grants to the state governments grew from ₦ 323.8 million in 1974 to ₦ 2,534 in 1979-80. Following the Revenue Allocation Act of February 1981 the revenue sharing system was as follows: total federal revenue ₦ 15,773.5 million, statutory grants to state governments ₦ 4,968.7 million (31.5 percent of the total), statutory grant to local governments ₦ 1,577.4 million (10 percent), and ₦ 9,227.5 (58.5 percent) retained as federal revenue.

The 1970s was a qualitatively different era. Following the termination of the war, the growth of the Nigerian economy was rapid. Between 1970 and 1976 GNP grew at a real annual rate of 7.4 percent, and GNP per capita at 5.4 percent per annum. Growth has been, moreover, accompanied by a significant sectoral transformation (Table 4.3). By 1975 agriculture had dropped by half from its 1963 place in the national economy and only accounted for 28 percent of national output while the proportion of the labor force remained high at 64 percent. Conversely, the contribution of petroleum to federal revenue and to GDP between 1964 and 1974 increased from 4 percent to 80 percent and from 3 percent to 46 percent respectively (Oyediran 1979, p. 69). These changes in sectoral constitution reflected, however, not simply a growth in nonfarm activities (notably mining and manufacturing) but a stagnant agrarian economy (Table 4.4). Between 1970 and 1976 total farm output in Nigeria fell by –0.2 percent; in part, this may be accounted for by the severe harvest shortfall in 1972 and 1973, but it is also a reflection of labor demand in other sectors, pricing policy, and changing forms of production in the countryside. In 1974 the food production index stood at the same level as 1960; over the same period the food import index had tripled.

TABLE 4.2
The Federal Budget Position 1970/71-1978/79

(million ₦)

	70-1	*71-2*	*72-3*	*73-4*	*74-5*	*75-6*	*76-7*	*77-8*	*78-9*
Revenue	756	1411	1390	2172	5177	5856	7070	8359	7252
Current Expenditure (a)	774	849	1021	1120	1912	3402	3574	4425	385
Current Surplus	–18	562	378	1051	3265	2454	3496	3934	3399
Capital Expenditure (b)	99	214	311	529	1684	3823	4913	5627	3742
Overall Surplus/Deficit	–117	348	67	522	1581	–1369	–1417	–1693	–343

Notes: (a) Excludes contributions to Development Fund
(b) Excludes Loans to States

Source: Central Bank of Nigeria, Annual Report, Nigerian Federal Office of Statistics.

TABLE 4.3
Sectoral Composition of National Output in Nigeria for Selected Years, 1960-75
(in percent)

Sector	*1960*	*1963*	*1970*	*1975*
Agriculture	64.1	55.4	43.8	28.1
Oil & Mining	1.2	4.8	12.2	14.2
Manufacturing	4.8	7.0	7.6	10.2
Building & Construction	4.0	5.2	6.4	11.3
Others	25.9	27.6	30.0	36.2
	100.0	100.0	100.0	100.0

Source: Federal Office of Statistics, National Accounts of Nigeria 1960/61-1975/76, Lagos.

TABLE 4.4
Sectoral Growth Rates in the Nigerian Economy for Selected Periods 1960-75 in Constant Prices
(in percent)

Sector	*1960-65*	*1966-69*	*1970-75*
Agriculture	2	−1	−1
Oil & Mining	38	8	12
Manufacturing	15	6	14.5
Building & Construction	10	1	21

Source: Federal Office of Statistics, National Accounts of Nigeria 1960/61-1975/76, Lagos.

The civil war, then, marked a watershed in the course of Nigerian development. From its prewar mercantile basis and a wholesale dependence on several agrarian export commodities such as groundnuts, palm oil and cotton, Nigeria emerged into the 1980s as a robust and outspoken member of a semi-industrial and capitalist periphery.

Yet growth patterns in the 1970s also generated substantial income disparities between sectors. According to Matlon (1981b, p. 324), between 1970 and 1975 per capita GDP measured in constant 1974-75 prices in agriculture remained virtually constant at ₦ 61 per capita compared to the increase in the national average from ₦ 137 to ₦ 189. Per capita farm incomes fell, therefore, from about 45 percent to 32 percent of the national average. Relative to per capita GDP in all nonfarm sectors, average agricultural output per capita fell 34 percent during the first half of the 1970s.

This transition is perhaps best illustrated by the remarkable transfiguration of Kano, whose condition will be analyzed below in greater detail. In 1963, with a population of just over a quarter of a million, Kano was a classically mercantile city specializing in the export of groundnuts. By 1980, the population was estimated to be in excess of 2 million with an industrial labor force of about 50,000. Kano has experienced a rapid proliferation of multinational investments and manufacturing, the internationalization of consumption styles among the urban rich, the commoditization of urban social relations, a sharp upturn in the numbers of a disenfranchised and militant "floating population," new waves of rural migrants from close settled zone and, not least, a corresponding increase in urban violence.

We are concerned here first with the manner in which these new social and economic contradictions, ushered in by the petroleum boom, have transformed the material circumstances of the Nigeria popular classes, and second with an assessment of the relationships between state society and economy for the 1980s in the light of these contradictions.

THE POPULAR CLASSES: EXPERIENCES AND RESPONSES DURING THE PETROLEUM ERA

Thus far we have argued that the period of military rule witnessed a rapid transformation of Nigerian economy and society, a transformation that was led by petroleum fueled economic development and directed by an increasingly interventionist state at and within all levels and sectors of Nigerian society. A volume addressing the political economy of Nigeria must assess the experience of the majority of Nigerians during this transformation in terms of its effect on their material welfare and life expectations, the quality of their lives and general social existence as well as their ability to participate in and to benefit from the political and economic processes underlying Nigeria's transformation. We do not disagree with the consensus of commentators who conclude that social inequality and a more unequal distribution of income has resulted from this transformation. Yet, at the same time, we hold that to analyze the concrete experience of Nigeria's majority (whom we designate as "the popular classes") requires that one specify an objective class location. "Popular classes" refers to Nigeria's rural and urban majority who are drawn from the peasantry, unskilled and semiskilled wage earners and the independent producers of the urban informal sector. For, despite Nigeria's considerable regional and ethnic variation, we shall argue that the combined activity of petroleum-led economic development and state intervention on behalf of the dominant capitalist classes has created new objective conditions of class differentiation and class formation.

Even though the peasantry is located in the rural sector and wage earners and independent commodity producers are located in the urban sector, and thus belong to different social classes, they share commonalities and social experiences that allow one to include them under the rubric of "popular." In selecting this rubric for the three classes rather than, for example, the Nigerian journalists' epithet "masses," our intention is to emphasize both the *objective* and the *subjective* concerns of these classes during the period of interest.

To comprehend why the term "popular" is appropriate one must examine the emerging cleavage between the dominant and subordinate classes. For an examination of the contemporary political economy of Nigeria reveals a process of rapid capital accumulation by the dominant class fractions: the administrative bourgeoisie who control the state's administrative and directly productive activities (e.g., petroleum, steel, irrigation schemes); the private sector bourgeoisie who accumulate wealth through trade, finance, state contracts, construction and industrial production; and the rising, highly educated professional and technocratic groups who mediate between the state and international firms, whose careers vascillate between state employment and servicing international firms, while at the same time, maintaining their own private firms and investments. If the petroleum boom has benefited anyone, then such benefits are located within this class frame rather than with the popular classes. For the popular classes, their common relationship to state and capital is one of *exclusion*, and this provides the foundation of their class unity.

To belong to the popular classes means that one does not have access to state patronage in the form of loans, contracts, import licenses, seats on the board of directors of joint state-multinational industries, or to any of the other legal and illegal sources of wealth that flow from linkages with the petroleum state. It is important to remember that since 1966 the dual processes of state centralization and increasing (federal) control of petroleum revenue has meant that the emerging bourgeoisie, in order to be successful, must gain direct or indirect access to state patronage of State controlled revenues broadly defined. Further, even once wealthy members of the popular classes do not possess sufficient amounts of capital to remain secure in the face of a rapid inflation, varying at an estimated annual rate of 20 to 50 percent during the era of the civil war and the petroleum boom. Again, in order for modest or petty capitalists to expand and to maintain their relative – and sometimes their absolute – level of wealth and social rank, they must gain access to the most lucrative investment opportunities, most of which require access to state power. Besides lacking state patronage and sufficient capital to allow independence, members of the popular classes lack the formal education (e.g., secondary school and above) that would allow them to take advantage of the opportunities for private accumulation, skilled state employment, or professional and technocratic employment in the private sector.

Within the space allowed here we cannot detail the particular features of petroleum-led capitalist development or the reasons that the Nigerian state plays the vanguard role in extending and deepening capitalist social relations of production, exchange and consumption in the interest of the accumulation needs of the dominant classes. Instead, we wish to emphasize that the differentiating effects of rapid economic growth and the experience of exclusion from the purported benefits of the petroleum boom have not only created a profound cleavage between the "haves" and "have nots" but, more importantly, for the subject matter of this essay – the popular classes – they create an objective set of inequality experiences that possess the potential to launch a popular political movement in the future. Therefore, our aim here is to describe the distributive effects of Nigeria's transformation on the popular classes, within their respective and urban sectors. And, at the same time, we intend to suggest how the popular classes have responded to these distributive effects by taking account of popular responses outside of the formal political party system that emerged during the late 1970s.

Conventional political analysts have noted that, despite increased income inequality, the elections of 1979 did not register an unambiguous class response on the part of the popular classes. Although we do not disagree that regional and ethnic affiliations remain strong in Nigeria, we reject any analysis of these continuing affiliations that depend solely on cultural value differences or which treat ethnic groups as primordial and closed social identities. Rather, ethnic and communal identities should be seen as dynamic, embedded in and altered by structural and historical processes of change in Nigeria, and in tension with emerging class identities. For example, colonial rule and associated processes integrated and thus created the contemporary Yoruba ethnic identity from diverse subethnic groups that were not integrated during the precolonial period. Similarly, among Muslim ethnic groups in the cities of the northern states, a Hausa-speaking Islamic communal identity is emerging among the popular classes of northern Nigeria. Indeed, we concur with Yusufu Bala Usman, when he excoriates Nigeria's political elites for dividing the popular classes by manipulating their fear of domination by alien religious and ethnic groups in order to preserve ethnic voting blocks. Ethnic identities are not Platonic essences that came into existence by metahistorical forces; rather, they are communal identities that were created historically by concrete historical processes – migration, state formation, Islamization, colonialism and the world economy. Given the reality of politics in a petroleum state like Nigeria, where the elites distribute patronage through ethnic networks, one should not be surprised that ethnic voting patterns were strongly represented in the 1979 election. But from the individuals' perspective, ethnic loyalty is a mode of resource acquisition, not necessarily a commitment to the primacy of ethnic over class politics.

With these issues in mind, let us review briefly the electoral results of 1979 in order to ascertain if, in the face of increasing inequality, the popular classes choose ethnic over class representation. As Bienen notes in his contribution to this volume, socialist parties with purely class appeal such as the Nigerian Workers' and Peasants' Vanguard Movement were not allowed to compete in the election. Indeed, the process was a closely managed affair of the dominant classes. It was only after an urban riot in Kano that the presidential candidate of the populist-socialist Peoples Redemption Party (PRP), Aminu Kano, was allowed to compete. What of the role played by the Nigerian trade union movement and the Nigerian Labor Congress (NLC) in the election? The answer is found in the Federal Military Government's recent reorganization of the trade union movement, which has prohibited it from participating in formal political party movements. In other words, the most powerful voice of urban wage earners, therefore, was not allowed to participate politically. At the same time, the conservative National Party of Nigeria (NPN), favoring greater foreign investment and viewed by most as the party of the emerging state and private bourgeoisie, was allowed to allocate offices for the forthcoming election on the basis of geography, such that the presidential candidate was to be chosen from the northern states. Clearly, this managed political affair *enhanced* ethnic politics first by eliminating class-oriented political parties and the labor movement, while allowing the NPN to engage in the same ethnic patronage as practiced by its predecessor, the Northern Peoples Congress (NPC) of the First Nigerian Republic.

Nevertheless, in spite of these managed obstacles to class politics, a populist, class-oriented political party (PRP) did win the state governorships in the states of Kano and Kaduna. Both are of course the two most developed northern states, which have directly experienced the effects of state intervention and petroleum-led capitalist growth and social differentiation. These victories, moreover, need to be seen in light of the fact that PRP candidates for legislative office were often disqualified just prior to the election, even after Aminu Kano was allowed to participate in the presidential election. Of course, the class orientation of this party was expressed in regional terms as a struggle between the commoners, the *talakawa*, and the aristocracy, the *sarauta*, and their "bourgeois" allies. Indeed, here is an excellent illustration of how a precapitalist inequality relationship between *sarauta* and *talakawa* informs the consciousness of the popular classes in those states where state intervention and capitalist development have been most intense, but was conspicuously absent in the more backward states like Sokoto and Bauchi, which are nonetheless characterized by the *sarauta-talakawa* cleavage. Finally, interpreters of the Nigerian political system who rely on ethnic and regional explanations must explain why the most economically backward northern states, which have always been described as the least modern, least educated, and generally most underdeveloped areas of Nigeria, should provide Nigeria with the most ideologically developed political parties: the PRP representing the left and the NPN representing the right.

For the popular classes, then, the elections of 1979 provided little opportunity to participate or to express their grievances. In what follows, we review those grievances, that is the social and material circumstances of the rural and urban poor, and then offer some examples of how the popular classes have responded to the new forms of inequality associated with the petroleum economy.

The Rural Sector

From the early 1950s up to the breakdown of civil authority in 1966, Nigeria pursued a limited import-substitution path in which the industrial proletariat constituted a small proportion of those actively employed and manufacturing represented only 4.8 percent of Nigerian national output in 1960. Conversely, agriculture accounted for 58 percent of GDP in 1964 and employed 70 percent of the active workforce. Furthermore, between 1960 and 1967 the volume of export crops grew at an annual compound rate of growth of 4-6 percent. Staple food output expanded more or less in tandem with population growth. Food and live animal imports were ₦ 21.2 million in 1967 (9.5 percent by value of total imports). The food production index grew from 82 in 1960 to 89 in 1967, and the food importation index over the same period actually fell from 105 to 99. Three-fourths of the food imports in 1966 and 1967 were processed forms of nutritionally "superior" food items: fish, wheat and flour, milk, and sugar. Indeed, based on the experience of the previous decade, Food and Agriculture Organization (FAO) projections in the mid-1960s estimated food surpluses for the 1970s simply by letting the food sector take care of itself.

And yet, the post oil-boom political economy of Nigeria is perhaps made especially distinctive by the extraordinarily sluggish performance of agriculture, more specifically, the total collapse of export production and spiraling food imports. Between 1976 and 1978 food production, in relation to population, was 89 percent of that between 1960 and 1970 (*West Africa* December 1, 1980). Over the period 1970-78, real food output per capita declined by 1.5 percent per annum; total food output has also been remarkably unimpressive (Table 4.5). Food imports have risen dramatically; in 1977 total food imports stood at ₦ 790 million (almost 11 percent of total imports) while in 1965 the food import bill was ₦ 46.4 million (8.8 percent of all imported commodities). The dependence of Nigeria on externally produced staples has grown markedly since 1972 (Table 4.6); in 1980 the Federal Government spent ₦ 1.5 billion on imported cereals (*West Africa* September 7, 1981). Furthermore, the staple imports have been subject to the galloping inflation of the 1970s, which in 1978 was running at 16 percent per annum. Rising food prices were thrown into sharp relief in 1977 with the scandalous marketing of imported rice, the landing cost of which was ₦ 15 per bag but which fetched in excess of ₦ 100

TABLE 4.5
Output of Major Food Crops 1971-79

	Guineacorn	*Millet*	*Rice*
1972	5794	2835	279
1973	2298	2391	447
1974	3125	3794	487
1975	4738	5554	525
1976	3325	4737	515
1977	3700	2950	579
1978	3770	3060	842
1979	3785	3100	1000

Note: Output in '000 tons

Source: Federal Office of Statistics, *Nigeria Quarterly Economic Review* (Nigeria), 1980.

TABLE 4.6
Food Imports: 1970-77

	1964-66	*1970*	*1972*	*1974*	*1977*
Total Food imports					
(₦ million)	46.4	57.7	95.1	154.8	790.3
Percent of Total	8.8	7.6	9.6	8.9	10.9
Wheat					
Quantity[1]	55.6	258.7	296.7	318.3	720.0
Value[2]	7.6	15.4	22.0	50.7	96.0
Rice					
Quantity	1.2	1.7	5.8	4.8	413.0
Value	0.2	0.1	1.0	1.4	155.0
Barley					
Quantity	no data	no data	no data	9.7	94.9
Value	no data	no data	no data	0.009	0.04
Maize					
Quantity[3]	no data	no data	no data	20,171.0	2,440.0
Value	no data	no data	no data	0.6	3.4
Fish					
Quantity	34.3	6.6	20.8	14.7	100.0
Value	14.3	2.9	5.3	7.4	71.0
Meat					
Quantity	0.5	–	–	0.4	23.0
Value	0.3	–	–	0.3	21.6

[1] In '000s of metric tons
[2] ₦ million
[3] In '000s of Kg

Source: Forrest (1981), Federal Office of Statistics.

because of speculative licensing and hoarding (*Washington Post* December 27, 1980). The agricultural export sector has quite literally fallen apart as producer incentives disappeared (Table 4.7).

As Nigerian agriculture stagnated, the provision of cheap food became ever more critical. The growth in oil revenue permitted the Nigerian government, however, much more flexibility in confronting the wage-food issue. Prices of bread were fixed, import duties on staples relaxed, and rising demand shifted to foreign sources because of the overvaluation of the Nigerian currency. As a World Bank

TABLE 4.7
Agricultural Exports 1972-77

Commodity	*1972*	*1973*	*1974*	*1975*	*1976*	*1977*
			('000 tons)			
Groundnuts, decorticated	106	199	30	–	–	8
Cocoa, raw	228	211	180	202	231	165
Palm kernels	212	137	185	173	257	169
Palm oil	2	–	–	–	–	–
Cotton, raw	1	8	–	–	–	9
Rubber	41	49	59	57	39	18

Source: Quarterly Economic Review of Nigeria, 1979.

report concluded, "the overvalued [naira] is consumer biased. The massive importation of rice and wheat keeps the price of these [commodities] lower than would occur under restricted imports or a land exchange rate" (IBRD 1978, p. 38). Yet dependence on imported foods was no solution, of course, since it was itself contingent upon expanding oil revenues. In any case, cheap imports further depressed local foodstuff production, and the low prices offered by the Marketing Boards had all but quashed export commodity production.

The Federal government accordingly confronted the food issue in the Third Development Plan (1975-80) which gave pride of place to agriculture and specifically food. The proportion of government spending in agriculture remained low – roughly 5 percent – but oil revenue permitted a huge increase in actual spending (Table 4.8). In spite of the priority of "ensuring food supplies in adequate quantity and quality to keep pace with increased population and urbanization" (Third Development Plan 1975, p. 65), it was also clear that the agricultural sector was still to be the bedrock of the cheap food policy and a source of foreign exchange revenue. Moreover, the vast majority of rural smallholders were profoundly marginal to revenue allocation. Of the total allocated capital of ₦ 3.1 billion in 1977, 30 percent went to massive irrigation schemes, 14 percent to direct production schemes under state management, and 10 percent to extension service and input. Since the famine, however, the Third Development Plan has provided the means for a

TABLE 4.8
Expenditure on Agriculture, by Major Expenditure Category
(₦ million)

	1977/78 Estimates (Recurrent & Capital)			
	Federal	*States*	*Total*	*Percent*
Extension service and input supply	34.0	89.1	123.1	(16.0)
Fertilizer purchases		43.0	43.0	(5.6)
Mechanization	0.9	33.7	34.6	(4.5)
Direct production schemes	11.1	47.2	58.3	(7.6)
Seed multiplication	2.8	18.9	21.7	(2.8)
Credit	16.0	11.2	27.2	(3.5)
Irrigation	182.4	45.2	227.6	(30.0)
Training	1.2	15.9	17.1	(2.2)
Marketing and storage	15.4	15.5	30.9	(4.0)
Miscellaneous	5.1	13.7	18.8	(2.4)
TOTAL CROPS	268.9	333.3	602.3	(78.8)
Livestock	20.3	77.4	97.7	(12.7)
Forestry	7.6	35.1	42.7	(5.5)
Fisheries	8.5	15.2	23.7	(3.1)
TOTAL AGRICULTURE	305.3	461.1	766.4	(100.0)
Less Federal grants to States			12.6	
TOTAL (net)			753.8	

Source: The Green Revolution, Lagos: Federal Ministry of Agriculture, 1980.

radical transformation of Nigerian agriculture, ostensibly to increase food supplies without increasing food prices.

More specifically the Nigerian state has embarked on a two pronged strategy. The first involves state production schemes often in concert with international finance capital and multinational agro-industrial concerns. And the second refers to the New Green Revolution strategy that (1) encourages the emergence of large-scale mechanized agriculture and (2) promotes differentiation within the countryside by attracting urban and administrative elites into production or appealing to rural "progressive farmers." This, then, marks a new phase of capital accumulation in Nigeria and a direct threat to the persistence of small-scale peasant production.

State Production and International Capital

The Third National Development Plan initiated increased involvement by Federal and State governments in the direct production of agricultural products, especially wage foods. In the early 1960s the Farm Settlement Schemes in Western Nigeria had established 1,500 acre farms for similar purposes, but by 1971 the Western Region Government had spent ₦ 16.4 million – 55 percent of total capital expenditure for agriculture – with almost no productive success. The new efforts were vastly expanded: government food companies, for example, were allocated ₦ 114.2 million. In the southern states government plantations and food companies will absorb ₦ 67.35 million from a total of ₦ 131.38 million on food crops. Three parastatals – the National Livestock Production Company, the National Grains Production Company and the National Rootcrop Production Company – are charged with accelerating food production through large-scale heavily mechanized productive units. The Grains Company has established 4,000 ha. farms that include storage and processing facilities. By 1980 food production farms had been established at Mokwa (Niger), Jema (Kaduna) and Ilero (Oyo); similar enterprises are under construction in Bauchi and Kano and should be completed in all the remaining states by 1982. The Livestock Company engages in cattle, pig farming and dairy production; three poultry hatcheries produce 5.4 million chicks annually, and state funded broiler factories are under construction at Agege and Port Harcourt.

Some of the most dramatic state involvements have been in large-scale irrigated agriculture which, by virtue of their size and cost, have frequently been joint ventures with international finance capital (especially the World Bank) or private European firms. In the 1970s three huge projects were initiated for the Chad Basin, the Hadejia-Jemaare valley and the Sokoto-Rima valley, which would create an irrigated area of 274,000 hectares by 1991 at a cost of ₦ 2.2 billion. The drive for irrigated agriculture is perhaps understandable in terms of drought risk, but the past performance of water control projects in the Middle Belt has been poor. More critically, irrigation psychology is closely linked to import substitution of wheat and rice for urban markets.

The recently completed Bakalori irrigation project 150 kms southeast of Sokoto provides a blueprint for these sorts of state funded enterprises. The impetus for Bakalori came from a FIAT-based bank consortium which is now in the hands of an Italian contractor (IMPRESIT). Two contracts for construction totaled ₦ 154 million to be completed by March 1980, but by January of that year costs stood at ₦ 350 million and construction was blocked by farmer opposition (*West Africa* August 28, 1978). Already, however, a consulting company (MASDAR) is encouraging a wealthy farmer class, and the state has established 350 ha. "development farms." Within a year of completion, some indebted farmers sold out to teachers, businessmen and officials.

The Bakalori experience, moreover, is not unusual. Wallace (1981) and Palmer-Jones (1980) have shown how the first phase of the Kano River Project at Kadawa, which involved the construction of the Tiga dam in 1974, has suffered from similar defects. The resettlement of 12,000 farmers at Tiga has resulted in a deterioration of material conditions for 43 percent of all settlers, most particularly felt as a lack of good farmland. As at Bakalori, downstreamers in the Hadejia valley have lost access to fishing and lucrative vegetable production. At Kadawa, south of Kano, tenure, labor and technical shortcomings have severely constrained the operation of the project; the project functions ineffectively but to the benefit of scheme workers, locally influential trader-farmers and to rich outsiders (Palmer-Jones 1980).

The production of wheat on the Kano River scheme is very costly and much more so than imported wheats. It will probably require high subsidies to cover recurrent costs. The production of wheat and tomatoes for urban markets conflicts with farmers' wishes to produce guineacorn, which is harvested after wheat should be planted. Wheat production is further constrained by untimely provision of tractor plowing and fertilizers and by inadequacies in the flow of water and the maintenance of canals. Yields are correspondingly low and uncertain. The scheme authorities also do not own the land and are therefore unable to direct the farmers to comply with their wishes. All this needs to be seen against the massive costs per hectare of irrigation agriculture: ₦ 2,000 at Bakalori, ₦ 1,750 in Chad (Phase 1) and ₦ 1,200 in Chad (Phase II), and ₦ 8,000 at Kadawa (Kano).

The state has also become heavily committed to estate sugar production; the Third Development Plan budgeted ₦ 350 million to three integrated projects in Gongola, Kwara and Niger states. In most cases, sugar production is closely linked to irrigation and dam construction; the huge Savanna sugar project at Numan, for instance, was tied to the ₦ 144 million Kiri dam on the Gongola River. Once again, however, the performance of estate agriculture has been poor; inflated technology prices, infrastructural bottlenecks and poor management and financing account for the huge delays and massive overspending. Expenditure on the Savanna Sugar Company alone stands at $412 million, yet the irrigation remains uncompleted and "there appears little likelihood of the sugar ever being competitive on the world market" (*Quarterly Economic Review* 3rd Quarter 1981, p. 20). Undeterred by these difficulties, the Nigerian government is going ahead with the $568 million Sunti sugar estate which will employ 4,000 people and ultimately produce 50,000 tons per year. The government's decision to acquire 90 percent of the equity from Tate and Lyle has halted production, however.

In many instances state capital has been supplemented by foreign or international finance capital. This is especially clear in the integrated rural development projects which we discuss in the following section. The Nigerian government has, however, also recently encouraged investment by private foreign capital in the agricultural sector. Nineteen joint ventures are already planned by companies from Brazil, Canada and Europe (*African Business* November 1981), and in July 1980 the U.S. Government and Nigeria signed a Memorandum to encourage American agribusiness, in conjunction with the U.S. Department of Agriculture, to invest heavily (*Foreign Agriculture* June 1981). By the mid-1970s, European firms had begun to invest in agriculture; the Bokko poultry farm in Plateau State was a joint venture between the state government and the German firm Rau Imex, while Danish and British companies had established pig farms near Kuru. In both instances, investment had encouraged vertical integration principally through encouraging local farmers to use hybrid maize as livestock feed. Further, in 1978 the Federal Commissioner for Agriculture informed a Dutch delegation that the recent Land Use Decree was a means by which large amounts of land required by foreign capital could be easily and cheaply mobilized for international investors.

The Green Revolution Strategy

In addition to a direct involvement in production, the Third Development Plan also provided for a huge expansion of capital expenditure for raising rural productivity and food production. The ₦ 750 million allocated to financing agricultural development since 1975 has seen an explosion of parastatal organizations concerned directly with subsidized credit, fertilizer, mechanization, integrated rural development, and land tenure changes. A major impetus for parastatal expansion was the food crisis itself. Early efforts, specifically Operation Feed the Nation (OFN) established in 1976 and the National Accelerated Food Production Program (NAFPP) founded in 1972, were designed to boost and mobilize individuals around the food issue. OFN was a largely propagandistic strategy directed at mass motivation and incentives. Almost 30,000 post secondary students were paid ₦ 96 per month to participate in rural production schemes though with very little effect and, in view of the minimal logistical and institutional support by the government, there is little evidence to suggest that OFN actually significantly raised food production. The NAFPP, conversely, aims specifically to stimulate production of rice, maize, sorghum, millet, wheat and cassava through integrated use of high yielding seed varieties, chemical inputs, credit and improved marketing. The program has concentrated on "packages of improved practices" or production kits ostensibly for small-scale producers. Expenditure in 1980 was ₦ 4 million. In addition, however, the state has constructed 380 agro-service centers to improve input delivery and technology transfer. Seed laboratories have been completed in Ibadan and Kaduna and a National Mechanization Center is in progress at Ilorin.

The entire program received further support in April 1980 with the establishment of the National Council for Green Revolution which, as a coordinating body, aims to "boost agricultural production and to ensure rural development through . . . agro-based industries [and] the construction of feeder roads" (*Africa Now* October 1981, p. 181). The new Green Revolution initiative is in fact building upon the prototypical integrated rural development projects (IRDPs) initially sponsored by the World Bank in the early 1970s. Since 1963, the World Bank has eclipsed USAID as the principal donor to Nigeria and up to 1978 had loaned $295 million to agricultural projects. By the late 1970s there were nine integrated rural development projects, each catering to 60-80,000 farmers. During 1980 other loans were negotiated with the World Bank for projects in Sokoto ($168 million), Bauchi ($132 million), Kano ($142 million) and Ondo (₦ 59.6 million), and the Federal Director of Rural Development has apparently been assured that the Bank will assist the multiplication of such projects to all states by 1983 (*West Africa* April 6, 1981).

In spite of the purported populist of smallholder focus of NAFPP and the IRDPs, the new Green Revolution package has important social and economic consequences for the countryside that threaten the persistence of the Nigerian peasantry. In attempting to capture rural producers through parastatal functions and subsidized inputs, the Nigerian government has actually encouraged large-scale production and promoted the participation of urban and rural elites in agricultural operations. In attempting to transform the forces of production by subsidization, the high demand for inputs discriminates against the rural poor irrespective of their appreciation of fertilizer or insecticide utility. The scarcity of inputs works in favor of the bureaucratic elites, influential merchant-traders and traditional aristocracies. The expansion of rural credit by the Agricultural Credit Guarantee Scheme, for instance, entailed ₦ 30.9 million in 1980 but only 42.5 percent were approved; 68 percent went to livestock and poultry production and 10 percent to mixed farmers both of which exclude the vast majority of small farmers (*African Business* November 1981). Of the ₦ 5.2 million available for food production, credit worthiness stipulations favored wealthy peasants. The experience of the cooperative movement in Nigeria over the last 20 years clearly shows how such potential benefits are usurped by influential kulaks. In his study of three villages in Kano State, Matlon (1981a) documents the substantially higher participation rate among village elites (*sarauta*, traders and bureaucrats) in government programs. In much of the North, village and district heads have huge discretionary powers in the selection of program participants, and Matlon estimates that of total supplies to the three villages "20% was diverted for the personal use of selected members of the elite" (Matlon 1981a, p. 352).

In spite of populist rhetoric, the agricultural development projects are also oriented to large-scale mechanized production. The average farm size in the Funtua project is 4.1 hectares but the project aims to convert "all progressive farmers into large scale [100 hectare] farmers" (D'Silva and Raza 1980, p. 285). In 1979 there were 186 large-scale farmers, 19,562 progressive farmers, and 66,438 traditional cultivators. Sixty percent of all extension visits concentrated on the progressive class, while the large-scale producers received intensive advice on design, implementation and supervision of farm plans. In any event, the project has actually failed to provide many of purported service benefits; in 1980 only 520 kilometers of road had been built, and few villages had significantly improved their water or electricity supply, post primary schools, or maternity centers since 1966. Additionally, if crop production has increased, it has not occurred in the projected fashion and prices have often been terribly depressed. In 1978/79 maize markets were saturated and farmers faced falling prices. Cotton has lagged behind expected growth trajectories. Contrary to expectations, sorghum has dominated local production. The project has also been hampered by cash flow problems, by budgetary overexpenditure, by poor marketing, and by low disease resistance among high yield varieties (HYVs). More critically for the small farmer, heavily indebted and incapable of obtaining inputs, the possibility of further impoverishment is high. A class of "overnight" farmers resulted from urban businessmen; civil servants and district heads have, conversely, been created by the liberal provision of subsidized inputs. As D'Silva and Raza wrote, "the emergence of a landless class is a possibility for the first time in the area" (1980, p. 295).

The new Green Revolution Strategy envisages a massive expansion of these schemes: between 1980 and 1985 a fivefold increase in cropped area by large scale irrigation, a threefold increase in sugar estates, and a fourfold expansion of large-scale mechanized farms. The World Bank projects – known officially as the Agricultural Development Project – will grow from 629,000 families (1980) to 3,831,000 (1985). A modified Green Revolution package will be supplied to the so-called residual Accelerated Development Area that will cover two-thirds of all Local Government Areas by 1983.

Distributional Consequences and Popular Response

As we have already implied, the distributional effects of these policies have not radically altered the pre-civil war rural-urban income imbalance and apparently have skewed income distribution within the rural sector. The recent International Labor Office (ILO) report estimated average rural income (at town prices) in 1977/78 at ₦ 128 compared to ₦ 559 in the cities; moreover, between 1973 and 1979 the rural-urban income gap widened from 1:4.7 to 1:6.1. Ladipo and Adesimi (1981) also estimate a worsening of conditions in the rural sector. Data on local or village-level income distributing is, of course, notoriously difficult to obtain. Such work as exists indicates pronounced inter-household inequality in the cocoa producing areas and some in the northern close settled zones. Moreover, Ladipo and Adesimi (1981, p. 310) believe, on the basis of data from Western and Oyo States, that the coefficients of rural income inequality for those with less than ₦ 500 per year (i.e., the vast majority of rural producers) actually worsened considerably between 1969 and 1975.

Naturally any mean statistic of rural income gives a misleading impression of the geographical distribution of rural poverty. In the mid-1970s Usoro (1978) identified four contrasting areas, all of which were economically vulnerable. First, the northern provinces are subject to periodic droughts and the threat of desertification where population densities are already close to carrying capacity. These areas had been hit badly by the famine of 1972-74 and are, in any case, characterized by considerable seasonal outmigration and limited off-farm income sources in districts without access to the restricted dry season irrigation. Second are the closely settled peri-urban regions subject to intense population pressure on land. Hill's study (1977) near Kano showed clearly how a significant proportion of Dorayi villagers were nearly landless and what debilitating circumstances were associated with limited nonfarm income. One-tenth of the community worked as wage laborers in menial urban occupations and an equal number of male householders desperately sought borrowed farm land each year. Poor families were quite literally too poor to migrate to new farmland with the result that demographic pressure on limited holdings actually increased. Similar land constraints are to be found in the densely settled areas of Anambra, Imo and Cross River States where poor farmers finance food purchases from sporadic palm oil production, petty trade or erratic wage laboring.

A third pattern consists of intense export commodity producing areas subject to economic shocks detonated by price fluctuations.

In the major cocoa regions, increased cocoa prices since 1973 have scarcely kept pace with rises in the consumer price index; the cost of cocoa farming, of food and of labor (the latter fueled by a high demand for casual labor in the urban construction industry) have all spiraled in the 1970s, and cocoa production has slumped accordingly. Drought and the rosette epidemic combined with low produce prices leveled groundnut production in the north, whereas palm produce, though increasing in value in real terms in the 1970s, has suffered from the high rates of general inflation since 1975. As produce prices plummet, the demand for off-farm income correspondingly increases; whereas in 1964 over 80 percent of household incomes in Uboma (Imo State) came from farming, in 1974/75 only 40 percent did so in three different Imo State communities (Williams 1980). Only the more fortunate, however, were able to benefit from the lucrative trade operations that accompanied the commodity boom. The rural poor faced admittedly rising rural wage levels but were nonetheless incapable of meeting rapidly inflationary food prices even though farm wages in some southern rural areas in the late 1970s were ₦ 5 per day, almost twice the government minimum wage (Clarke 1979). Between 1975 and 1980, the price of staples in rural areas increased by almost 150 percent.

And finally, Usoro noted those peripheral districts often with sufficient land but lacking good road access to markets, such as Idah in Benue State, Wasinmi in Oyo State and lands along the eastern frontiers of Cross Rivers. Of course, some farmers with access to lowland (*Fadama*) or market gardens profited from the expansion of purchasing power among the urban middle classes and civil servants. Equally, declining staple food production and volatile market prices during the 1970s brought windfall profits to intensive food exporting regions such as southern Katsina and Lafiya, but speculative profits accrued to large scale urban and rural wholesalers rather than to direct producers.

Although many rural surveys suggest that income and landholding irregularities in Nigeria are not oppressive (especially in the North in relation to the South), it seems clear that the poorest third of rural households remain especially vulnerable and have little to show materially from the oil boom. Clarke's (1979) study of Ifetedo south of Ife, for example, shows marked income differences between community members and migrant tenant farmers; the estimated income of the average farmer was ₦ 348 per annum but only ₦ 159 per annum for tenants. Village studies in Sokoto, Zaria and Kano also reveal marked inequities where market access, lowland irrigation and craft production were limited (Norman et al 1976; Matlon, 1981b). Hill's survey near Kano estimated that 36 percent of all households owned only 4 percent of the total farmland, each with less than one acre per household which is clearly incapable of provisioning domestic subsistence demands. Clough's (1979) study in an intensive millet producing area of southern Katsina also indicates high inequality. The wealthiest 10 percent of the farmer-traders owns 40 percent of the land. Clough suggests that the extent of inequality has increased concurrently with the emergence of a prosperous farmer-merchant class who has bought and rented a large proportion of the better farmland at the expense of poor and middle peasants.

All this suggests a reproduction crisis among the rural poor who find themselves increasingly on Lilliputian holdings, incapable of fulfilling domestic food needs and resorting to wage laboring to secure socially necessary income. Among this class, borrowing and debt become essential to meet reproductive requirements which can act as a source of surplus extraction for those to whom they are indebted. Sharp seasonal price swings for grains, for example, mean that the rural poor may engage in distress sales at harvest, yet are projected back into the market six months later when staple prices are 50 to 100 percent higher. Merchant wholesalers are able to use debt relations and seasonal price variations to accrue large speculative profits which can be reinvested in lucrative trade sidelines such as livestock (Watts, forthcoming). Invariably, the poor with limited access to the state and to remunerative off-farm income sources can only reproduce themselves by scavenging among the slim, trickle-down pickings of the petroleum economy.

These trends should not obscure the real and obvious material deprivation of many rural producers. Indeed, if Matlon's (1981a) survey of three Hausa villages in 1974-75 is at all representative, levels of absolute poverty in the rural sector are shockingly high. Eighty percent of households were not self-sufficient in domestic food production, and 20 percent of families experienced caloric deficits of 15 to 25 percent. According to Matlon, there was "a serious degree of absolute impoverishment among the poorest 30-40% of households" (1981a, p. 339). The ILO report estimated 4 million rural households were below their poverty data line in 1978, an increase of 25 percent over 1973. Crude death rates among the 1- to 4-year age group is still in excess of 20; life expectancy at birth remains less than 50 years; and the daily per capita calorie supply as a percentage of the 1977 FAO requirement was only 83 percent (World Bank 1981).

These conditions have been met with increased popular protest. This is perhaps most explicit in the urban areas not only with rising crime and violence among the popular classes but the recurrent successes of the Nigerian labor movement in securing significant wage increases through the Adebo and Udoji Commissions. In the rural sector, peasant resistance to the state is grounded in the individualized nature of household production and already violent rural responses to statist intervention have surfaced. In May 1980 14 farmers were killed and 200 arrested on the Bakalori irrigation project after they had blocked roads and occupied offices following a compensation dispute (*West Africa* May 12, 1980). Further, the success of the Peoples Redemption Party in the 1979 elections in Kano and Kaduna states suggests that the 1970s saw a broadening of the sociological basis of peasant resistance. The PRP Governor of Kano State, Alhaji Abubakar Rimi, has already claimed that his party has enabled the rural producer to remove the shackles of the "traditional [rulers], the Alkali [and] the police, who have been the state instruments of his oppression" (*West Africa* October 20, 1980). In addition, the PRP Governor of Kaduna State, Alhaji Balarabe Musa, in direct contradiction of the Federal Minister of Agriculture, voiced his untrammeled opposition to the World Bank rural development projects, which will:

> merely serve a handful of large-scale farmers who are basically urban dwellers, but who have taken away most of the benefits at the expense of the small peasant farmers in the villages (*New Nigerian* November 21, 1980).

The attempt at land nationalization with the Land Use Decree of 1978 was marked by considerable rural agitation, especially in the south, while attempts to use cheap female wage labor on some of the Northern irrigation schemes have met with fierce resistance and strike behavior (Jackson 1978).

The Urban Sector: an Overview

The forces that have brought state intervention and peasant differentiation in the rural sector have also had an impact on the urban sector by increasing the rate at which peasants migrate to Nigeria's already swollen cities. Without a reliable census we must simply estimate the rate of urban population growth. Within the major urban centers – Lagos, Ibadan, Kano, Kaduna, Port Harcourt, Onitsha – the annual rate is at least 7 percent and perhaps as high as 10 to 12 percent. An International Labor Office study (1981) estimates that the urban poor have doubled during the 1970s. And, given the significance of the Nigerian economy within the West African region, the urban population now includes millions of aliens from neighboring states. The bias of state and private sector investment toward urban centers ensures that the drift to urban areas will continue, as construction industries among others promise to employ large numbers of short-term unskilled workers. Reliable estimates put the proportion of Nigeria's urban population at about 30 to 24 percent of the national population, depending upon one's population estimate.

The rapid expansion of the urban population is characteristic of all cities of Nigeria, even within rural and backward states like Gongola or Bauchi where rural migrants are attracted to the administrative centers which receive some state capitalist investment. Since the onset of the petroleum boom one can discern three major areas of urban growth in Nigeria. Without rival the most important urban center is metropolitan Lagos. It has grown from about 1 million at the beginning of the Nigerian Civil War (1967) to over 5 million at present. It is not difficult to explain the rate of growth of Nigeria's largest commercial, industrial and government center. Besides serving as the administrative center for the increasingly centralized federal government as well as the Lagos State government, metropolitan Lagos accounts for about 60 percent of all modern sector industrial employment. Here, those who live at the highest international standard of consumption meet those who live at one of the lowest, one that approaches levels attained in Asian cities. Congestion, traffic, flooding and urban violence have risen astronomically during this period.

The petroleum and natural gas resources of Nigeria have stimulated urban growth in the second growth area southeast of Lagos in the cities of Benin, Warri and Port Harcourt. Since the basic state industrial investments – petroleum refineries, petrochemical industries and steel – are located in this triangle, urban growth has soared. Port Harcourt's population, for example, ". . . has galloped from under 200,000 in 1969 to about 800,000 in 1977, [but] infrastructural facilities and housing have remained at almost 1969 levels, thus creating one of the worst urban crises in the country after Lagos" (Ogbonna 1979, p. 197). The new industrial city of Warri presents the same picture, but its crisis is more extreme because it has changed from being a tiny inland river port with a population of 55,254 to "the fastest growing city in the country after Lagos" with an estimated population of 400,000 in 1977 (Ogbonna, p. 198). Of course, such rates of urban growth result in chronic overcrowding, squatter settlements, declining public sanitation and great increases in social inequality. Part of the problem in the petroleum production region arises from the high wages and salaries paid to workers employed in the highly internationalized enclave economy that is typical of petroleum production worldwide.

The third urban concentration of importance emerged along the Kaduna-to-Zaria axis that connects with Kano, the regional economic center for the northern states of Nigeria. Petroleum revenues redistributed from Lagos have been invested in a refinery and petrochemical complex at Kaduna and a capital intensive irrigation scheme immediately south of Kano city. All three cities have attracted industrial development from local, state and international sources. Industry is oriented toward import substitution, food and raw material processing, and the production and servicing of agro-industrial production. Infrastructural investments in communications between the three cities, measured in airports, motor roads and railway facilities, have expanded the role of these cities as commercial distribution centers for the northern states. With Kano's population approaching an estimated 1.5 to 2 million and Kaduna's roughly 1 million, together with Zaria's population of about 400,000, this highly urbanized corridor possesses an urban population of nearly 4 million. As in Lagos and Warri, congestion, poor public health and an appalling quality of urban life abound.

Let us briefly examine the situation in Kano, the oldest and largest of these three cities making up the northern corridor. As in all of Nigeria, the urban poor have increased, but housing is expensive as it is scarce. Kano has no modern sewage disposal system, peasant lands around the perimeter of the city are devoured by real estate speculators, and state policies designed to compensate the dispossessed peasant offer prices well below market value, usually termed a disturbance fee. Thus the city growth rate is a function of rural to urban migration as well as the engulfment of densely settled peasant communities surrounding the ancient Muslim city center. Indeed, it is the tension between older urban social processes that emerged out of an earlier Muslim mercantile era and the more recent growth of inequality and internationalized consumption standards that distinguishes Kano from other major urban centers in Nigeria.

As we mentioned earlier, Kano serves as a center of Islamic radicalism with both socialist and "fundamentalist" tendencies represented in a political tradition that both champions the cause of the commoners – the *talakawa* – and historically has resisted external political authority whether from Kaduna during the First Republic or from Lagos during the current period. Its traditional role as a precolonial Muslim urban center with strong Islamic and commercial connections to rural and urban centers in the wider region means that emigrants to Kano have expectations about the quality of urban life that are derived from Muslim norms of charity and income redistribution. But the Kano of the petroleum era does not satisfy the expectations of impoverished emigrants who usually follow traditional Islamic or commercial networks into the city. Of course, what they discover is a city radically modified by industrial estates and construction projects, new roads that cut through wards of the old city, and an unprecedented inequality of wealth as well as a new life style among the dominant classes that is oriented toward internationalized consumption rather than Muslim patrimonial styles (Lubeck 1982). Equally important, the price of food, housing and other minimal necessities, that once were easily redistributed in ways governed by the Islamic norms of charity, have risen and/or become marketized to such a degree that large numbers of the destitute are no longer absorbed by the informal mechanisms of the past. As we shall illustrate below, both "popular" expectations and recent inequity contributed to a violent upheaval during December of 1980.

Urban Life for the Popular Classes: Issues of Income Inequality

Let us turn to the urban material and social conditions as actually experienced in everyday life by wage workers, independent commodity producers and the floating population of Nigeria's urban poor. As we noted earlier, all research indicates that the gap between the wealthiest and poorest classes has widened since the onset of the petroleum economy. Yet, to accept the published data on income distribution that is based either on tax data or formal sector (e.g., government and corporations) income data is misleading and most importantly, seriously underestimates the level of income inequality as well as the distribution of wealth across Nigerian classes. Why is this so? To answer this question one must first realize that income distribution studies depend upon published income statements, rather than evidence for the actual amount of wealth owned by particular income strata. In Nigeria, the wealthy do not report their legitimately earned income through trade, real estate or other forms of profit; and the state is unwilling or unable to control this practice. Note that illegally gained wealth, an important source of income for many individuals if Nigerian commissions of inquiry are to be believed, is an additional source of income that falls outside of these studies. Even if one ignores illegally gained income, the merchant-industrial bourgeoisie who are the wealthiest in Nigeria fall outside of the formal taxation system, and thus their incomes are not registered for any income distribution study.

Notwithstanding the problems of illegality and the nonreporting of income, state sponsored credit and loan schemes allow them to speculate in real estate at state expense. In fact, such credit is a form of income subsidy. Moreover, according to the ILO study on Nigeria, upper level salaried employees are not registered for taxation in the same proportion as are the lower income groups within the formal, enumerated sector. For example, while analyzing tax data, the researchers discovered that most (90 percent) unskilled and semi-skilled workers were "netted" by the Pay As You Earn (PAYE) tax system. But when they examined the figures for the class composed of professional, management and administrative personnel, the number of taxpayers in this category were undercounted; in their estimation, this class . . . "must have included over three times as many persons at that time" (ILO, p. 234).

For all of these reasons, any income distribution study for Nigeria *must* underestimate the real degree of income inequality in contemporary Nigeria, a fact astutely assessed by the urban popular classes – wage earners and independent commodity producers – and by members of Nigeria's educated elite. The Adebo Commission described the tension generated by the maldistribution of wealth after the civil war and prior to the petroleum boom in a way that is even more relevant today. After noting the problem of equality and the suffering of the lower income groups during and immediately after the civil war, the commission noted:

> It is clear not only that there is intolerable suffering at the bottom of the income scale, because of the rise in the cost of living, but also that the *suffering is made even more intolerable by manifestations of affluence and wasteful expenditure which cannot be explained on the basis of visible and legitimate means of income*. (Their italics.) [First Report of the Wages and Salaries Review Commission Fed. Min. of Information, Lagos, 1971, p. 9.]

Nor, to their credit, have Nigerian observers ignored the hidden bias of state expenditure and subsidies in favor of the dominant classes. Sada, for example, shows how the maldistribution of sanitation services favors the affluent areas of Lagos, and how state urban transportation investments exploit the lower income groups and favor the elite class:

> In spite of the traffic problems and the obvious problems of accessibility by the low income (earners) from Mushin, Shomulu, and so forth, to government offices in Lagos, the federal government still felt convinced that the appropriate location for the interim federal Secretariat should be farther down in Ikoyi. After having set this location, a multimillion naira set of overhead roads and bridges were built to link Ikoyi with Victoria Island to enhance the accessibility of the resident elites to the Secretariat. Thus, while taking care of the elite class who were supported by car loans and allowances from the government, the low income class – most of whom are not being paid any type of transport allowance – were left without adequate consideration. Thus, the low income worker in the government service now must spend more money on his journey to work while the elite administrator spends less since the Secretariat has been brought nearer to his home. (Sada 1981, p. 286.)

Sada concludes his analysis of government investment by noting that since a greater proportion of the benefits of government are enjoyed by the elite class, it can be inferred that the greater the government investment the wider the gap in income distribution in the cities. Space does not permit us to provide more examples, but the bias of state investment in areas such as housing, roads and industries is virtually always in favor of the urban elites.

The Quality of Urban Life for the Popular Classes

Having reviewed the distribution of income among the urban classes, let us turn to issues referred to as the quality of urban life. Here we refer principally to housing, malnutrition, health, community life and the general issues of life changes and personal safety. Given the prevailing rate of urban growth described, housing is a serious problem. Currently, the best evidence available is contained in the ILO study, which suggests a significant deterioration in residential standards since Independence: rents have soared such that the poor spend 30 to 40 percent of their income on housing. Furthermore, the proportion of households living in a single room has increased markedly since 1970 when over 72 percent of Lagos, 69.9 percent of Kano and 51 percent of Port Harcourt urban residents fell into this category. By 1977, for example, the proportion of households living in a single room in Port Harcourt had increased by 12 percent to over 63 percent (Ogbonna 1979, p. 199). The federal government's planning target of two persons per room looms distant from the current estimated 3.6 per room. There is no relief on the immediate horizon, for ". . . most new housing has been for the middle- and high-income groups. Low income migrants tend either to hire single rooms or build substandard squatter dwellings. . . . and in the crowded cities, many are sleeping in the open air" (ILO, p. 120). The period between 1960 and 1975 witnessed almost complete state neglect of urban issues. Loan allocations averaging 30,000 to 35,000 naira increased from 200 in 1972 to a mere 800 in 1976; almost all went to the rich.

Sanitation and health have also deteriorated in urban areas because of overcrowding and the absence of public sanitation facilities such as a comprehensive urban sewage system which all Nigerian cities lack. The generalized result, of course, is widespread, appalling filth and endemic disease: during the rainy season flooding, the mixture of raw human waste and surface water is nothing short of a nightmare. According to the ILO study: "Emptying pails outside the house is still the predominant method of human waste disposal in urban areas. . . . In 1975 49 percent of urban dwellers used the pail system . . ." (ILO, p. 121).

The responsibility for this situation rests with the federal government which, during the 1957-80 period of the Third Plan, allocated 1.4 percent of capital expenditure to sanitation though implementation was much lower still. While Lagos receives great coverage in the international press for its sanitation problems, the situation is serious in the more arid regions of the north. In Kano, for instance, deep burrow pits, once used to mine clay for building material, collect stagnant water which is employed for domestic purposes. One can regularly observe toilet pipes flushing into these pits at one end while simultaneously observing the urban poor bathing and laundering clothing at the other. Water borne diseases – hepatitis, cholera and intestinal disorders – are endemic.

The quality of urban life has deteriorated in other ways: the urban water supply is unable to reach its limited capacity because of crowding and breaks in the power supply. Again, according to the ILO study, ". . . crimes against the person more than trebled between 1960 and 1975 . . ." (ILO, p. 132), and armed robbery is now a serious problem in cities, especially Lagos. Most importantly, for the popular classes, all of these developments have undermined the quality of urban community life which, prior to the oil boom, expressed a vitality even under the conditions of material poverty.

Popular Responses to Inequality

We have outlined the class and social situation in which the urban popular classes struggle in order to obtain subsistence and to create the social conditions for family and community life. As we have illustrated, the petroleum boom has brought great inequality to Nigeria's urban inhabitants. Given Nigeria's tradition of militant trade unionism, one may argue that the conditions of labor, if not the real wage rate for unskilled workers, have improved marginally during this period. But, for the urban majority who labor in the informal sector as independent commodity producers, only the most fortunate among them appear to have benefited. The reason for this fact resides in the nature of the informal sector itself. Independent producers who trade, repair, service and produce at the small-scale industrial level are in competition with each other in a market that allows unlimited entry of new and marginal producers. New entrants to the urban labor force usually begin as wage workers or apprentices in the informal sector. Thus it functions as an informal educational system for trade and small-scale industries. Both profits and wages are low relative to merchant industrial capital. Again, it is not that the producers of the informal sector do not provide essential services and products that are necessary for the material reproduction of Nigerian cities; rather, these producers gain little because of the underdeveloped technology and low productivity that characterizes the sector as a whole. Oftentimes, lines of production or services that become profitable are absorbed by a more efficient firm and plied with capital from merchants or credit from industrial firms. Bread baking, for example, has become much more heavily capitalized and thus, to a significant degree, has moved out of the informal sector. In an economy in which direct state subsidies, joint venture monopolies and tariff protection characterize the modern formal sector industries, the opposite holds for state support of informal sector producers. Yet, despite this discrimination, informal sector producers remain unorganized as a political force and have been largely ineffective in protesting the state's relative neglect of their specific needs.

Although formal sector wage workers constitute a distinct class, their social existence is aligned with producers in the informal sector. The evidence presented by Peace for Lagos and Lubeck (forthcoming) for Kano confirms that most informal sector wage workers and most independent producers identify with the struggles for higher pay waged by formal sector counterparts. Why should this be true? Not only do wage workers pass through the informal sector at some time during their working careers, but they compete in similar market conditions for housing and subsistence and thus share the same urban squalor as informal sector producers. Much of their social existence, then, is shared, even though the working conditions of wage workers is radically different from independent producers. Since a large proportion of independent producers produce goods or services for wage workers, i.e., wage goods, members of the informal sector have a material interest in the success of wage earners' struggles for higher pay. Community, ethnic and other social ties that arise from common residence reinforce the solidarity of these two popular classes, especially when juxtaposed against the immediate material circumstances of the dominant classes.

Wage workers in the state and private sector, especially in manufacturing, have created a militant tradition during Nigeria's short national history. Nationwide general strikes occurred in 1964, 1971, 1975 and 1980. In addition to the national strikes, industrial disputes are commonplace in the Nigerian industrial sector. For example, the central bank reports hundreds of thousands of man-days lost during the 1970s, and these figures unquestionably undercount the actual number of strikes, many of which go unreported: 144,881 man-days in 1974; 435,493 in 1975; 213,186 in 1976, and, for the first six months of 1978, 200,374. Hence, class action at the workplace is quite advanced even though wage workers have not translated this energy into political activity, again, in part, because of the banning of trade unions from formal political party activity. Table 4.9 presents food prices in relation to the beginning wage for industrial workers in the city of Kano and indicates that the real wages of workers have not kept up with the rise in the cost of food among other wage goods like housing.

TABLE 4.9
Food Prices and Wages in Kano 1971-80

	Price in Naira				*Percent increase*
Commodity	*1971*	*1975*	*1978*	*1980*	*1971-80*
Millet (measure)	.17	.50	1.10	1.20	605
Rice (measure)	.83	1.60	2.50	5.50	562
Sorghum (measure)	.21	.50	1.00	1.00	376
Starting wage	.87	1.75	2.25	3.85	342

Source: Lubeck (forthcoming).

The Nigerian Labor Congress: Prospects for Popular Leadership

Thus far we have analyzed the distributive effects of the petroleum boom on the urban popular classes. Though strong in number, the independent producers of the informal sector do not appear to form a class that is capable of serving the political needs of the popular classes. In contrast, the wage workers of the formal sector have responded to the inequality and deteriorating social conditions of the urban dwellers with a militancy unmatched by others. But until now the power of the wage earning class has been limited to the economic rather than the political sphere. Let us briefly review how this economic focus emerged.

Prior to the reorganization of the trade union movement during the last years of the military government, trade union organization was fragmented into overlapping and often competing industrial unions that were often affiliated with foreign international trade union organizations, especially those organized by the anticommunist business unionist International Confederation of Free Trade Unions (ICFTU) or the Prague based and pro-Soviet World Federation of Trade Unions (WFTU). In practice, both international federations funded the operation of their local congresses, the United Labor Congress (ICFTU) and the Nigerian Trade Union Congress (WFTU). Both because of the lack of rank and file control and because of the corruption within the delegations, the competing congresses were unpopular with trade union democrats, nationalists and militants who favored trade union unity.

The move by the military government to reorganize the competing unions into 42 national industrial unions came only after trade union leaders attempted to form an independent yet unified national trade union congress, a move occasioned by the death of a trade union militant. The resulting organization, however, was banned as "undemocratic" by the military government. Here one should note that many Nigerian scholars and trade union militants believe that the "independent" Nigerian Labor Congress formed by the unified congresses was banned precisely because it represented a unified threat to the interests of the dominant classes during the elections for a return to civilian rule. After banning the independent Nigerian Labor Congress, the military government attempted to appoint national secretaries to head the newly reorganized unions in a move that clearly emulated state "corporative" strategies used by authoritarian

Latin American regimes. But trade union resistance has, however, been strong enough to resist this cooptation strategy.

When the reorganized trade unions were instituted under a NLC with an elected leadership and a state appointed administrator, the new policy appeared to be ambiguous. On the one hand, the trade unions were organized into 42 centralized and noncompeting unions; monthly union dues amounting to naira 1.50 per worker were automatically deducted for financing the unions, and laws allowing workers to join unions were enforced for the most part by the state and federal governments. On the other hand, trade unions have now become dependent upon the state for financial support in the form of initial grants and for enforcement of compulsory check-off of union dues. The question remains whether the state has successfully incorporated the trade unions into an economic and essentially nonpolitical posture within Nigerian politics. Nonetheless, the NLC successfully waged a general strike for higher minimum wages during May 1981 while the number and sophistication of trade union members has clearly increased significantly during this period.

Popular opposition to the dominant classes has assumed less organized forms and rested within the economic rather than the political arena. Independent producers often protest government action insofar as it affects their immediate interests such as market fees or squatting privileges. Yet, the ability of the state to contain and to push Nigeria's militant trade union movement into an apolitical stance is much more questionable. Given the conditions that we have described here, it is likely that organized labor will discover a way to participate in the political party deliberations planned for the 1983 elections. But for the most part, one must look outside of the formal political party institutions in order to understand and to observe the response of the popular classes to the new forms of inequality emerging in contemporary Nigeria.

CONCLUSIONS

The civil war and oil have laid a new foundation for the political economy of the Nigerian state. The expanded role of federal expenditure and state capital has provided a major filip to capitalist development and class formation though these new tendencies have also involved international capital at all levels of the economy. We have emphasized the burdens imposed on the popular classes by this transformation and the responses it has elicited. But the important question that remains is whether the Nigerian state is capable of managing this transition and accommodating the new contradictions associated with a palpably changing social field of force.

In one respect, the new fiscal allocation indicates a massive commitment to social transformation. The Fourth Development Plan (1981-85) envisages a huge total expenditure of ₦ 82 billion of which total government expenditure is ₦ 70.5 billion (*West Africa* September 28, 1981). Priority will in fact be given to agricultural production (15 percent of capital resources) and processing, which are expected to grow at an annual rate of 4 percent. The 1981 capital estimates allocated ₦ 1.62 billion to agriculture and the appropriations to the Agricultural Credit Guarantee Scheme were doubled in October 1981 to ₦ 208 million (*Nigeria Newsletter* #75). Yet the capability of the state to effect a complete and rapid social transformation is effectively constrained in three ways. The first is the managerial incapacity of the state apparatus that is the expression of its own class constitution. As Joseph (1978) points out, during the 1970s there was a huge spending spree, thoroughly disorganized and chaotic, in which civil servants, technocrats and merchant capitalists channeled state revenues into their own coffers. In the course of events, millions of naira have mysteriously disappeared or surfaced in Swiss bank accounts. "Oilgate" and endemic corruption and patronage color the vastly inflated federal and state bureaucracy. In 1979, for example, the Public Accounts Commission reported that the Nigerian Customs and Excise could not account for ₦ 8 million in missing vouchers, the Ministry of Finance had no listing of ₦ 2 billion of state investments (1970-74) and, in a condemnation of bureaucratic management, high ranking civil servants had completely ignored the direction of routine duties (*West Africa* November 9, 1981). Indeed, the almost anarchic manner in which the state functions contributes precisely to its limited political capacity.

The second is the critical issue of state capability and weakness in relation to popular dissent, perhaps the most startling example of which was the "Yan Tatsine" millenarian movement of December 1980. As a militant Islamic sect under the leadership of their prophet Alhaji Mohammed Marawa, it attempted to take over the Friday Mosque in the old city of Kano with the intention of seizing control of Kano. Blocked from reaching the Friday Mosque by the police, the 'Yan Tatsine took over a school, fought with and killed at least two policemen, and then retreated into the 'Yan Awaki section of the old city. There they fortified their area, seized from 50 to 65 hostages and prepared to fight the authorities for their religion. After ten days of widespread disorder marked by vigilante groups seizing alleged followers, protracted fire fights between the police and the 'Yan Tatsine, and the breakdown of public order, the Nigerian army was called in on December 28. The army leveled the area and drove the rebels to a village outside of town where their leader died and a large number of his followers were either killed or captured. A tribunal of inquiry has gathered evidence and testimony from hostages and followers, and estimates of the loss of life vary from 1,000 to 10,000.

Significantly, the social and political views of the movement are related to the name *tatsine* which refers to the Hausa word "to damn," in this case invoking the leader's preaching style during which he damned all those who concerned themselves with modern materialism. His followers were told to carry only enough money to satisfy their needs for one day. Consequently, during his stay in Kano – he had been expelled from the city around 1962 as well as from other Nigerian cities – he and his followers verbally and sometimes physically attacked merchants and landlords and seized property in the area of 'Yan Awaki prior to the confrontation of December.

In sum, 'Yan Tatsine involved an overt critique of the materialism and inequality that has accompanied the petroleum boom in Nigeria. The movement was not solely a lower class revolt, but it was directed against the wealthier classes of Kano and especially those who ostentatiously exhibited Western consumptionist styles of life. The followers of the movement were largely *gardi*, a Hausa term meaning an unmarried man who wanders from community to community studying the Koran. The same institution also served as the base of the recruitment of industrial labor in Kano. Instead of begging with humility, however, the 'Yan Tatsine seized property and damned the affluent consumers of "modernization." It appears that Marawa's recruits were drawn from the large floating population of displaced and wandering vagabonds who assume the status of Koranic students or *gardi*. 'Yan Tatsine, in other words, was expressive precisely of the despair and frustration arising from the post oil transformation of Hausaland and is symbolic of the extent to which the Nigerian state must now confront and mediate glaring class antagonisms.

The third aspect of state weakness is the dependence on oil revenue itself. Nigeria faced a financial crisis in 1977/78 precisely when crude oil output fell by 29 percent from 2.23 billion b/d to 1.57 billion b/d. The recent slump, however, caused by an oil glut in relation to economic recession in the EEC and North America, is much more serious. Production fell from 2.09 billion b/d in January 1981 to 0.64 billion b/d in August; the loss in oil revenues is expected to be about ₦ 4.3 billion for 1981 (*West Africa* September 28, 1981). In August, Nigeria actually reduced the price of its oil by $4 per barrel by which time foreign exchange reserves were supporting the import bill. The bulk of the Fourth National Development Plan is, of course, expected to come from the oil sector. Not surprisingly, the fiscal crisis has resulted in an austerity budget for 1982, and President Shagari has already forced the government to prune $1.5 billion from planned expenditures (*African Economic Digest* October 30, 1981). Most publicity has been given to the civil service cuts but the larger cuts must come from the delaying of capital projects; one-third of the planned projects are likely to be withheld and significantly the River Basin Development Authorities have already been cut from ₦ 1.55 billion to ₦ 0.21 billion (*African Economic Digest* October 2, 1981). Though Nigeria is considered to be under-borrowed internationally, it remains unclear what the vulnerability of oil dependence might mean for the continuing social transformation.

NOTES

The majority of references in this chapter may be found in the sections entitled, "Current Works on Nigeria – Economy/Agriculture."

The naira (₦) was officially worth $1.53 at the end of 1981.

5

STATE STRATEGIES TOWARD NIGERIAN AND FOREIGN BUSINESS

Adeoye A. Akinsanya

Recent literature on "dependency" and "under-development"[1] has indicated, indeed, suggested that some less developed countries have but a margin of choice or area of maneuver through the exercise of public policy in creating successful indigenous capitalist economic development or at least in ensuring that the activities of foreign owned enterprises in the "commanding heights of the economy" are not at variance with the goals and aspirations of the host government, namely, raising the living standards of the masses of the people. A range of policy instruments is increasingly being used or applied to *enhance* national control over private foreign investments and, at the same time, give opportunities for the development and expansion of indigenous public and private enterprises.

This study examines the experience of Nigeria which, particularly in the postcivil war period, has taken various measures to increase the involvement or participation of its nationals in the economic life of their own country. This chapter is divided into three parts. Part I examines the various attempts made by various Nigerian governments at balancing the dual aims of (1) economic development and industrialization through private foreign investors; and (2) economic development and industrialization through the expansion and encouragement of indigenous enterprises and capital. Part II takes a look at government investment in industry as well as government control of industry, and Part III examines the future of public and private enterprise in the light of Nigeria's experience at implementing the Nigerian Enterprises Promotion Decrees of 1972 and 1977.

I

Given the peaceful transfer of political power from the colonial oligarchy to the Nigerian "founding fathers," it is not difficult to assume that an independent Nigeria would offer private enterprise an expanded field of operation within the context of a "mixed economy" (see Post 1964). This is made clear in policy statements by government leaders at the federal or regional levels. Some of these call for mention here. First, while a Federal Government White Paper presented to the Nigerian Parliament declares that a "mixed economy" is envisaged for the country, in the sense of having both public and private sectors overlap in several areas, the Sessional Paper indicates that private enterprise is "responsible for the preponderant part of the economic activity." Second, allaying the fears of alien investors with respect to the security of their investments, a statement issued by the Federal Government indicated that there are

> no plans for nationalising industry beyond the extent to which public utilities are already nationalized . . . Should this occur then fair compensation assessed by independent arbitration will be paid.[2]

Third, speaking before the Federal Parliament four years after independence, the country's Prime Minister, Sir Abubakar Tafawa Balewa reiterated his government's determination to maintain a "liberal" (i.e., "open-door") policy toward private foreign capital:

> It must be obvious. that no Nigerian can be content so long as any major sector of the economy is controlled by foreigners. But we are realists and we say that so long as there is a dearth of Nigerian capital, so long must there be an opportunity for foreign capital in Nigeria. We do not seek the withdrawal of foreign capital from any area of the economy before Nigerian enterprise is able to replace it. When the time for withdrawal has come, due notice will be given (Proehl 1965, p. 159).

But 1952-1959 was a period of "regional competition . . . in carrying on public relations activity directed at . . . attracting investments to their respective regions," and it witnessed a steady stream of official missions abroad to Western European countries "to stimulate trade and investment" (Coleman 1963, p. 390). Thus, before independence, Nigeria demonstrated a capacity to attract substantial private foreign investments. To be sure, the magnitude of Nigeria's dependence on foreign capital is revealed by the fact that 40 percent of the funds for the 1955-1962 Economic Development Plan had to be secured from abroad. More illuminating, the plans for financing the First National Development Plan (1962-1968) called for an expenditure of $1,892 million, one half of which ($949.2 million) had to come from external loans and grants while 30 percent ($560 million) represented direct foreign investments, and the balance was to be raised internally (Anglin 1964, p. 249; Coleman 1963, p. 385).

CREATING A FAVORABLE INVESTMENT CLIMATE IN NIGERIA AND THE DEBATE ON NATIONALIZATION

Whereas state policies directed at private foreign capital were aimed at encouraging foreign enterprises to participate in industrial activities and moving foreign capital out of retail, semiwholesale and other commercial and service enterprises that it was felt that indigenous businessmen could reasonably carry out, those policies directed at Nigerian businessmen were meant not only to provide capital and technical advice but also to expand the base and increase the number of indigenous capitalists. Since State policies toward indigenous and private foreign investments do, and may change *with* time, it is fair to say that the best source of guarantee of "international minimum treatment" for privately owned property is the Nigerian Constitution which, under Section 30(1), provides *inter-alia* that

> No property, movable or immovable, shall be taken possession of compulsorily and no right over or interest in any such property shall be acquired compulsorily in any part of Nigeria except by or under the provisions of a law that –
>
> (a) requires the payment of adequate compensation therefor; and
>
> (b) gives to any person claiming such compensation a right of access, for the determination of his interest in the property and the amount of compensation, to the High Court having jurisdiction in that part of the country.

Although Constitutions can be amended, the constitutional provision relating to the safety or security of privately owned property or the payment of "adequate compensation" in the event of nationalization out of "public necessity" is carried over to Section 40(1) of the 1979 Constitution and applies to Nigerians and aliens alike.

Now let us look at various policies enunciated or formulated to stimulate private foreign investments. That the Nigerian "nationalists" and the Colonial Department of Commerce and Industry were agreed on the desirability of industrialization, there is no doubt. To many Nigerian nationalists, industrial development is not only a means for improving the living standards of their peoples; industrialization is also a tool for building national strength and prestige as well as an asset in international politics. The first concrete action taken to stimulate direct foreign investment in Nigeria, however, was the Aid to Pioneer Industries Act, No. 10 of 1952. Under this Act, companies investing in industries designated as "pioneer" were given relief from the payment of company tax for a period of two to five years depending on the volume of investment. Other concessions included claiming offsets in future taxable years for losses incurred during the tax holiday period and the writing-off of the full amount of capital expenditure during the latter period in subsequent taxable years.

This act was followed by an avalanche of legislation directed specifically at stimulating direct foreign investments and protecting local industries. The relief under the Industrial Development (Income Tax Relief) Act of 1958 takes the form of complete exemption from income tax for a period of two to five years, depending on the volume of investment. The minimum investment required is ₦ 10,000, but at least ₦ 20,000 investment is required to qualify for the maximum period of five years. The relief is available only to pioneer companies, namely, public companies which have been awarded pioneer certificates and are operating in an industry which has been declared a pioneer industry. Any company operating in a pioneer industry wishing to enjoy Income Tax Relief (ITR) has to apply for a pioneer certificate, each application generally being considered on its own merits (Phillips in Teriba and Kayode 1977, pp. 233-51).

These liberal industrial legislations were all features depicting the federal government as a secondary and tertiary party in its efforts to promote industrialization within the private sector during the initial "open-door" phase which coincided roughly with the period 1947-1962. The inducement guarantees were provided by all the regional governments. With respect to the guarantees for private foreign enterprise in the former Eastern Nigeria, the then Premier, Dr. Nnamdi Azikiwe, said:

> The only way of attracting these industrial development pre-requisites from overseas is to ensure for those who provide them instinted co-operation, confidence, security and opportunities to earn adequate rewards for their capital and skill . . . and we are against arbitrary nationalization (Usoro in Teriba and Kayode 1977, p. 65, n. 4).

Undoubtedly, the incentives provided by policy achieved its objective of stimulating the development of private foreign enterprises in the country. Between October 1946 and March 1958, 1,027 companies were registered as opposed to 182 in the previous decade, whereas twenty-six industries were declared "pioneer" industries between 1955 and 1957 as opposed to one that was granted "pioneer" status in 1955.

Aside from economic inducements ranging from complete tax exemptions to generous depreciation allowances, the rules relating to private foreign investments contain guarantees of fair compensation in the event of nationalization, remittance of profits, nondiscrimination, and fiscal stability. Our main concern here is with the issue of guarantees against nationalization. Although it is true that no one, today, seriously questions the right of a State to nationalize – expropriate privately owned property located within its territorial jurisdiction – the main factor responsible for the dearth of private foreign capital in less developed countries (LDCs) has been the fear of nationalization. Because of this, most LDCs have provided legal guarantees of fair compensation in case of expropriation. References have been made to the policy statement made by Sir Abubakar and to the provision of the Nigerian Constitution guaranteeing the payment of "fair" or "adequate" compensation in the event of nationalization out of "public necessity." Nevertheless, the problem of creating a climate conducive to attracting direct foreign investments became a public issue, indeed, a subject of a full-scale debate at the Federal Parliament in November 1961, and it involved the question of guarantees against nationalization. This is very significant because although the Action Group (AG), and the National

Council of Nigerian Citizens (NCNC) advocated "democratic socialism" and "Fabian socialism" respectively, there appeared to be no real conflict over these terms and the question of nationalization during the 1959 federal election campaign. In fact, the prevailing opinion by 1957 seemed to regard Nigeria as a "haven" for direct foreign investments:

> Our Governments have no plans for nationalising industry beyond the extent to which utilities are already nationalised. Nevertheless, they are anxious that there should be no doubt in the minds of overseas entrepreneurs that Nigeria would provide adequate safeguards for the interests of investors in the event of any industry being nationalised in the future. Should this occur, then fair compensation assessed by independent arbitration will be paid (Epelle 1960, p. 244).

For various reasons (see Mackintosh 1966, pp. 427-60), the early 1960s saw a shift in the policy of the AG when its leader, and Leader of the Opposition in the Federal Parliament (House of Representatives), Chief Obafemi Awolowo, enunciated at the March-May session of the House what has come to be regarded in Mexico and the Andean Common Market countries as a policy of *investment and divestment*. He urged that Nigeria, in attracting direct foreign investments, should say "in effect to foreign investors 'come to our aid in the meantime but in due course we will buy you out' " (Phillips 1964, p. 108). As was expected, Chief Awolowo's statement prompted leading political figures to make statements clarifying Nigeria's position with respect to private foreign investments. In New York, the leader of the Northern Peoples Congress (NPC) and the Premier of the former Northern Nigeria, Sir Ahmadu Bello noted that:

> The scope for development is so vast, and the needs for new capital so great, that we should be acting to our own serious detriment were we foolishly to start nationalisation which would cut off at once the help we so much require (ibid).

In his own statement, the leader of the NCNC and the then Premier of the former Eastern Nigeria, Dr. Michael Okpara, said that his party was not planning any nationalization; like Sir Ahmadu he added that Chief Awolowo's statement "cannot aid in the wooing of outside capital in Nigeria" (ibid). Both Sir James Robertson, the outgoing

Governor-General, and Dr. Azikiwe, his successor, issued warnings against statements that would have the effect of driving and scaring away foreign investors.

Replying, Chief Awolowo asserted that nationalization could not totally be ruled out, and this led Chief Festus Okotie-Eboh, the Federal Minister of Finance, to warn against "wild statements" which damage Nigeria abroad, and to name-calling by Dr. Okpara who charged that "those who are advocating nationalisation are communists and they should have the courage to say so" (ibid).

Contributing to the debate on the 1960 Federal Budget at the House of Representatives, Chief Okotie-Eboh lambasted those advocating a policy of nationalization. He expressed the view that the Federal government's role in industrial development was that of "pump-priming," adding that where direct government (public) investment was necessary, the aim should be to sell out to private investors at the earliest possible moment (Blunt in Teriba and Kayode 1977, p. 81). On the demands for public control of the insurance industry, he had this to say:

> This is a very serious matter. We all know that nationalization of industry is akin to communism (Several Hon. Members: No, No!) Yes, it is. This sounds all very simple but this simplicity is most misleading. First, this talk of nationalization is dangerous to our economy. All the Governments (of the Federation) have publicly declared that no steps of further nationalization beyond various public utilities will be undertaken. It is therefore shameful that the Leader of Opposition (Chief Awolowo) who had been heading a Government and who is a party to this assurance comes here to call upon this Government to nationalize insurance which is a private enterprise (Shame, shame!) The new talk of further nationalization can only frighten off those who wish to invest in Nigeria. Thus, the first point is that his suggestion is economically dangerous. The second point is that insurance business is highly technical (Blunt in Teriba and Kayode 1977, p. 81).

But the debate on nationalization was far from coming to an end because, while presenting the Supplementary Appropriation Bill in the first Parliament in an *independent* Nigeria, Chief Okotie-Eboh noted that he found it "most distressing" that "people who should know better are propounding new and dangerous philosophies" which include "loose talk of Nigeria being in the pocket of Britain, economically, politically and otherwise," and "talk of nationalisation." He said:

> Nothing . . . is more likely to deter potential investors than a threat that, once their investments have matured into a successful enterprise, they will be expropriated. No amount of talk of just and fair compensation can fully eradicate this fear (Phillips 1964, p. 109).

He rejected attempts made at using Great Britain as an example of nationalization to be compared with Nigeria:

> In Britain, a highly developed economy had already emerged before certain basic industries were taken by public corporations. A new nation like Nigeria cannot be built on the basis of nationalisation. I need, perhaps, only refer to the examples of America and Canada to illustrate how rapid and orderly development has been achieved by private enterprise efforts, including a large measure of foreign capital, but without the over-hanging threat of nationalisation (ibid).

Concluding his attack on proponents of the policy of nationalization, Chief Okotie-Eboh noted that:

> Nationalisation, based on quasi-Communist ideas, is alien to our philosophy. It is in direct conflict with the farsighted statement of foreign investments to which all the Governments of the Federation have fully and freely subscribed (ibid).

Replying, Chief Awolowo agreed that LDCs need the "requisite" foreign investment climate, and it is because of this that the Nigerian Governments "have made provisions for aid to pioneer industries and also for granting new enterprises tax-free holidays when they are established in this country." He noted, however, that these inducements did not rule out the possibility of nationalization. He then advised that Nigeria should borrow a leaf from other LDCs such as India, Burma, Ceylon (Sri Lanka), Siam and Indonesia which have nationalized industries, and in spite of nationalizations, "foreign investors . . . flock" to these countries (ibid).

That the issue of nationalization would continue to be a subject of much public discussion was made clear when, in delivering his First Speech from the Throne as the Governor-General, Dr. Azikiwe reiterated the 1957 policy statement on foreign investment signed by the Heads of Governments of the Federation. He said: "My Government has no plans for the nationalisation of industry to any greater extent than the public utilities of this country are already nationalised" (Phillips 1964, p. 110). However, when the Motion of Thanks on the Speech from the Throne was proposed, Chief Awolowo put forth an amendment to the effect that "the declaration regarding nationalisation contained in the Speech neither represented the true wishes nor accords with the best interests of the people of Nigeria" (ibid).

Because many voices began to be heard in support of nationalization, Chief Okotie-Eboh who, incidentally was the Leader of the Government Business in the Federal Parliament, announced that the Federal Government would permit a Motion on Nationalization to be debated in the November 1961 session of the Parliament if proposed by the Opposition. On November 19, 1961, Chief Awolowo moved that:

> this House approves in principle the nationalisation of basic industries and commercial undertakings of vital importance to the economy of Nigeria (Proehl 1965, p. 163).

Specifically, he advocated the nationalization of all mining, the merchant marine, insurance, foreign owned plantations, and "all pseudo-extractive and secondary industries like the timber and plywood industry. . . ." Chief Awolowo started from the premise that "nationalisation is the cornerstone, and an indispensable tool of the politico-economic system called socialism." Nationalization, he said, was necessary to combat the *three* traditional evils of capitalism. First, capitalism "of necessity, places a newly emergent and underdeveloped nation, such as ours, in a state of defenseless servitude" because aliens control not only the "commanding heights of the economy" but also distributive trade. Second, capitalism generates "excessive self-interest and utter disregard and disdain for the interests of others." Third, capitalist agents of production – labor, land, capital and entrepreneurship – Chief Awolowo maintained "are rewarded, not for what they actually do or produce, but in accordance with what the harsh remorseless and impersonal and outdated mechanism of supply and demand dictates." Thus, the laborer, although "indispensable to society, gets low wages" because what he supplied is "unusually plentiful in relation to demand" (Phillips 1964, p. 111).

Undoubtedly, the most definitive policy statement with respect to nationalization on behalf of the Federal Government was that made by Chief Okotie-Eboh when he proposed an amendment to Chief Awolowo's Motion on Nationalisation (Proehl 1965, p. 163):

> That this House
>
> (i) Resolves that the nationalisation of industries and commercial undertakings beyond the extent to which public utilities, shipping, Airways, Railways, Power, Communications and Marketing Boards are already nationalised is not in the best overall interests of Nigeria;
>
> (ii) Welcomes the review of company and other legislation now being carried out by the Federal Government and other measures to ensure that such undertakings are conducted in the best interests of Nigeria;
>
> (iii) Welcomes the increasing participation by Nigerians in the ownership and direction of such undertakings; and
>
> (iv) Deplores irresponsible statements on nationalisation which have recently been made in Nigeria and overseas.

Defending the Government's Counter-Motion, Chief Okotie-Eboh raised five "major practical objections" to nationalization. First he cited the shortage of qualified Nigerians to run "nationalized" enterprises, necessitating the recruitment of expatriates to manage these enterprises. Hence, it is uneconomic to nationalize foreign owned enterprises. Second, he contended and rightly too, that the limited financial resources of the Government, must be "deployed to build up the basic infrastructure" and not used as compensation to the dispossessed owners. Third, he argued that nationalization "adds nothing whatsoever to the growth of the economy, whether by increasing our productive capacity, making new opportunities for employment or in any other way, to take existing concerns into state ownership." Fourth, nationalization, he said, would discourage *Nigerian* private investment. This would occur because past policies directed "primarily towards foreign investment" but also toward Nigerian private investment "have achieved a wide measure of success in creating a climate favourable to private investment in Nigeria." Fifth, he maintained that

> we all know that at least until such time as our resources are adequate to sustain our further growth and development, there will be a continuing need for foreign investment in the private and productive sectors of our economy if economic growth is to be maintained and improved (Phillips 1964, p. 112).

Emphasizing his fifth "major practical objection," the Federal Finance Minister noted that it would be difficult if not impossible to attract investment or aid from international financial institutions or "friendly governments" if they felt "that we were using our own limited resources to buy out undertakings rather than deploy them in ways which would contribute directly to the growth of our economy." He added, and this is very significant, "friendly Governments might well question the desirability of imposing additional burdens upon their own tax-payers to assist Nigeria in those circumstances" (ibid).

As if to demonstrate official opposition to public enterprise in general, Chief Okotie-Eboh maintained that "almost" all the statutory corporations existing in Nigeria "pay exhorbitant salaries and they are invariably not properly *managed.* This is a statement of fact" (ibid).[3] Furthermore, he said that through taxation "we already enjoy a forty percent share in the profits of all companies operating in Nigeria without risking a penny of our own limited financial resources in them." To sum up, he said that he was not arguing whether nationalization was good or bad in general; he maintained that nationalization in Nigeria will not "secure an improvement in the lot of the mass of our people." Nevertheless, for several reasons not derived from hostility to private enterprises the government may participate in some enterprises. The enterprise may fall within an area of economic activity in which foreign control or foreign capital participation is not desired, and while it is open to Nigerian capital participation, indigenous capital is simply inadequate or not forthcoming.

From the policy statement made by Chief Okotie-Eboh, the views expressed by Dr. Okpara denying that the NCNC ever stood for nationalization as well as the statement by Chief Samuel Akintola, the then Premier of the former Western Nigeria, that industrial development was the province of private enterprise, it is basic that the attitude of the Nigerian governments is in practice one of *opposition* to State intervention in the economy except when such interventions are in the "public interest" (whatever that means), or for national security or economic development. Furthermore, the persistent pressure for the industrialization and "Nigerianization" (or indigenization) of the economy has led to demands for the protection of *indigenous* businessmen against foreign competition and the activities of foreign owned enterprises operating in Nigeria as well as for opportunities for Nigerians to buy shares in enterprises established with government assistance.

To be sure, a number of trends and attitudes can be discerned in the debates on nationalization. First, those advocating the nationalization of the "commanding heights of the economy" saw nationalization as a means of wresting foreign control of those sectors of the economy. Second, nationalization was seen as an essential prerequisite of socialism while others defined socialism as excluding nationalization. Third, and this is very significant, "we find demands for socialism combined with nationalistic demands for government support for Nigerian private enterprise . . . For most politicians, private enterprise was acceptable if it was Nigerian, unacceptable if it was foreign-owned. Socialism meant nationalisation if one was talking of expatriate business, but meant private enterprise if one was referring to Nigerian-owned business" (Blunt in Teriba and Kayode 1977, p. 84). As the Opposition Chief Whip, Chief Akin-Olugbade put it, "there will . . . be no need to nationalise if the economy of the country is in the hands of the indigenous Nigerians" (ibid). Fourth, by reiterating the pledge that only public utilities will be subject to nationalization, the Nigerian government was, by no means, saying that it would enter into or initiate enterprises that are not public utilities. During consideration of the Insurance (Miscellaneous Provisions) Act of 1964 in March 1964 by the Federal Parliament when members expressed the views that the insurance industry should some day be nationalized, Chief Okotie-Eboh had this to say: "I must say . . . that we do not contemplate in this country, the nationalisation of insurance business. . . . Nationalisation is not our policy. . . . It is not the policy of this Government to nationalise any private industry. When the time comes for us to set up our insurance business, we will do so" (Proehl 1965, p. 165). The Federal Government adhered strictly to this policy of non-State intervention in the insurance industry until the seventies when it not only established the National Insurance

Corporation of Nigeria (NICON) but also acquired 60 percent equity interests in foreign owned insurance companies.

So much for the debate on nationalization. The point that we want to stress here is that much importance is still given to foreign capital in the Nigerian economy. Consistent with the policy guaranteeing "international minimum treatment" for direct foreign investment, such as "adequate compensation" in the event of nationalization "on grounds or reasons of public utility, security or national interests," Nigeria voted for several United Nations General Assembly Resources on Permanent Sovereignty Over National Resolutions stating that a State exercising the right to "nationalise, expropriate or transfer ownership of foreign property," shall pay the deprived owner "appropriate" or "possible" compensation (see Akinsanya 1979; 1980, pp. 48-68). Although it could be argued that these resolutions are merely recommendations and therefore have *no* legal force, the point is that resolutions dealing with legal matters constitute evidence of State practice, and may well in time acquire the character of customary international law. In any event, Nigeria's adherence to these resolutions merely reflects what is Nigerian law, namely, the provision of the Nigerian Constitution providing for the payment of "adequate compensation" in cases of compulsory acquisition (i.e., nationalization). For example, when the Nigerian Government nationalized shipping and airlines, and took over a majority interest in Cable and Wireless Limited, the evaluation of the nationalized assets was carried out by third parties, the compensation figure was reached by agreement between the parties, and it was paid in convertible currency. Additionally, Nigeria concluded an Investment Guarantee Agreement with the United States on August 28 and December 24, 1962, and again on August 3, 1974.[4] The Preamble to the Agreement talks of the

> conscious . . . need for attracting investors of the United States of America as a means of promoting industrial growth and transferring desired technological skills. . . .

The Agreement provides insurance coverage to United States investors against *inconvertibility*. Under it, Nigeria recognizes the subrogation of the United States to claims of its nationals "to any right, title or interest in assets expropriated or assets rendered useless by reason of expropriation." Nigeria also accepted international arbitration if both parties could not resolve (through negotiations) disputes arising from the interpretation of the Agreement. To reassure alien investors of the security of their investments or at least "international minimum treatment" of private foreign investment, Nigeria signed the World Bank Convention on the Settlement of Investment Disputes Between States and Nationals of Other States on March 18, 1965 and became a party to the Convention when the Convention entered into force on October 14, 1966.[5] Finally, Nigeria joined other African, Caribbean and Pacific (ACP) countries in concluding with the ten-member European Common Market the Lome Conventions I and II, which, like the World Bank Convention, were essentially instruments for the promotion and protection of direct foreign investments (see Akinsanya 1976a; 1979; Zartman 1971).

GOVERNMENT POLICIES ON INDUSTRIALIZATION, POLITICAL CLIMATE AND PRIVATE FOREIGN INVESTMENT

We have examined efforts made by the Nigerian Governments to create a favorable climate for private foreign investments in the name of *economic development* and *industrialization*. Nigerian industrial policies from 1947 to 1974 (when the Nigerian Enterprises Promotion Decree of 1972 came into force)[6] can be viewed as having passed through three distinct but interrelated phases: the initial "open door" phase, 1947-1962; the realization phase coinciding with the First National Development Plan, 1962-1968; and the transitional phase, 1970-1974.

As has been correctly asserted, one distinguishing feature of the "open-door" phase was the philosophy of welcoming any industrial development activity and the drive toward frequent overseas inducement campaigns (by official regional delegations) for the establishment of industries backed by liberal industrial legislation such as the Aid to Pioneer Industries Act 1952; Industrial Development (Import Duties Relief) Act 1957; Income Tax (Amendment) Act; Industrial Development (Income Tax Relief) Act 1958; and Customs (Drawback) Regulations 1958. During this phase, the government acted not only as a primary party in the process of industrialization; it also acted as a secondary and tertiary party through official control and administration policy by its use of such weapons as taxes, subsidies, tariffs and licensing. During the second phase, although much emphasis was still placed on private foreign enterprise, the First National Development Plan document indicated that it was "the intention of the governments to enable Nigerian businessmen to control increasing portions of the Nigerian economy."[7] What characterized these two phases was the encouragement not only of private foreign investments either solely or in partnership with Federal or regional public corporations but also the development of public corporations operating industrial concerns (Akinsanya 1978). The transitional phase, however, saw a policy shift in the drive toward industrialization. Whereas the first two phases saw the private sector leading the public sector in the drive toward industrialization, the transitional phase witnessed a policy enunciated to bridge the gap betwen the two sectors. During this phase, alien investors were put on notice that they could no longer be given unqualified guarantees against "nationalization." In fact, the Second National Development Plan document asserted that "it is vital . . . for government to acquire and control on behalf of the Nigerian society, the greater proportion of the productive assets of the country." The authors of the Plan contended that ". . . Government will seek to acquire, by law, if necessary, equity participation in a number of strategic industries that will be specified from time to time. . . ."[8]

A number of factors accounted for or favored direct foreign investment in industrial enterprises in an independent Nigeria. According to one study, they included

> the cordial and peaceful atmosphere in which Nigerian independence was granted in 1960, the impression of political stability left by British administrators in the minds of British and other foreign private investors, the regional structure of the country . . . and foreign businessmen's experience of successful business associations (Usoro in Teriba and Kayode 1977, pp. 66-67; see also Hakam 1966, p. 54).

To be sure, while regional rivalry for concrete evidence of "development" militated against national economic planning and led to wasteful duplication in the establishment of industrial enterprises at a time when capital was considered one of the major constraints to development, it indirectly encouraged and promoted substantial private foreign capital investments (Dean 1974). Added to these factors are "the increased encroachment of nationalistic attitudes on economic matters, the introduction of liberal credit facilities advanced mostly to Nigerian politicians-cum-businessmen. . ." (Usoro in Teriba and Kayode 1977, p. 67). The result was that foreign owned enterprises such as the giant United Africa Company Limited withdrew from the distributive trade and the service industry and moved into the industrial sector of the economy.

We have indicated above that whereas the period 1947-1968 was a period during which measures were taken to attract and promote private foreign investments, the post-civil war period witnessed the promotion of industrial investments not only by the government but also by Nigerian business particularly through the provision of credit facilities by the Federal Government owned banks as well as financial institutions established by the Federal Government, such as the Nigerian Industrial and Development Bank (NIDB), Nigerian Bank of Commerce and Industry (NBCI), and the Nigerian Agricultural Development Bank (Akinsanya 1983). This policy shift has been attributed to a number of forces including the demands of the Nigerian bourgeoisie, the experience of the civil war, increasing government revenues particularly from the oil sector, increasing improvement in manpower and technology, the emergence of technocrats who are more committed to national planning and a strong federal government, and the coming to power of the "men in uniform" (Akinsanya 1976b; 1977). It is small wonder that the Federal Military Government allocated the third highest investment of ₦ 172.2 million or 8.4 percent of the public sector investment to industry in the Second National Development Plan 1970-1974 in contrast to the ₦ 3.8 million or 2.9 percent of total public capital expenditure allocated to trade and industry in the 1955-1961 Plan.

The policy shift to which reference has been made was reflected in a series of legislative decrees promulgated by the Federal Military Government led by General Yakubu Gowon. The first is the Nigerian Enterprises Promotion Decree of 1972 (Decree No. 4), otherwise known as the Indigenisation Decree. Under the Decree, which came into force on April 1, 1974, twenty-two small-scale enterprises (such as bread and cake making, candle manufacture, laundry and dry-cleaning) listed in Schedule I were reserved exclusively to Nigerians. In thirty-three enterprises listed in Schedule II, the Decree provides that Nigerians must have 40 percent equity participation.[9] Other enterprises not listed in either Schedule I or Schedule II, namely, enterprises requiring high-level technology, could be operated by alien investors without Nigerian equity participation. In addition to the Indigenisation Decree, the Federal Military Government (FMG) acquired 55 percent equity interests in petroleum production and 60 percent equity interests in petroleum distribution while it nationalized Esso Standard Limited, paying ₦ 3.175 million as compensation. Apart from directing the Central Bank of Nigeria (CBN) to underwrite stocks or shares that could not be acquired by Nigerians pursuant to the indigenization policy and aside from directing commercial banks through the CBN to allocate a higher percentage of their credit to businesses in which Nigerians held a controlling interest, the FMG acquired 40 percent of the equity interest of all foreign owned banks with a view to influencing their loan policies, perhaps at the board level. More significant, the Federal Military Government established the NIDB, NCBI and the Nigerian Agricultural Development Bank to provide credit facilities to Nigerian businesmen pursuant to the Indigenisation Decree. Furthermore, in addition to establishing the National Insurance Corporation of Nigeria (NICON), the Federal Military Government acquired 49 percent equity interests in all foreign owned insurance companies.

Because of the sharp criticisms levied against the Indigenisation Decree, for example, that the scope was not sufficiently wide and that it could hardly reduce overall alien control of the Nigerian economy; because of acts of omission and commission by public functionaries charged with the responsibility of implementing the provisions of the Decree; and because the powers vested in the Nigerian Enterprises Promotion Board were not sufficient enough to deal with alien investors frustrating the intentions of the FMG "to promote greater and more effective participation by Nigerians in the economic life of the nation. . . ." or at best that the powers did not seem to have been fully exercised, the Federal Military Government, led by General Murtala Mohammed, appointed the Industrial Enterprises Panel to investigate the implementation of NEPD 1972 and recommend amendments to the Decree as well as the level of Nigerian participation in Schedules I and II enterprises. As a result of the Report of the Panel, which has not been made public to date, the FMG led by General Olusegun Obasanjo promulgated the Nigerian Enterprises Promotion Decree 1977 (Decree No. 3 of 1977) on January 3, 1977 and made it retroactive to June 29, 1976.

Under the Decree, enterprises operating in Nigeria were again classified into three groups: Schedules I, II, and III. Schedule I covers forty enterprises considered to be within the "competence" of Nigerians to manage. Consequently, they were reserved *exclusively* for Nigerians. As it turns out, they include those enterprises in which Nigerians were *already* playing a dominant role. Listed under Schedule II were fifty-seven enterprises, and Nigerian equity participation was set at 60 percent. And, under a newly specified Schedule III were thirty-nine enterprises requiring 40 percent Nigerian equity participation. Finally, because of the need to control what is essential for running the economy, the FMG increased its equity interests in foreign owned insurance from 49 percent to 60 percent under the Insurance Decree of 1976 and also its equity interests in foreign owned banks from 40 percent to 60 percent.

We have argued elsewhere (Akinsanya 1981a; 1983) that the indigenization of private foreign investments under the Nigerian Enterprises Promotion Decrees of 1972 and 1977 have not really enhanced national control over the economy nor do the Federal Government's majority equity interests in petroleum production and the service industry (insurance and banking) necessarily confer effective control on the FMG over the operations of the joint ventures. What indigenization seems to have accomplished is to "secure a certain position for a growing local elite of private entrepreneurs whilst at the same time preserving the dominant place for foreign capital elsewhere in the industrial sector" (Collins 1975, p. 144). Indeed, an analysis of the provisions of the Decrees and official statements issued to clarify the rationale behind indigenization does not seem to indicate any intention on the part of the Nigerian Government to reduce the role of alien investors in the economy.

THE STATE AND THE DEVELOPMENT OF NIGERIAN PRIVATE ENTERPRISE

Having examined the position of the Nigerian governments with respect to private foreign investment, just how much contribution did the State make to the development of Nigerian private enterprise? The view of many students of the industrialization process is that historically,

> the integration of tropical Africa with the international capitalist system (through colonialism) can be assumed to exclude the possibility of a nationalist capitalist pattern of development (First 1970, p. 100).

Hence, as Arrighi rightly noted,

> thanks to the grip of the international corporations on African economies, tropical Africa may not produce more than a satellite, subordinate lumpen bourgeoisie, less able to stimulate economic growth independently of these companies (Arrighi and Saul 1972).

On the national bourgeoisie, Frantz Fanon said:

> The national bourgeoisie, which takes power at the end of the colonial regime, is an underdeveloped bourgeoisie. Its economic power is almost nil, and in every case it cannot be compared with that of the metropolitan bourgeoisie, in whose place it means to place itself. . . . The national bourgeoisie has the mentality of men of affairs, not of captains of industry.

This explains why they confused economic control with political control during the struggles for colonial freedom, assuming that if political independence was won, it automatically meant economic control as well. But they were wrong. The point we want to emphasize is that at independence:

> The power base of the new State and what stability it achieves must be sought in a consistency between the interests of the corporations and groups other than the feudal landowning or bourgeoisie, which themselves do not exist or are insufficiently solid to constitute the power base (First 1970, pp. 456-57).

Reference has been made to the period 1947 and 1955 which falls within what has aptly been described as the "open door" phase of the period of industrialization and coincided with the Colonial Government's "Ten Year Programme of Development and Social Welfare for Nigeria." This period witnessed the sustained effort by the government to encourage private investment; more significant, in order to attract private foreign capital, particularly in infrastructural development, the Government published for the benefit of prospective investors a booklet entitled *Opportunities for Overseas Investment in the Federation of Nigeria.* For a variety of reasons, the discussion of which need not detain us here (see Akeredolu-Ale 1972; Akeredolu-Ale in Teriba and Kayode 1977), foreign owned enterprises rather than Nigerian owned enterprises availed themselves of these investment opportunities. The result was that while private foreign investors dominated the economy including the distributive trade, no large Nigerian capitalist class emerged during this period. In fact, as we have demonstrated above, the policy of the government during the period 1947-1962 was that of non-State intervention in the economy other than in the areas where public utilities were already nationalized. This policy continued during the next phase of the period of industrialization, 1962-1968, when the authors of the First National Development Plan (p. 60) indicated that a policy will be adopted

> to enable Nigerians to participate to an ever increasing extent in the *ownership*, *direction* and *management* of Nigerian industry and trade.

To be sure, the Plan document stated that it was "the intention of governments to enable [Nigerian] businessmen to control an increasing portion of the Nigerian economy" (p. 24).

The year 1968 marked a policy shift from foreign capital although whatever policy was adopted was consistent with the free enterprise system. The 1962-68 Plan document (p. 21) asserted that "Governments are convinced that no amount of Government activity can effectively replace the private (foreign) sector." In that year, the Companies Decree (Decree No. 51 of 1968) was promulgated by the Federal Military Government. The Decree embodies the legal requirements for the incorporation of various companies. The Decree:

1. States the patterns for the sale of shares and debentures of registered companies
2. Provides for compulsory inspection and stipulates the arrangements for amalgamation, reconstruction and the modes of winding up registered companies (*Offical Gazette Supplement* 1968, pp. A191-458).

More significant, all foreign companies operating or wishing to establish and operate any business in Nigeria must be incorporated as Nigerian companies before commencing such a business. In the case of insurance companies, the Insurance Companies Regulation of 1968 specified the different classes of insurance business that could be operated, the mode of operation, and the process of registration.

The shift in governments' accommodationist attitude toward foreign capital although still within the orthodox framework of the free enterprise system was manifested in the Second National Development Plan 1970-1974 (p. 289) in which it was asserted that

> The Government will seek to acquire, by law of necessity, equity participation in a number of strategic industries that will be specified from time to time. In order to ensure that the economic destiny of Nigeria is determined by Nigerians themselves, the Government will seek to widen and intensify its positive participation in industrial development.

This policy shift was demonstrated when the Federal Military Government not only promulgated the Nigerian Enterprises Promotion Decrees 1972 and 1977 on February 28, 1972, but also acquired majority interests in petroleum production and distribution and all foreign owned banks and insurance companies.

II

We have come now to an examination of the issue of the State's intervention in the economy. In examining this issue, several questions come to mind. First, why should the State intervene in the economy? Second, how much place should be given to private enterprise if the State must play a major role in the development of industry? Third, what are the issues involved in the economic development of a less developed country like Nigeria.

Undoubtedly, the Nigerian founding fathers were committed to a policy of industrialization wherein the government must play a major role in the country's industrialization and developmental process. It seemed to have been accepted as a matter of fact and, indeed, principle, that the government must be responsible for developing the infrastructure and the public utilities upon which industrial growth depends. More important, because of the dearth of private (foreign and local) capital, it is then obvious that investment must come from government (public) sources. Aside from being committed to a policy of industrialization, the Nigerian founding fathers also had the desire to indigenize or Nigerianize the economy. In a letter to A. K. Blankson, describing how he had been humiliated by a Manager of the First Bank of Nigeria (formerly Bank of West Africa or Standard Bank of Nigeria), Dr. Azikiwe noted:

> it dawned on me that the struggles for Nigerian freedom had many fronts, and that political freedom was not enough; economic freedom must be won also (cited in Post 1964, p. 172).

Thus, although the Nigerian governments made sustained efforts to attract private foreign capital during the first two phases of the period of industrialization, namely, 1947-1968, they were equally aware of the dangers and consequences of allowing foreign control of the economy. As the World Bank Survey of 1954 observed: ". . . the development agencies have sometimes . . . discouraged the entry of foreign capital by their cautious attitude, reflecting the uncertainty of Nigerian political leaders about the extent to which they wish foreign capital to participate in industrial expansion" (cited in *National Development Plan 1962-68*, p. 28). Finally, the Nigerian leaders also believed that it was not enough to indigenize the economy; they believed that the management-level positions of those sectors of the economy under public control must also be indigenized or Nigerianized. Here a distinction is being made between *ownership* and *control*. Whereas ownership is vested in the shareholders, control is wielded and exercised by the management, which need not own any share capital in the enterprise. It was small wonder then that there were persistent demands to Nigerianize all the top-level posts in the country's public services and public enterprises (see Akinsanya 1973).

Some authorities have recognized the role of public enterprise in a country's developmental process. Writing as early as 1959, Hanson (p. 23) observed:

> Whatever the ultimate perspective may be, the country anxious to develop economically has no alternative but to use public enterprises on a considerable scale, at the very least in order to 'get things going.'

> How much is left for private initiative will depend, partly on ideology, but to a much greater extent on social and economic circumstances.

To be sure, the extent and pattern of government's participation in the industrial sector varies from country to country and depends on the country's political and economic circumstances. In most free-enterprise economies, certain industries such as public utilities are State owned and largely on economic grounds. These are publicly owned, first, because they are essential sectors of the national economy. Since private enterprise is not run for philanthropic reasons and since the services rendered by these industries cannot be charged directly to the consumers, it was felt, at least on political grounds, that they are better run as State monopolies. Second, certain industries are State owned because they entail a huge capital outlay that is beyond the means of any single private company in the country concerned. Third, certain industries are State owned for reasons of national security.

There are other industries owned by the State on economic and noneconomic grounds, for example, banking, insurance and mining. In LDCs, measures have been taken by the government largely to increase indigenous participation through direct government ownership and control of key sectors of the economy, lest the control of such sectors by alien investors should cast shadows of economic dependence and neocolonialism (see Akinsanya 1981b). In other cases, certain industries which are considered socially desirable but not economically profitable are undertaken by the government. However, much of government investment in the manufacturing sector is essentially promotional, that is, much government investment is made in the manufacturing sector largely because of the need to attract industries to some areas, usually economically "depressed" areas or to encourage the development of certain strategic but capital intensive and high risk industries. Again, government may enter into joint ventures with private foreign enterprises partially because these enterprises usually make this a condition for investment and, partially, because the government sees it as a means of increasing national stake in industrial production and direction. Finally, government assistance in the form of loans and technical and management services is given to small-scale indigenous industrialists, largely as a means of promoting and developing indigenous enterprises and thus increasing national stake in industrial production.

But just what is the Nigerian experience? We have indicated that one major policy objective of the Nigerian governments is to industrialize as a means of promoting rapid and orderly economic growth. We did make the claim that, until 1970, the strategy of the government was to rely almost entirely on private enterprise, albeit private foreign enterprises, as the engine of growth, and to this end, various incentives and guarantees were provided by the Nigerian governments to attract direct foreign investments, particularly in the manufacturing sector. The Nigerian governments, however, were concerned primarily with the development of economic infrastructure and the operation of public utilities. Speaking on the Government's Counter-Motion on Nationalisation, Chief Okotie-Eboh made clear the Federal Government's position on the State's intervention in the economy:

> we accept the necessity for measures to ensure that all economic activity in Nigeria is carried on in accordance with our own best interests and that, where those interests conflict with those of any other person or country, Nigeria's interests must prevail. At the same time, we do not believe that in order to achieve these aims it is necessary, or desirable, for the State itself to own and operate every important organ of economic activity (Proehl 1965, p. 163).

On many occasions, public functionaries have made statements to the effect that the Nigerian governments "have no plans for nationalising industry beyond the extent to which utilities are already nationalised" and most important, that "fair compensation assessed by independent arbitration will be paid" in the event of any industry being "compulsorily" acquired out of public necessity.

Essentially, the establishment of public enterprises in Nigeria is the product of the country's political and economic circumstances. Nigerian public enterprises can be classified into five groups. First are public utilities created to run enterprises formerly under the control of a Government Department; the objective is largely to free such commercial undertakings from civil service control and red-tape. These include the National Electric Power Authority (NEPA), a merger of the Electricity Corporation of Nigeria (ECN), and the Niger Dams Authority (NDA); the Nigerian Coal Corporation, the Federal Corporation of Nigeria (formerly the Nigerian Broadcasting Corporation); the Nigerian Ports Authority (NPA); and the Nigerian Railways Corporation (NRC).

A second group comprises development and finance corporations established by both the regional (State) and federal governments:

1. to undertake those projects for which individual initiative and private capital are not forthcoming; and,
2. to undertake those types of enterprises for which the minimum economic unit and, so, the capital requirements are large (Akinsanya 1981a).

More often than not, development corporations have entered into joint ventures with privately owned enterprises with rich successes, and they have, on their own operated certain projects, and these have been financial disasters (Akinsanya 1978; Agunpola in Teriba and Kayode 1977). These corporations included the Western Nigeria Development Corporation (WNDC), the Western Nigeria Finance Corporation (WNFC), the Eastern Nigeria Development Corporation (ENDC), the Northern Nigeria Development Corporation (NNDC), and Northern Development (Nigeria) Limited. They have also been used as avenues for diverting public funds into party/private coffers (Mackintosh 1966, pp. 295, 452-53, 524, 526). Third are public enterprises established by the regional governments in fields where government was not previously active. Their *raison d'être* is partly to meet some social need and partly to encourage and provide a model for private enterprises operating in these fields. Such enterprises include the Western Nigeria Housing Corporation which has provided loans for building residential houses at the Bodija Estate. Fourth are enterprises established for reasons of national security or to increase the international prestige of Nigeria. Examples of this group are the Nigerian Security, Printing and Minting Company, the Nigerian External Telecommunications Limited, the Nigerian Airways, the Nigerian National Shipping Lines and the Nigerian Television Service.

Fifth are public corporations established for specific purposes. For example, the Nigerian Industrial and Development Bank (NIDB) was established by the Federal Government in 1964 to provide loans and equity finance for Nigerian entrepreneurs and encourage the inflow of private foreign investment into Nigeria both by borrowing in the international capital market under government guarantee and by investing directly in foreign sponsored projects. Again, the Nigerian Bank of Commerce and Industry (with an authorized capital of ₦ 50 million) and the Nigerian Agricultural Development Bank were established by the Federal Government to provide equity capital and funds by way of loans to Nigerian entrepreneurs and associations, pursuant to the Nigerian Enterprises Promotion Decree of 1972 while the Nigerian National Oil Corporation (NNOC), later the Nigerian National Petroleum Company (NNPC), and National Insurance Corporation of Nigeria (NICON) were established at a time when the Federal Military Government decided that it was opportune to enter into oil production and the insurance industry respectively.

In essence, several reasons can be adduced to explain the State's investment in industry particularly in the post-civil war period. Perhaps, a major reason is that public ownership is perceived as a vehicle for accelerating economic development. Another reason for government's investment program is to increase substantially the low percentage contribution (less than 10 percent) made by the manufacturing sector to the Gross National Product. Third, the military regime (1966-1979) was a period in Nigeria's developmental process when certain industries were regarded as "strategic," and the government, for reasons of economic nationalism, felt that it should have controlling interests in such industries. More significant, public ownership of strategic industries was considered essential not only because of the need to maximize local retention of profits and increase the net industrial contribution to the national economy but also because of the consequences of foreign control of "strategic" sectors of the economy.

It has been asserted that until 1970 the strategy of the Nigerian government was to rely almost entirely on private (foreign) enterprise as the engine of growth. Private enterprise was encouraged, first, by the economic infrastructure provided by the government; second, by the provision of incentives, financial and other forms of assistance to private firms; and third, by the government entering into joint ventures with private investors. These efforts, however, did not prevent public ownership of certain sectors of the economy through the instrumentalities of public enterprises. As the First National Development Plan document (p. 362) emphasized:

> Nigeria's economy is a mixed one. The Governments have taken an active part not only in providing the social but also the basic economic services, such as electricity and ports. They also intend to participate in the operation of various industries, such as a steel plant and an oil refinery. The attitude of the Government of the Federation, however,

> is entirely pragmatic and accepts the desirability of a mixed economy. At the same time, the Governments are convinced that no amount of Government activity can effectively replace the efforts of a broadly based and progressive private sector.

Under the Second National Development Plan 1970-74, however, provisions were made at the federal and state levels (by the Supreme Military Council) for public ownership of at least 55 percent of the equity interests in the following industries: iron and steel, petrochemical industries, fertilizer production, and petroleum production and distribution. Additionally, the government reserved the right to acquire at least 30 percent of the equity interests of other large and medium sized industries such as plantation production of export crops and basic raw materials for the food processing industry and the forest product industries as well as building and construction companies. It should be noted here that until the military regime, and except for the experience during the civil war (Onege in NES 1975), the Federal Government (which has exclusive authority over mining under the Constitution) refrained from direct participation in the extractive industry, principally because of the high risks and complex technology involved, and partly because it required a huge capital outlay. The result was that the Nigerian extractive industry was exclusively dominated by private foreign capital: Shell-BP (British); Agip/Phillips (Italian/American); Mobil (American); Gulf (American); Texaco (American); and Elf (French). But by the early seventies, the Federal Government was participating directly and indirectly in the exploration and production of mineral wealth through the establishment of the NNOC (under the Nigerian Oil Corporation Decree 1970), later renamed the Nigerian National Petroleum Company which was mandated to go into oil exploration and mining and through acquisition of majority equity interests in all foreign owned oil producing companies. For example, the Federal Government through the NNPC expended over ₦ 400 million in acquiring 60 percent equity interests in all foreign owned oil producing companies (NNPC 1978, p. 12).

An examination of the First and Second National Development Plan documents indicates that ₦ 449.238 million represented planned capital expenditure on public utilities, mining and extraction and manufacturing during the 1962-68 Plan period whereas ₦ 412.090 million represented planned capital expenditure for these three sectors during the 1970-74 Plan period. The breakdown for each sector is shown in Table 5.1.

Additionally, capital investment programs were formulated for these sectors under the 1975-80 Third National Development Plan. Data available to us indicate that ₦ 298 million was expended by the Federal Government between 1975-78 to acquire 60 percent equity interests in foreign owned oil producing companies (Table 5.2).

For many reasons, which include inadequate capital (largely as a result of decreasing oil revenues, graft and corruption, and reckless spending by the military) and lack or shortage of appropriate manpower to conduct feasibility studies and carry out project evaluation, various planned capital investment programs of the Federal and State Governments could not be implemented. More important, in spite of government's expressed determination to participate actively in the mining industry (particularly crude petroleum) and although the Federal Government has acquired 60 percent equity interests in all foreign owned oil producing companies, the industry remains virtually under foreign control. In any event, government investment in the industry, for example, during the Second National Development Plan period, was *insignificant* compared, for example,

TABLE 5.1
Federal and State Capital Investment Programs under the First and Second National Development Plans 1962-74

	1962-68 Development Plan (₦m)	*1970-74 Development Plan (₦m)*
Public Utilities	300.88 (310.16)*	204.78
Mining and Extraction	1.232 (0.414)*	35.172
Manufacturing	147.126	172.138

*Figures in parentheses represent actual (rather than planned) expenditure.

Source: Teriba and Kayode (1977, pp. 312-15).

TABLE 5.2
Federal Government Expenditure on Equity Participation in Foreign Owned Oil Producing Companies

Year	*Amount*
1975	50,768,871
1976	203,783,544
1977	–
1978*	43,092,000
	297,643,415

*Estimates

Source: Nigerian National Petroleum Corporation (1978, p. 12).

with manufacturing. Out of a total investment of over ₦ 570 million planned for the mining industry during the 1970-74 Plan period, government investment stood at ₦ 35.172 million or about 6 percent of the total, and out of a total investment of about ₦ 928 million planned for the manufacturing sector during the same period, government investment stood at ₦ 172.138 million or 18 percent of the total. Additionally, the performance of many public industrial enterprises leaves much to be desired (Akinsanya 1981a).

Thus, in spite of efforts made by the Nigerian governments to make investments in what have been regarded as strategic sectors of the economy, such efforts have not altered the strong dominant position of the private sector controlled by foreign capital. Perhaps this can be attributed largely to the fact that planned and actual government investments in these areas have been inadequate. What this has meant is that the Nigerian economy is a mixed economy with the private sector always being the dominant sector.

GOVERNMENT CONTROL OF INDUSTRY

We have advanced some reasons for State's intervention in the economy particularly in the post-civil war period. The measures taken by the Nigerian Government to control the industrial sector of the economy are *diverse*. We shall be concerned only with physical and financial controls and controls in the area of foreign exchange and management.

Physical Controls

Mention has already been made of the provisions of the Companies Decree, 1968 (Decree No. 51 of 1968) as well as the Nigerian Enterprises Promotion Decrees of 1972 and 1977. One of the ways by which the Kenyan government accomplished the "Kenyanization" of the economy was the refusal to renew business or residence permits. Thus, the indigenization program of the Kenyan Government was carried out without causing major economic dislocations and causing much anguish to the Kenyan Asians.[10] In Nigeria, the issuance of licenses has been used by the Government not only to direct businesses to areas of priority ("depressed" areas) but also to regulate business activities. Again, some Customs Regulations issued by the military regime either required that licenses be obtained before the importation of certain goods or specifically prohibited their importation. Although these regulations were issued primarily to conserve foreign exchange, they were used by the Government to control the volume and direction of trade. The Government of President Shehu Shagari, however, has come a long way in liberalizing the importation of what is considered "essential" commodities, such as rice, stockfish, poultry and poultry feeds, indeed, in making Nigeria a "dumping" ground for goods that have been and can be produced in the country given careful and proper planning and execution.

But the principal measure through which the Federal Military Government sought to influence the conduct of enterprises operating in Nigeria was the Price Control Decree 1970 (Decree No. 33 of 1970), amended by the Price Control Decree, 1971 (Decree No. 3 of 1971), which again was amended by the Price Control Decree, 1977 (Decree No. 1 of 1977). The principal Decree stipulated the commodities to be sold at prices fixed by the Price Control Board (at the federal level) and the Price Control Committee (at the state level); it made it not only illegal for any person to sell, agree to sell or offer to sell controlled goods at a price exceeding the controlled price but also outlawed the hoarding of such goods. That the PCB was unable to prevent the continuing rise in prices of goods is much to be expected, particularly given the excess of demand over supply. The result is that the principal Decree was three times amended: first, in 1971; second, in 1977; and third, prior to returning power to the civilians on October 1, 1979, when the military regime *decontrolled* the prices of virtually all goods under the provisions of the Price Control Decree 1977.

In order to regulate the exploitation of the country's vital and irreplaceable natural resources, the FMG promulgated the Petroleum Decree, 1969 (Decree No. 51 of 1969) and the Oil In Navigable Waters Decree. The Petroleum Decree states that nobody shall explore, prospect for, or mine petroleum in Nigeria or in the country's territorial waters without a license. More significant, the decree regulates the importation, storage, sale and distribution of petroleum and petroleum products in the country. In addition to issuing guidelines for field operations, exploration, and the maintenance of boreholes, oilwells and drilling rigs, the Oil In Navigable Waters Decree, 1968 makes provisions for the protection of productive trees and the prevention of pollution of Nigeria's inland waters and rivers. But when oil spillage resulting from the operations of a major foreign oil company (Texaco) in the River State was reported in the country's newspapers, the government of President Shagari did not take any punitive action against the company. It could not have taken any punitive action against a company in which it had 60 percent equity interests! All the Government did was to provide financial assistance to the Rivers State government while the oil company provided what was considered in the Nigerian press very insulting: some bags of rice!

Finally, in order to remove two complaints generally leveled against insurance companies, namely, unnecessary procrastination in making payments of claims against them and arbitrary increases in premium rates payable by the insured, the Insurance Decree 1976 (Decree No. 59 of 1976) was promulgated by the Federal Military Government. The Decree repealed the Insurance Companies Act of 1961 and the Insurance (Miscellaneous Provisions) Act of 1964. While re-enacting some of the provisions of these Acts, the Decree not only prescribes additional measures for the registration of insurers but also makes provisions for the licensing of insurance agents and the registration of insurance brokers. More significant, it sets a *time limit* within which motor-accident claims are to be settled, and it also prohibits general increases in premium rates except with the prior approval of the Government.

Financial Controls

Through a number of Banking Decrees, the Federal Military Government made use of the banking industry to impose controls in the industrial sector of the economy. For example, whereas the Banking Decree of 1969 was promulgated to restore confidence in the banking industry so that it could play the vital role earmarked for it in post-civil war Nigeria, it was used by the government to extend its control to all facets of the industry. The Banking Decree:

1. makes it compulsory for all banks to be incorporated in Nigeria;
2. stipulates the conditions for the granting of a licence to operate a banking business, namely, a minimum paid-up share capital of ₦ 0.6 million in the case of indigenous companies and ₦ 1.5 million in the case of foreign companies;
3. requires the prior approval of the Central Bank of Nigeria before any licensed bank can open or close branch offices within and outside Nigeria;
4. stipulates that every licensed bank must maintain a minimum holding of cash reserves, specified liquid assets, special deposits and stabilisation securities with the Central Bank (Teriba 1969).

In fact, some of the provisions of the Decree were directed at preventing the growth of mushroom banks.

The Federal Government also attempted to influence bank loans to industries through the Central Bank of Nigeria. In 1972, for example, the Central Bank directed that at least 40 percent of all bank loans and advances should be made available to Nigerian borrowers; it also directed that commercial banks should hold at least 40 percent of their liquid assets in Treasury Bills and Certificates and money-at-call. The Government also directed the Nigerian Industrial and Development Bank (NIDB) to grant up to 80 percent of its loans to Nigerian owned companies.

Control of Foreign Exchanges

Because of persistent balance of payments problems, the Federal Government took several foreign exchange control measures that directly influence the industrial sector. Then came the civil war (1967-1970) which meant more stringent foreign exchange control measures. The Exchange Control Order of 1971 provides that the payment on goods under Schedule I[11] can be made with the consent of the Central Bank 90-180 days after their importation into the country while payment on capital goods under Schedule II can be made with the consent of the Central Bank. The credit terms for imported plant and machinery range from between ₦ 50,000-₦ 100,000 to ₦ 2 million, and the corresponding payment periods range from one to seven years. Payments for imported capital equipment, plant and machinery valued at less than ₦ 50,000 can be made if such goods were imported under Schedule I. In order to avoid delays and excessive interest payments on imports on deferred invoices, the Federal Government upgraded most of the goods from the 180-day schedule to the 90-day schedule (Teriba and Kayode 1977, pp. 328-29).

We have indicated elsewhere that one major incentive for direct foreign investments in many LDCs is that their investment laws make adequate provisions for the repatriation of capital and profits (Akinsanya 1981b). Until 1967, Nigeria permitted free transferability of currency to the Sterling Zone while the transfer of currency for "non-resident capital investment" and "approved status" required the approval of the Federal Ministry of Finance. Since 1967, the rate at which foreign companies can repatriate their profits and dividends has been strictly regulated by the Federal Government: foreign companies have been permitted to repatriate in full dividends made up to the end of 1971 and about 50 percent of the 1972 dividends. Because of the Federal Government's Guidelines on Productivity, Prices, and Incomes, companies operating in the country can only declare a total dividend of 25 percent on share-capital at the Annual General Meeting of the Shareholders.

Indigenization of the Management Positions of Nigerian Companies

Because Nigerian leaders believe that it is not enough to indigenize the economy and that the management-level positions of enterprises operating in the country must also be indigenized if ownership of the means of production is to be meaningful, measures were taken to regulate the composition of the management-level positions of industrial enterprises. To this end, the Nigerian Immigration Law of 1962 makes the following provisions:

1. That any foreign individual seeking employment in Nigeria except those to be employed by the Federal Government must obtain the written permission of the Chief Immigration Officer.
2. That an alien may not, solely or in partnership with any Nigerian, establish or acquire any enterprise on the basis of limited liability in Nigeria without the written permission of the responsible Minister.
3. That any Nigerian wishing to employ an alien must forward an application to the Chief Immigration Officer indicating the provision to be made for his repatriation and dependents.

Again, in order to ensure that Nigerians hold top management positions in public and private enterprises, an Expatriate Quota Allocation Board was established by the Federal Military Government. This policy was reiterated in the Second National Development Plan 1970-74 (p. 295) when the Federal Government announced that in order to "reduce" the "earnings leakage" resulting from the employment of aliens "who receive considerable sums in form of salaries and allowances," it would intensify "efforts to ensure, not only that high-level Nigerian personnel are employed by private industry, but also that they are given responsibilities commensurate with their training and experience." When the Federal Government acquired 60 percent equity interests in foreign owned oil producing companies, banks, and insurance banks, such controlling interests were reflected in the composition of the Boards of Directors of such enterprises. But such controlling interests were not matched by increased indigenous representation at the management level, thus making Federal Government's control rather ineffective. Similarly, majority equity control by Nigerians in privately owned enterprises is not matched by increased indigenous representation at the management level. Three possible reasons can be adduced for the predominance of expatriate staff at the management level of public and private enterprises. The first is the acute shortage of high-level manpower required to cope with the rapid economic growth achieved during the 1970s and planned for the 1980s. Second, the Nigerian owners of privately owned enterprises seemed to have been more concerned with efficient "management" and "running" of such indigenized enterprises rather than the indigenization of personnel. Third, the Federal Government indicated, when it was acquiring majority interests in foreign owned enterprises, that it had no intention of interfering with the management of the joint ventures, and it certainly kept its own side of the bargain – *pacta sunt servanda.*

III

In concluding this study, it is in order to examine the future of public and private enterprise in the light of Nigeria's experience at implementing the Nigerian Enterprises Promotion Decrees of 1972 and 1977. Notwithstanding the pious declaration of the Federal Military Government that the *raison d'être* for promulgating the indigenization decree is to ensure "greater and more effective participation by Nigerians in the economic life of the nation" and, in doing so, consolidate Nigeria's political independence, as various studies (Collins 1975; Akinsanya 1983; Biersteker in this volume) have shown, the indigenization of private foreign investments under the Nigerian Enterprises Promotion Decrees of 1972 and 1977 has not really enhanced national control over the economy nor does the Federal Government's majority equity interests in foreign owned oil producing and insurance companies and banks necessarily confer effective control of the Government over the operations of the joint ventures. In the first place, various measures have been devised by alien investors, with the tacit support or connivance of Nigerians or Nigerian officials, to ensure noncompliance with the provisions of the Indigenisation Decrees. Second, whatever elements of control that go with 60 percent equity interest in indigenized enterprises are weakened by the atomistic nature of indigenous equity shareholding. Third, while the Federal Government's majority of equity interests in local subsidiaries of transnational corporations are reflected in the composition of their boards of directors, such controlling interests are not matched by increased indigenous representation at the management level. In essence, although the headquarters of the joint ventures are in Lagos, the headquarters of the former parent companies retain *de facto* control in joint ventures in which they are, technically, junior partners. Furthermore, the problem of control is compounded by the fact that the Federal Government concluded management contracts with its junior partners, meaning, first, that the former managerial powers of the TNCs remain unsailable; second, that the Federal Government is heavily dependent on the TNCs for the provision of specialized and technical services and usually upon payment of a large fee.

Thus, although the Federal Government took measures under the Nigerian Enterprises Promotion Decree 1977[12] against "undue" concentration of wealth among very few Nigerians; and although General Gowon declared, in his 1974 Budget Speech, that "it has never been, and it cannot be, the intention of the Federal Military Government merely to create avenues for a few individuals to grow rich excessively and easily on account of the indigenisation," the view shared by students of Nigerian political economy is that what indigenization seems to have accomplished is to "secure a certain position for a growing local elite of private entrepreneurs whilst at the same time preserving the dominant place for foreign capital elsewhere in the industrial sector" (Collins 1975, p. 144). As has been noted by Oyebode (1977, p. 7), indigenization "has been a calculated attempt to transfer economic power and consequently political power to a microscopic minority of Nigerians, i.e., the propertied few who could gain access to bank loans, sometimes in fact using their future share certificates as collateral security." He added (p. 15), and this is very significant:

> The Nigerian Business Enterprises Decrees of 1972 and 1976 . . . when taken in a holistic framework amount to no more than the indigenisation of the exploitation of the Nigerian nation and resources by the affluent members of the national bourgeoisie.

Another observer (Akeredolu-Ale in NES 1975, p. 69) has noted that:

> There have been reports of over-subscription in the case of every company which has offered its shares to the Nigerian public. . . . [however] we find that the shares have gone in the main to those of us who either had personal savings or had effective access to money from institutional lenders or had both. It also follows that the shares have *not* gone to persons who had no savings and no effective access to institutional loans. Of course, those who have acquired the shares are, by and large, the elite (persons already in business as proprietors, or hired executives, in the civil service, in the Universities, in the armed forces, in various professions) and that those who have not are the teeming thousands of poor urban workers and the millions of peasants and other rural persons.

Of course, it has been claimed that the Indigenisation Decree was not really meant as a tool for achieving egalitarianism and, thus, it should not be criticized for not achieving what it was not meant to achieve. It was small wonder that Onoge (in NES 1975, p. 60) asserted that "the main thrust of the decree . . . is to legitimise the capitalist road of development." Whether the Indigenisation Decree was meant as a tool for achieving "egalitarianism" is certainly not the concern of this study. But there is no doubt that whatever it is that the Decree was meant to achieve was inconsistent with the goals and objectives of the Second National Development Plan 1970-74 (which incidentally was the forerunner of NEPD 1972), namely, building Nigeria into: (a) a united, strong and self-reliant nation; (b) a great and dynamic economy; (c) a just and egalitarian society; (d) a land of bright and full opportunities for all citizens; and (e) a free and democratic society.

As for the place of private foreign enterprise in the economy in the light of the experience gained under the NEPD of 1972 and 1977, there is no doubt that its place remains unassailable. As indicated elsewhere (Akinsanya 1983), an analysis of the provisions of the Decree and official statements issued to clarify the rationale behind indigenization does not seem to indicate any intention on the part of the Nigerian Governments (even in the post-military era) to reduce the role of alien investors in the economy. For example, Section 7 of the NEPD of 1977 states that notwithstanding the scheduling of business enterprises and the provisions relating to them:

> any alien who immediately before the commencement of this Decree was the owner or part-owner of any body corporate carrying on an enterprise the business of which comprised enterprises specified in Schedules 1, 2, and 3 of the Decree or in any two of these Schedules may after the appointed date continue to be owner or part-owners of such body corporate if –
> (a) the annual turnover of the body corporate was not less than ₦ 25,000,000;
> (b) the business of the body corporate was being carried on in not less than 10 states in the federation;
> (c) the equity participation of Nigerian citizens or associates is by the 30th of June 1977 not less than sixty percent.

Obviously, the provision of this Decree can only encourage continued alien ownership and participation in the economy. It was small wonder that foreign investors and their home States have generally welcomed the provisions of the Decree. More significant, various Nigerian governments have welcomed private foreign investors into the country either as partners with local businesses or public agencies, all in the name of "development." At the same time the Federal Government, by amending the Nigerian Enterprises Promotion Decree of 1977 has, in fact, created a new investment regime, giving primacy to private foreign capital. This situation is likely to continue and certainly will be welcomed by foreign investors as well as investor States, particularly the United States. Whether the situation will continue indefinitely will depend on the extent to which the Unity Party of Nigeria (UPN), by no means a "socialist" party although drawing its support through programs that have a populist appeal, overcomes the contradictions of being a *mass* party and an *elite* party at the same time. This is because the UPN is the only party that appears to be in any good position to challenge the National Party of Nigeria (NPN) which, to all intents and purposes, is a party representing business interests and will be at the helm of affairs at the federal level until October 1984, *ceteris paribus*.

To sum up, we have been examining State strategies toward Nigerian and foreign business. We take a look at various measures taken to attract and promote private (Nigerian and foreign) enterprise. We also examine government investment in industry and government control of industry, particularly the reasons advanced for public investment in the industrial sector and government control of industry. The concluding part of the study examines the future of public and private enterprise in Nigeria in the light of Nigeria's experience at implementing the NEPDs of 1972 and 1977. Although Nigeria remains a "mixed economy," private (foreign) enterprise still plays a dominant role. Regarding the impact of the NEPDs of 1972 and 1977 on Nigerian politics, the acquisition of shares under the Nigerian Enterprises Promotion Decrees is obviously and certainly grossly *unfair* and, *potentially, politically* dangerous. Akeredolu-Ale (in NES 1975, p. 70) has noted, and rightly too:

> In transferring the bulk of the acquired shares into the hands of the elite rather than into those of the masses the line which has been drawn and which has separated the have-much from the have-little will be further thickened. Such enhanced economic inequalities are likely to produce social polarisation. Access to wealth and poverty will tend to become increasingly hereditary within particular social groups, the broadest demarcation being between the elite and the masses. Frustration and discontent among the masses will tend to accumulate and reach very high levels in the next few years, and will almost certainly

> reach explosive levels among Nigerians who will be alive some twenty-five years from now. Of course, the concentration of discontent among the general population will also systematically weaken the people's motivation and undermine the nation's development capacity all along.

Interestingly enough, this issue was discussed at the plenary session of the forty-nine member Constitution Drafting Committee. The CDC rejected the Report of one of the Sub-Committees that post-military Nigeria should adopt "socialism" as a State policy, adopting instead what has come to be known as Fundamental Objectives and State Directive Principles which, regrettably, are not justiciable. Essentially the problems associated with inequities and uneven distribution of the national wealth remain *unresolved* and will probably remain so for a long time in Nigeria.

NOTES

The majority of the references in this chapter may be found in the section entitled, "Current Works on Nigeria – Business."

1. See B. Van Arkadie, "Foreign Investment and State Enterprise: An African Context," paper presented at IDEP-IDS-CLASCO *Conference on Strategies of Economic Development in Africa Compared with Latin America*, United Nations African Institute for Economic Development and Planning, Dakar, September 4-17, 1972, IDEP/ET/ES/2347-36; B. Warren, "Myths of Underdevelopment, Imperialism and Capitalist Industrialisation," 81 *New Left Review* (September October 1973):3-45; R. First, *The Barrel of a Gun: Political Power in Africa. and the Coup d'Etat* (Penguin, 1970), p. 100; G. Arrighi, "International Corporations, Labour Aristocracies and Economic Development in Africa," in *Essays on the Political Economy of Africa*, edited by G. Arrighi and J. Saul (New York: Monthly Review Press, 1972).

2. See United Nations, *United Nations Economic Commission for Africa: Report on Investment Laws and Regulations in Africa*, E/CN.14/INR/28, October 30, 1963. Reprinted in 3 *International Legal Materials* (March 1964): 198.

3. Ibid. Emphasis added. On the general problems of evaluating the performances of public enterprises, see Akinsanya 1981a.

4. Initially, the Nigerian Government was reluctant to sign such an agreement because it was "an infringement of sovereignty." It agreed to sign after the United States Government committed itself to providing £80 million for the implementation of the First National Development Plan 1962-1968. Some Latin American nations have not concluded Investment Guarantee Agreements with the United States because they do not recognize the subrogation of the United

States to the claims of its nationals for "assets expropriated or rendered useless by reason of expropriation." See "Investment Guaranties Agreement Between the United States of America and Nigeria, Signed at Lagos August 3, 1974, With Agreed Minute," *Treaties and Other International Acts Series 8012.*

5. See "Convention for the Settlement of Investment Disputes Between States and Nationals of Other States," 60 *American Journal of International Law* (October 1966): 892-911; P. C. Szasz, "The Investment Disputes Convention – Opportunities and Pitfalls," 5 *Journal of Law and Economic Development* (Spring 1970): 23-44; A. Broches, "The Convention on the Settlement of Investment Disputes Between States and Nationals of Other States," 2 *Recueil des Cours* (1972): 333-410.

6. See Federal Republic of Nigeria, *Supplement to Official Gazette Extraordinary*, No. 10, Vol. 59, February 28, 1972, p. A. 18.

7. See Federation of Nigeria, *National Development Plan 1962-68* (Lagos: Federal Ministry of Information, 1962), p. 24.

8. Federal Republic of Nigeria, *Second National Development Plan 1970-74* (Lagos: Federal Ministry of Information, 1970), p. 289.

9. The Decree also provides that the enterprise in Schedule II must have a capital of over ₦ 400,000 ($764,000 or an annual turnover exceeding ₦ 1 million ($1.8 million).

10. See Akinsanya, 1981b; F. Woodridge and V. D. Sharma, "The Expropriation of the Property of the Uganda Asians," 14 *Indian Journal of International Law* (January/March 1974): 54-69.

11. Goods for which payment can be made 90 days after their importation included day-old chicks, milk, salt, cement, sugar, baby foods, drugs and pharmaceuticals, fertilizers and chemicals for agricultural purposes and essential raw materials. Other goods were required to be paid for after 180 days.

12. Sec. 11(1) of the Nigerian Enterprises Promotion Decree 1977 (Decree No. 3 of 1977).

6

INDIGENIZATION IN NIGERIA: RENATIONALIZATION OR DENATIONALIZATION ?

Thomas J. Biersteker

During the 1970s there was a growth in the role of the state and an assertion of economic nationalism throughout Africa. As in the rest of the developing world, most national states have increasingly assumed regulative, welfare, and planning functions, and the state has become a major (if not *the* major) economic actor in many countries (Stepan 1978). At the same time, policies of economic nationalism (nationalization and indigenization) have become widespread in Africa, and most host countries have levied increasingly stringent regulations on the operations of foreign firms (Bergsten, Horst, and Moran 1978).

Both the growing role of the state and the assertion of economic nationalism have taken place in an international environment characterized by the breakdown of the post-World War II hegemonial dominance of the United States (Gilpin 1975). The convergence of these interrelated trends has created both new policy opportunities and the appearance of a real change in the position of many poor countries in the world economy. This is especially true with regard to the relationship between transnational corporations and the state in the Third World. The growth of state involvement in the national economy and the increase in the frequency and extent of regulations affecting foreign firms have created the impression that it is the transnational corporation, rather than the nation-state, that is increasingly "at bay" in the contemporary world economy.

Nigeria appears to be no exception to these global trends. As a member of OPEC, it has been at the forefront of the confrontation with the transnational corporation. It has relied on this experience in its expansion of state involvement in the economy, notably in the petroleum and related petrochemical sectors. Direct state involvement has also increased in other areas of the economy as well (notably in mining, utilities, banking, insurance, vehicle assembly and agriculture). Although Nigeria has historically offered potential investors a number of investment incentives, a basic objective of its foreign investment policy since the end of the civil war in 1970 has been to increase indigenous control over economic activities. There have been recurring pressures for the indigenization of personnel, and later, of share capital in virtually every foreign company operating in the country.[1] There have also been intermittent, but significant, limitations placed on the repatriation of profits and dividends from Nigeria.

A closer examination of the sources of and responses to Nigeria's indigenization program provides an illustration of the extent to which its growth of state power and assertion of economic nationalism may prove, however, illusory. Rather than increasing national control over its economy, Nigeria's indigenization exercise may actually have reduced it.

SOURCES AND OBJECTIVES OF INDIGENIZATION

Although Nigeria's most far-reaching and controversial indigenization decrees were promulgated during the 1970s, there is a long history of indigenization pressures in the country. Proposals for increasing Nigerianization of the economy were first incorporated in official policy statements describing investment opportunities for potential investors during the late 1950s. A national committee to promote the Nigerianization of business enterprises was created by the colonial government in 1956 (Hoogvelt 1979). The 1958 Tax Relief Act required transnational corporations seeking "pioneer" company status both to increase Nigerian ownership and personnel and to use Nigerian materials in production. However, it was not until after independence that significant legislation was passed. After being supported in principle in both the first national development plan and in a 1961 House of Representatives resolution, provisions for increasing Nigerianization were codified into law in the 1963

Immigration Laws. The stringent set of controls and regulations established quotas for expatriates working for newly established transnational corporations and were designed to increase Nigerian participation in the highest levels of management.

There has been a broad base of popular support for any assertion of economic nationalism in Nigeria since independence was attained in 1960. Indigenization has been justified as a response to popular pressures, and public support has consistently been mobilized in defense of the exercise. It would be misleading and inaccurate, however, to suggest that indigenization has been pursued as a response to broad-based public pressures. Such a response would imply a commitment to an egalitarianism that was neither a central motive nor objective of the indigenization exercise (Aboyade 1974b; Asiodu 1974).

On the contrary, from the time of its inception during the 1950s the indigenization process in Nigeria has stemmed from two primary sources with different and occasionally contradictory objectives. Indigenization has been instituted by an amenable military elite in response to intermittent, but recurring pressures from an indigenous economic elite. Nigerian businessmen had been agitating for protection against competition from foreigners in the distributive trade since the late 1950s (Hoogvelt 1979). This agitation became more insistent during the six years of civilian rule after independence in 1960 (Asiodu 1974). It was not until after the Nigerian civil war, however, that indigenous businessmen found a Nigerian government with the wilingness and ability to carry out a more comprehensive indigenization program.

The Federal Military Government had experienced the consequences of excessive reliance on foreign governments and transnational corporations during the Nigerian civil war. The indecision of transnational oil companies about whether to make payments to the Federal Government or the Biafran government had a significant impact on the military rulers and created serious doubts about whether transnationals could be trusted (Collins 1975). The civil war also encouraged the growth of state involvement in the economy to manage the war effort. The general strengthening of the state increased its confidence against foreign involvement in the Nigerian economy.

The civil war also fostered the rise of a new bourgeoisie who accumulated "easy wealth" by supplying equipment and war material to both the Biafran and Federal governments. Since this bourgeoisie did not owe its wealth to foreigners, it could afford to fan the flames of popular nationalism and put pressure on the state to Nigerianize the economy after the war (Onoge 1974). There is a great deal of evidence that indigenous businessmen applied increasing pressure on the Federal Military Government for an indigenization program during this period. Alhaji Aminu Dantata, Kano State Commissioner for Trade and Industry in 1972, commented that "by promulgating the decree the Federal Government has done what businessmen themselves wanted so badly for several years past." P. C. Asiodu, former Minister of Mines and Power, suggested that "it was in the period between 1968 and 1971 that the widest consultations were undertaken leading to the promulgation of the Enterprise Promotion Decree of 1972."

The influence of these pressures on a military elite increasingly distrustful of foreign capital led to the announcement of the Nigerian Enterprises Promotion Decree in 1972. The central objectives of the 1972 decree reflected the dual sources of support for indigenization from the government and local business community. The central objective of the Federal Military Government was to obtain Nigerian control over the economy in general, and over strategic enterprises, in particular. Former Head of State Yakubu Gowon described the objective of the decree as "consolidating our political independence" and many observers have viewed it as an assertion of economic nationalism or an anti-dependency measure in response to the civil war experience. Paul Collins (1975) maintains that the decree was meant to give Nigerians greater involvement in economic and commercial affairs. In mid-1972 the Federal Commissioner for Trade Briggs (*West Africa* June 23, 1972) said the goal of indigenization was to "make the country's economy truly Nigerian," and E. O. Akeredolu-Ale (1976) suggested that indigenization was inspired by a desire to reduce Nigeria's external dependence.

At the same time, local businessmen wanted a protected niche in the economy free from foreign competition and a share of the proceeds of the most successful (foreign dominated) sectors of the economy. Both of these objectives were consistent with the Federal Military Government's objectives of increased national control over the Nigerian economy. Sule Kolo, Nigeria's High Commissioner to the United Kingdom in 1972, commented (*West Africa* June 23, 1972) that the indigenization decree was aimed at small expatriate concerns in trade and services that "excite resentment among rival indigenous enterprises" (Kolo 1972). Accordingly, much of the pressure from Nigerian businessmen in 1972 was directed mainly against the Lebanese controlled commerce and retail sector (Turner 1976; Williams 1976). This explains why these commercial activities were reserved for 100 percent local participation, while many of the largest European and North American based transnationals were not at all affected by the different schedules established in the 1972 decree.

The 1972 Nigerian Enterprise Promotion Decree stipulated that, by March 1974, no person other than a Nigerian citizen could be the owner or part-owner of enterprises in 22 selected industries in Nigeria (called Schedule I industries). The industries affected included small, labor intensive manufacturing and local service-related enterprises, many of which were already predominantly Nigerian in 1972. The 1972 Decree also stipulated that aliens could not participate in 33 other industries (called Schedule II industries), in which the paid-up share capital of the enterprises was less than £200,000 (Nigerian) or the turnover of the enterprise was less than £500,000 (Nigerian), whichever the Nigerian Enterprises Promotion Board (NEPB) deemed appropriate. The NEPB was granted sweeping discretionary powers to administer the Decree's provisions.

Enterprises exempted on the basis of their size were required to make available to the Nigerian public up to 40 percent of their total equity. The businesses in this second schedule included construction firms, some large import substitution industries, and wholesale and retail distributors. Because of the 1972 decree's exemption of large-scale enterprises in its Schedule II list of industries, most transnational corporations were not required to make available more than 40 percent of their total equity to the Nigerian public. A great number of Nigeria's largest and most important manufacturing industries (tobacco and textiles, for example) were completely unaffected by the 1972 Decree.

The release of a government White Paper on the implementation of the decree in 1975 revealed that only one-third of the affected enterprises had complied fully with the decree's provisions. Thereafter, pressures for increased indigenization reached a peak. The new Obasanjo government responded in less than a year with an extension of the 1972 decree, first announced in June 1976 and formally promulgated in January of 1977. The Nigerian Enterprises

Promotion Decree of 1977 reorganized the Board responsible for implementing the decree and increased its discretionary powers to inspect enterprises, conduct prosecutions, and seal up the premises of offending enterprises. In addition, 20 new industries were added to the list of Schedule I industries to be completely indigenized in ownership. Among those industries added were the wholesale distributors of local manufactures and other locally produced goods, major retail stores with an annual turnover of *less* than ₦ 2,000,000 ($3.3 million), commercial agents such as manufacturers' representatives, and most commercial transportation companies. Thirty-three new industries were added to the second schedule, and the mandatory sale of shares was raised from 40 to 60 percent. Among the most significant of the new activities added were banking (commercial, merchant and development banks), insurance, shipping agencies, food manufacture, basic iron and steel manufacture, and petrochemical industries. A third schedule was added to the revised decree which listed all remaining industries and required that they make available 40 percent of their equity to Nigerian subscribers. The Schedule III enterprises include the largest transnationals in tobacco concerns and textile firms, previously exempted from indigenization, as well as high technology enterprises. Thus at present, only enterprises engaged in single, nonrenewable projects are exempt from indigenization. All other enterprises are required to make at least part of their equity (a minimum of 40 percent) available to Nigerian subscribers. Thus the 1977 decree clearly contains more far-reaching and stringent regulations than the 1972 version of the decree which exempted most of the largest and most important transnational corporations.

The extension of the indigenization decree in 1977 once again reflects the dual sources and changing objectives of the military and business elites in Nigeria. The Obasanjo government of the late 1970s was more strongly committed to an ideology of economic nationalism than their predecessors in the Gowon government.[2] Accordingly, the revised decree was quite explicit about the desire to obtain control over important aspects of production. Included among the basic objectives of the 1977 Nigerian Enterprises Promotion Decree are ". . . to advance and promote enterprises in which citizens of Nigeria *shall participate fully* (italics added) and play a dominant role . . ." and ". . . ensuring the assumption of the control of the

Nigerian economy by Nigerians in the shortest possible time" (Federal Government of Nigeria 1977, p. A19).

In addition to being explicit about its objectives, the Nigerian government appears to be serious about its intention to obtain control over important aspects of production. Indigenization is the most prominent component of Nigeria's foreign investment policy, and there is no evidence of either internal bureaucratic opposition to the decree or a tendency to trade off compliance with indigenization for other ("more important") concessions from transnational corporations.

Having already reserved a protected niche for commercial and low-technology activities in the 1972 decree, indigenous business modified its objectives and pressed for a larger share of the proceeds of foreign enterprises located throughout the economy with the extension of the decree in 1977. Since most of the share capital offered by transnational corporations in 1972 was heavily oversubscribed, the 1977 extension of the indigenization program offered investment opportunities for businessmen left out of the original exercise. It also provided investment opportunities for Nigeria's newest economic elite which developed during the oil boom of the mid and late 1970s.

These objectives were broadly consistent with, but more limited than, those of the Federal Military Government in 1977. While the central objective of the government decree was control of the economy and full participation by Nigerians, some of the strongest backers of indigenization among Nigeria's economic elite were more interested in a share in the proceeds of the economy than control of the economy. Some indigenous businessmen have expressed concern about the growth of public sector (state) acquisitions during indigenization, reflecting an uneasiness in the alliance between the state and local capital in Nigeria.[3] When this divergence of objectives is accompanied by a sophisticated array of transnational corporate responses to indigenization, the program can be effectively neutralized.

Responses to Indigenization

Nigeria appears to be a model case of the growth of the state and an assertion of economic nationalism. It is frequently cited as an illustration of these phenomena.[4] The state is gradually assuming a greater role in economic activities, the number of state corporations is growing, more stringent regulations affecting the transnational corporation have been enacted over time, and a majority of the equity of new operations is being acquired by the state and indigenous local investors. Not only has there been a marked increase in the frequency of state actions designed to control the operations of transnational corporations since 1970, but these actions give the appearance of being increasingly effective. According to official government reports, 1,858 firms have complied with indigenization requirements since 1972, selling over 500 million shares valued at more than 472 million Naira (more than $800 million). There have been very few instances of overt conflict between transnationals and the Nigerian government,[5] and virtually every transnational operating in Nigeria has complied with the equity sharing requirements of the recent decrees. In addition, Nigeria appears to fit the model of a gradual and incremental shift in the balance of bargaining power in the direction of a host country. Its successive indigenization decrees have required a gradual increase in the number of economic activities affected as well as in the amount of equity that must be shared with local capital.

Despite this apparent growth of state power, transnational corporations are still quite eager to invest in Nigeria. The "gold rush" of the mid-1970s, when foreign investors could recover their entire investment in one or two years, is over. However, most foreign executives currently working in the country maintain that there is ample room for new firms not interested in a quick return but in a longer term profitable investment in one of the fastest growing markets in the world. Only two of the hundreds of large, transnational corporations operating in the country have chosen an "exit" option and pulled out of Nigeria as a result of its increasing demands on foreign operations. And a number of the largest transnational corporations in the world not already operating in Nigeria are contemplating direct investments there. New foreign capital has continued to flow into Nigeria at an annual average of $331 million during the 1970s. It increased from $305 million to $377 million after the 1972 indigenization decree but declined to about $200 million immediately after the 1977 decree. It has risen even further in the wake of the return to civilian rule in October 1979 to a total of $595 million in 1980.[6]

Why should transnational corporations be so eager to invest in a country in which the state is imposing increasingly stringent controls on their operations? The explanation of this apparent paradox is that transnational corporations are not yielding managerial control. The sharing of equity directed in Nigeria's indigenization effort is not equivalent to the sharing of control in the newly established joint ventures. Virtually every transnational corporation involved in Nigeria has found ways to neutralize the indigenization requirements. The specific strategy or combination of strategies varies from firm to firm; however, they are all designed to ensure a minimal loss of control over the operations. Transnational corporations either (1) fight to retain a majority of the equity, or (2) find ways to retain control with a minority share of the equity.

This conclusion is based on detailed interviews conducted during July and August of 1979 with senior executives of twenty-three of the largest transnational corporations operating in Nigeria.[7] When asked to characterize the outcome of the indigenization process, not one of the executives of the thirteen firms in the sample which were reduced to a minority equity shareholding position was concerned about having lost managerial control over their Nigerian operations. A few minor changes had taken place since indigenization (more expenditure on housing schemes and other employee benefits, for example). However, there was virtually no concern expressed when asked specifically about loss of control over day-to-day operations. Several company executives said they would not stay in Nigeria if they were to lose control over their investments. At least eight of the remaining ten firms in the sample should have yielded a majority of their equity to Nigerian subscribers according to the 1977 decree, yet have managed to obtain exemptions (or find other ways) to avoid becoming minority shareholders.

There are as many different strategies to avoid losing control as there are transnational corporations investing in Nigeria. Only a handful of the major transnational corporations have chosen "exit" or "voice" options as responses to Nigerian indigenization, often with deleterious consequences, as Citibank and American International Insurance have discovered. Most have chosen a variety of other options, ranging from benignly legal strategies to blatantly illegal ones. Most of the transnational corporations choosing to remain in Nigeria have employed one or a combination of several of the following strategies to ensure that Nigeria's indigenization program will not alter control of their operations.

Public Sale of Shares

Several executives explained how they encouraged the public sale of their share capital to ensure that there would be no single indigenous subscriber with a bloc of shares comparable to the 40 percent retained by the transnational corporation. As one executive advised, "Once you've made the decision to go public, spread your shares as widely as possible." Another added, "the broader the distribution, the easier it is to control the operation." In part, this strategy was unintentionally encouraged by the 1977 Indigenization Decree which attempted to prevent the huge concentrations of shareholding among a small number of Nigerians that had accompanied the 1972 decree. The transnationals most likely to favor this strategy include the most visible and best known manufacturing firms with a long-term presence in Nigeria. Manufacturers of well known consumer products are most likely to attract a broad range of shareholders necessary for the effectiveness of this strategy.

Technical Services Agreements

A second way for minority partners to retain control over their Nigerian operations is to negotiate a technical services agreement with their Nigerian partners that provides the transnational with responsibility for technology choice, maintenance and innovation. Agreements for the training of personnel can also ensure that the structure and standard operating procedures of the former transnational remain unchanged. As one executive confidently responded to a question about his parent firm's ability to control its Nigerian operation with only 40 percent of the equity: "It's because of our technical expertise. . . . We still train all the managers." The negotiation of technical service arrangements is becoming an increasingly important aspect of the changing bargaining relationship between states and transnational corporations. This strategy is particularly prevalent among large, transnational banks and manufacturers engaged in high-technology activities.

Negotiate Exemptions

A number of transnational corporations have simply tried to negotiate themselves into exemptions from certain of the requirements of the indigenization decrees. Many have negotiated extensions for compliance with the provisions of the 1972 and 1977 decrees. Others have negotiated themselves into different schedules (requiring less of a commitment of capital to local subscribers, 40 percent as opposed to 60 percent). Some have negotiated complete exemptions from the indigenization decrees altogether. One executive commented: "This is a beautiful place for business, because everyone keeps talking . . . everything is in flux, everything is negotiable. That's why you need a hustler, an expeditor." Transnationals in the oil industry and those operating in industries with very little international competition have found it easiest to negotiate exemptions. Companies involved in one-time contractual arrangements with the government also rely on negotiating exemptions. As one executive described his negotiation with government officials: "I told them, you either want the product or you don't. Don't force the issue." He complained that indigenization would disrupt the tight schedule the government had imposed on the project and was granted an exemption from indigenization in his firm's contract. Although this strategy has worked for transnationals in oil, for those with few competitors or for those receiving government contracts, it has not been as successful when attempted by large, diversified manufacturing firms or by insurance companies.

Two-Company Strategy

Many of the larger, diversified manufacturing transnationals in Nigeria have responded to indigenization with a two-company formula. Since the Nigerian government has classified economic activities into categories (or schedules) requiring 40 percent, 60 percent and 100 percent local equity participation, diversified manufacturers have similarly divided their own operations. They have completely sold any subsidiaries requiring 100 percent local participation and have formed two subsidiaries for their remaining product lines or economic activities. In one subsidiary, the transnational retains 60 percent of the equity and organizes the production for the products assigned to this category (or schedule) by the indigenization decree. The economic activities in which transnational capital is restricted to 40 percent are organized in a second subsidiary in which local capital has 60 percent of the shares.

In this way, the transnational corporation retains uninhibited control over all of its product lines assigned to the subsidiary in which it holds 60 percent of the shares. Control is exercised over the other subsidiary in several ways. The two subsidiaries are usually established with identical organizational structures – and often have overlapping memberships on their boards of directors. In most instances, the same indigenous partners hold the local equity in each of the subsidiary companies. It is not unusual for the subsidiary in which the transnational holds the minority equity to negotiate a technical services agreement with the subsidiary in which it holds majority equity. Often, the two companies exist almost exclusively on paper. Only one factory is constructed, with one administrative building containing two incorporated companies. The physical proximity of the two companies (usually across the hall) also facilitates control over the subsidiary in which the transnational holds only 40 percent of the equity.

In most "two-company" arrangements, the subsidiary in which the transnational has a minority equity position manages the distribution, sales, and servicing for the products produced by the other subsidiary. The two-company strategy can also provide other benefits in addition to retaining control for transnationals. According to one executive, "It also facilitates splitting government contracts between the two companies, thus minimizing our Nigerian tax liability in respect of such contracts."

Fronting

"Fronting" generally refers to the placing of Nigerians in positions of apparent ownership or responsibility, when in fact they are only operating as cosmetic "fronts" to provide legitimacy for the continued presence and dominance of foreign capital. Such overt instances of "fronting" are specifically prohibited by the 1977 indigenization decree and are relatively rare. Less overt forms of fronting are, however, much more common.

In their efforts to retain control over their operations in Nigeria, most transnational corporations search for local partners and managers who conform to their business interests and standard procedures. This makes good business sense for the transnational corporations because it minimizes local conflicts. Critics of the transnationals describe this phenomenon as the grooming of a "comprador elite," whose primary allegiance is to the interests of international capital. With either interpretation, it is a modified form of fronting whenever it is deliberately employed by transnationals to retain control over the operations in which they have been reduced to a minority equity position.

Most foreign executives advise potential investors in Nigeria to take care to choose the "right" local partners. One emphasized the importance of "making the right selection," while another recommended that new ventures should look for "sensible" directors. One pragmatic American executive summed up his company's policy as one of "looking for noncontroversial people with money." An oil company executive provided a more detailed recommendation:

> Make investments with the most powerful people (not so that they control operations . . . so that they can provide access). It's important to spread your risk. This [Nigeria] is the most corrupt country in the world . . . therefore, it's necessary to buy protection.

Several foreign executives commented that they deliberately have "no management role by their Board of Directors." One company memorandum assigned specific weights to the contributions it expected from its local partners. The financial resources and the political clout and connections of the local partners were valued most highly and each assigned a weight of 40 percent. Within the remaining 20 percent, the management ability and knowledge about manufacturing were least valued and each was assigned a weighting value of only 2 percent.

Similar procedures are employed in the selection of local managers by transnational corporations. Choosing the "right" local managers for the firm often involves grooming them in the training programs offered by transnational companies and "bringing them up through the ranks." Unlike their local partners, local managers often have to be trained to be sure they share the transnational's business objectives and conform to their standard operating procedures. To ensure that the Nigerian managers exert very little influence over company policy, they are often given virtually no management responsibilities.

Another way to ensure that local managers or partners present no serious threat to the control of indigenized firms is to make them personally dependent on their foreign partners. Transnational corporations can accomplish this by guaranteeing the bank loans required by their local partners to buy into the company. Some firms even go as far as making contractual agreements with their Nigerian partners guaranteeing that commercial, financial and technical management is the responsiblity of the transnational corporation, that the Managing Director is appointed by the foreign partner, that the use of the transnational's trademark can be discontinued at any time at its request, and even that the company can be liquidated if the transnational loses control of the management.

Change Voting Rules

A much less subtle but still legal way to maintain control over a subsidiary is to change its voting rules. Several transnational firms have made changes in their company charters prior to indigenization which ensure that no important policy changes can be made without their support after they have sold a majority of the equity to local subscribers. The usual formula is to raise the number of votes required for passage of any major motions from a simple majority to two-thirds or three-fourths. As one executive described his company's policy: "We don't want to give the control of the company to Nigeria at the present time. The company can write voting rules any way it wants." An internal memorandum from another transnational corporation was equally explicit. It identified a number of measures to ensure that it would retain "a suitable measure of control over its investment." Among them were proposals to amend the Articles of Association (i.e., charter) of its Nigerian subsidiary "so that no decision can be taken without [our] consent, i.e., 2/3 or 3/4 majority required" in the company's general meeting. The Articles were to be similarly amended for board meetings "so that all decisions require the affirmative vote of at least one of the non-resident . . . appointed Directors, i.e., affirmative vote of 6 Directors."

A variant of this strategy is to change company standard operating procedures in ways that minimize the prospects for Nigerian influence in management. For example, one company simply began to hold fewer board meetings after indigenization and shifted many of its important decisions to other branches of the firm.

Divide the Board

A somewhat more malicious, but still legal, strategy for maintaining control is to select board members from different ethnic groups with the hope that disputes between them will distract them from trying to manage the company. This is not a very widely employed strategy. Only one of the 23 firms interviewed suggested that it was able to retain control by neutralizing its indigenous board members, "playing Hausas and Yorubas against each other." Most transnational corporations select board members from all regions of Nigeria, but they do so in self-defense to ensure that they are not closely identified with a single ethnic group in the country.

Add Extra Expatriates

Among the illegal strategies occasionally employed by transnationals in their efforts to retain control is the addition of expatriate employees without official work permits to key positions of the firm. The Nigerian government specifies strict expatriate quotas for each foreign investment, and most transnationals do not exceed them by bringing in expatriate employees on tourist or other visas that explicitly prohibit accepting employment in the country. However, there are ways around the expatriate quotas for large, diversified investors. One transnational corporation obtained permission to sponsor what it claimed were "necessary," but were in fact "redundant," expatriate employees for one of its subsidiaries in Nigeria where it has majority control of the city. Once these expatriates were in the country, they were simply transferred to another subsidiary of the same transnational where it held only a minority of the equity.

Bribing

When asked about the extensiveness of bribery in Nigeria, one senior executive replied, "Any successful business is a dirty operation." Bribery certainly is widespread in Nigeria, particularly in the granting of large, multimillion dollar contracts. Although none of the executives interviewed admitted paying any bribes themselves, one was able to quote the going rates for certain permanent secretaries and another commented, "Personally, I don't know how we got our contracts. . . . (pause) . . . I haven't asked . . . (pause) . . . I don't want to know." The senior expatriate executives of a transnational corporation rarely are involved directly in the handling of bribes. They usually provide their Nigerian managers with vague directives to "get the job done," expecting them to make use of their local connections and do not bother to ask them how they managed to do it.

The bribing of government officials can be used to retain control in the face of indigenization pressures. Special exemptions from certain aspects of the indigenization decrees can be "negotiated," and a number of firms are keenly interested in ensuring that their new product lines are classified in the schedule of the decree that requires that they make available only 40 percent of their total equity to local subscribers. Bribery, however, is probably more common in the awarding of contracts than it is in the granting of exemptions from the indigenization decrees. There are simply too many other means available to maintain control.

Unilateral Violation of Law

A handful of transnational corporations have retained control over their Nigerian subsidiaries by only partially complying with or by totally ignoring Nigeria's indigenization requirements. The construction industry is classified as a Schedule II activity, an area where foreign capital cannot exceed 40 percent. However, at least one large transnational construction company has retained a majority of the equity, selling only 40 percent to local subscribers. Its senior executives know they are in violation of the decree but are not concerned about the consequences:

> There have been no objections raised yet with distribution requirements. We expect some in the future, but nothing much will change for a few years.

The company is fully willing to comply with the decree when confronted by the government. In the meantime, however, it is not going out of its way to raise the issue and is operating in Nigeria with a clear majority of the equity.

Another form of unilateral violation of the law is much more widespread. A number of international banking agents, shipping agents, and representatives for international airlines contend that the indigenization efforts should not apply to their activities. Since most of them have no equity in the country, there is some basis for their position. Nevertheless, several have been informed that they are in violation of Nigerian law and have chosen to ignore requests that they file papers with the Nigerian Enterprises Promotion Decree Board. As one executive confidently put it:

> We have never properly registered with the NEPB, never produced a balance sheet for them. If they pursue it, we'll pay the penalties for not filing. Or we could type up the documents later, say the NEPB lost the copy we sent them, and produce an "original."

It should be emphasized that this type of strategy (and arrogance) is restricted to transnational corporations with very little at stake in Nigeria.

In conclusion, the range of strategies available to transnational corporations is impressive. By employing benignly legal methods (such as encouraging a wide distribution of shares) or blatantly illegal ones (such as bribery) transnational corporations have had little difficulty retaining effective managerial control over their Nigerian operations in the face of Nigeria's "assertion of economic nationalism." As well as Nigeria may appear to fit the model of a growth in the role of the state and economic nationalism, transnational corporations show no signs of being held "at bay" in the country.

CONCLUSIONS: RENATIONALIZATION OR DENATIONALIZATION?

The responsive (and defensive) capacities of transnational corporations have quite effectively neutralized the state's objectives in Nigeria.[8] The indigenization exercise has failed to ensure that Nigerians "participate fully" or "play a dominant role" in the enterprises that have been Nigerianized. Indigenization has also done very little to increase Nigerian control over the economy in general. More than majority equity participation is required to ensure "the assumption of the control of the Nigerian economy by Nigerians."

Essentially, indigenization has shifted the financial risk burden of new and existing investments onto Nigerian investors without any appreciable increase in their control over the enterprises. Rather than import capital or obtain it from local sources on their own, transnational corporations have been provided with capital from Nigerian shareholders or partners.

The opportunity costs of indigenization are also very high, especially in light of the state's objective of increasing Nigerian control over the economy. Indigenization makes possible the purchase of shares from transnational corporations, enterprises with the best reputation for a safe, profitable return. Since Nigerian society is pervaded by the idea that "foreign is better," indigenization inevitably encourages investments in transnational corporations. There are no counterincentives for investments in indigenously controlled enterprises, hence the program undermines the basis of accumulation by a national, capitalist class. Although some pockets of local accumulation exist, a risk-averse, profit maximizing Nigerian investor will buy shares in foreign owned and dominated concerns. Indigenization thus encourages a comprador role for local business in a society already plagued by strong comprador tendencies.[9] Accordingly, indigenization may have contributed to a *decrease*, rather than an increase, in Nigerian control of the economy.

Although the state's objectives of increased Nigerian control of the economy have been effectively neutralized, the objectives of local capital have fared much better. Local businessmen have obtained state sponsorship in their bid to create a protected niche reserved for their enterprises in the distributive and commercial sectors of the economy. They have also succeeded in obtaining state sponsorship in their efforts to secure access to a share of the proceeds of the enterprises in the dynamic sectors of the economy under the control of transnational corporations. Since they are largely satisfied with a comprador role and function (and never really wanted to control foreign enterprises in the first place), most indigenous businessmen have attained their essential objectives through the indigenization exercise.

Local capital has thus been engaged in a dual alliance with the state, on one hand, and with foreign capital, on the other. At one level, local capital has been allied with the Federal Military Government in support of a policy of indigenization. Both local capital and the state have employed the rhetoric of economic nationalism to mobilize support for the exercise, but only the state has pursued that objective with any conviction. Local capital has been able to attain its more limited objectives without going as far as assuming control over the indigenized enterprises. At another level, local capital has been allied with foreign capital in the latter's efforts to neutralize the state's objectives. The modified form of "fronting" taking place in Nigeria requires the cooperation of a transnational corporation interested in maintaining control and a local partner satisfied with a largely intermediary function (providing information about local markets or important political connections). Similarly, a change in the voting rules or unilateral violation of the law require cooperation between local businessmen unwilling to report violations and transnational corporations willing to commit them. It is not just their "cleverness" that enables transnationals to neutralize the Nigerian indigenization program. They also require the assistance of their local allies from the Nigerian private sector.

Although Nigerian indigenization is broadly supported as an assertion of economic nationalism, the divergent objectives of the state and local capital, combined with the responsive capacities of transnational corporations, have contributed to a decrease, rather than an increase, in Nigerian control of the Nigerian economy. Indigenization may appear to reflect a growth of state power and an assertion of economic nationalism in the Third World. Upon closer examination, however, these global trends appear illusory in the Nigerian case.

A POLICY POSTSCRIPT: WHAT COULD BE DONE . . .

Nigeria's present approach to indigenization is seriously flawed; however, that should certainly not lead one to conclude that the program should be scrapped altogether. The broad outlines of an alternative approach can be sketched which offer the promise of an indigenization program that does not necessarily result in a decrease in Nigerian control of the economy. Assuming that the Nigerian state wants to increase indigenous control of the economy and has no intention of departing from a capitalist or market approach to its national development, there are several measures that could be considered.

According to the analysis summarized in the preceding pages, one of the central flaws of the existing indigenization program is the extent to which it provides an incentive for the misallocation of local capital. Purchasing shares from transnational corporations is less risky and more likely to be profitable than investing in the productive enterprises of local entrepreneurs. The dividends received from such activities are most likely to be used for immediate consumption, the purchase of land, or reinvestment in other transnational corporations. A revised indigenization progam could attempt to reallocate local capital toward investment in sectors of the economy which could lead to accumulation by a national capitalist class.

To accomplish this, the government could begin by taxing the dividends and other payments of the transnational corporations to their local partners and shareholders. Transnationals could be asked to withhold a certain percentage of their dividends and payments and provide them to the government. Perhaps the NEPB could be upgraded to perform the task of monitoring and recording the amounts withheld. The NEPB (or other entity created for this purpose) could then identify sectors, projects or enterprises from which it appears local capital investment will lead to accumulation. If local businessmen chose to invest in these "approved" areas, an income tax credit could be granted up to the amount withheld from their dividend payments from transnational corporations. Thus, by taxing the dividend income of local businessmen, the state could encourage reallocation of private sector investment away from comprador, intermediary activities toward productive investments with a potential for indigenous accumulation. The state could encourage the emergence of effective local competitors to foreign capital in a number of strategic areas.

If an indigenization policy could be developed incorporating some of these ideas, the holding of shares of transnational corporations could become less profitable relative to investment in activities that lead to local accumulation. Some state protection or subsidies might be required to assist the establishment of local investments in certain areas (especially in those areas currently dominated by foreign capital). This proposal has advantages over a program of direct state subsidies or investment in such areas, however. State subsidies could be derived directly from revenues obtained from the dividend tax which are not redistributed as tax credits. Such a program would avoid reliance on state oil revenues for financing local capitalists who have already received a disproportionate share of support from the state as a result of the indigenization process of the 1970s.

Although a great many details would have to be worked out, this proposal has the potential to construct an indigenization program in Nigeria that does not facilitate a denationalization of the economy. It will not solve all of the problems identified with the present approach to indigenization. Comprador tendencies among the local business elite would undoubtedly remain, and transnational corporations would continue to control the most important aspects of their enterprises. This proposal would, however, offer an improvement to the existing approach to indigenization by providing a basis (within the confines of a capitalist approach to development) for increasing local control of the national economy.

A proposal of this sort would most certainly encounter strong opposition from Nigeria's current comprador business class. There is little likelihood that the current civilian regime would embark on an indigenization program of this kind. The state is now less autonomous than it was under military rule, more penetrated by representatives of local capital, less nationalistic, and accordingly less concerned with increasing local control of the economy. However, the longer the present approach to indigenization remains unchanged, the further the denationalization of the Nigerian economy is likely to proceed.

NOTES

The assistance of Marc R. Cohen with the research and conduct of interviews in Nigeria was indispensible and is gratefully acknowledged. An expanded version of this paper (with a more extensive theoretical and less policy-oriented discussion) will appear in Paul M. Lubeck (ed.), *The African Bourgeoisie: The Development of Capitalism in Nigeria, Kenya and the Ivory Coast*, forthcoming.

The majority of the references in this chapter may be found in the section entitled, "Current Works on Nigeria – Business."

1. The term "indigenization" is used to distinguish this general policy from its more specific form, "nationalization." Indigenization of share capital refers to the requirement that shares be sold to indigenous subscribers in the local private *or* public sector. "Nationalization" requires that the shares be sold to the public sector only.

2. The ideology of economic nationalism was also useful for providing legitimacy and broad based support for a regime in power less than two years and already shaken by the assassination of its Head of State, General Murtala

Muhammed, in February 1976.

3. Some observers of Nigerian indigenization have suggested that indigenization has been a deliberate attempt by the state to create a national capitalist class in Nigeria. The successive federal military governments had no objections to capitalism or capitalist development. However, a capitalist bourgeoisie was already present lobbying for its protection and assistance, not for its creation. Indigenization has thus far been only an inadvertent or unintentional effort on the part of the state to create a capitalist class in Nigeria.

4. For example, Bergsten cites Nigeria's indigenization program as an illustration of growing economic nationalism in the third world (Bergsten 1974), and Evans devotes a section of his concluding chapter of *Dependent Development* to apply his triple alliance ideas to Nigeria (Evans 1979, pp. 309-314).

5. The well publicized experience of the American-International Insurance Group appears to be an exception.

6. These data are obtained from the IMF's monthly *International Financial Statistics* (IMF, various years).

7. The interviews were conducted with the most senior foreign executives in 23 of the largest transnational corporations in Nigeria. Eighteen of the firms interviewed are included in the U.N. Center for Transnational Corporations list of the 200 largest enterprises in the world. Seven of the firms were engaged in banking activities, 7 in manufacturing, 4 in petroleum or petrochemical activities, 3 in consulting firms, 2 in services, 2 in construction and 1 in insurance. The total number of activities in this itemized breakdown exceeds 23 because a number of transnational corporations have established diversified investments in Nigeria and therefore operate in more than one sector.

8. The "state" is not defined here solely in terms of its relationship to a dominant class. Rather, it is considered an analytically separable entity composed of the principal institutions of the governmental apparatus (the military, police, civil service, and administrative bureaucracies). The state has a monopoly on the legitimate use of force within a given territory and also has a financial basis of support through taxation.

9. Although Nigerians have historically played an intermediary role in West African trade and commerce, it would be a mistake to suggest that their present approaches to transnational corporations simply reflect an inability or an unwillingness to play any other role today. See especially E. O. Akeredolu-Ale, *The Underdevelopment of Indigenous Entrepreneurship in Nigeria* (Ibadan: Ibadan University Press, 1975), and Thomas J. Biersteker, *Distortion or Development? Contending Perspectives on the Multinational Corporation* (Cambridge, MA.: The M.I.T. Press, 1978) for examples of Nigerian capabilities in the performance of productive and nonintermediary functions in economic activities.

7
NIGERIA IN THE INTERNATIONAL SYSTEM

Timothy M. Shaw

In a world economy that is basically reliant on oil. Nigeria's economic and strategic importance is enormous. . . . Increasingly, Nigeria's wealth and position has immensely enhanced her political and strategic importance in Africa and world politics. A strong member of OPEC, a pioneer and stabilizing force in the OAU, a member of the Non-Aligned Nations, a co-founder of ECOWAS, Nigeria is slowly but assuredly emerging as a major factor in the global power calculus.

– Nigerian Fourth National Development Plan

Our economy is still oriented outwards and locked into dependence on the West. . . . Our ruling class appears to be largely confined to the role of ensuring the existence of the political conditions of accumulation. Many are quite happy riding piggy-back to affluence on Western capital. . . . We have performed poorly in our quest for development . . . economic failure poses problems of legitimacy for those in power.

– Claude Ake 1981a, p. 1163

[On] the subject of my inaugural lecture – "Necessity and Freedom in Nigerian Foreign Policy" – I shall say a few words why I have chosen it. . . . The first is the lack of purpose and consistency in our foreign policy since the mid-seventies. The second has been the tendency of the

Some elements of this chapter are taken from "Introduction: Nigeria as Africa's major power" and "Nigeria in world politics: contemporary calculations and constraints" in Timothy M. Shaw and Olajide Aluko (eds.) *Nigerian Foreign Policy: alternative perceptions and projections* (London: Macmillan, 1982).

> Nigerian government and some powerful sections of the public to overestimate our ability to influence external events, and perhaps shape world events in our own image. An example of this was the recent statement of the Minister of External Affairs, Professor Ishaya Audu, that Nigeria was "longing to become a world super-power soonest." The third is the psychological trait among Nigerian leaders and some sections of influential opinion-moulders that we have a great deal of freedom of maneuver in the conduct of our external relations.
>
> – Olajide Aluko 1981a, pp. 9-10

In the present perplexing period in world politics, Nigeria's position in the world system cannot be ignored; for as Andrew Young (1981, p. 654) has recognized, "Nigeria is in some important respects Africa's most powerful nation." The Federal Republic of Nigeria had, of course, always been *primus inter pares* in postcolonial Africa, but international recognition of its power potential increased dramatically along with the price of oil in the mid-1970s. The OPEC induced shock waves broke over the global economy just as Nigeria was recovering its political poise and its petroleum production following the 1967-1970 war with Biafra.

Almost overnight Nigeria's image underwent a transformation from one of a "sleeping giant" (although at times the giant's "sleep" was quite disturbed) to one of an "OPEC major" (see Herskovits 1975 and 1977-78). And although its effective influence did not change quite as far or as fast as its imputed image, nonetheless, Nigeria's position in world politics was more elevated and ensured at the end of the 1970s than was imaginable at the start of the decade. Andrew Young (1981, pp. 654 and 656) reflects a widespread appreciation of Nigeria's centrality on the continent as the 1980s open: "Nigerian power must be of special concern to the United States. . . . Nigeria will remain important to the United States, as the chief economic partner in Africa and a key political ally."

The unexpected euphoria of the late 1970s, however, has yielded to a greater degree of modesty and scepticism in the early 1980s. It is not just that global conditions have become less favorable for Nigeria – especially the transition from a liberal Democratic to a conservative Republican administration in the United States – but Nigeria's inability to make its will felt has been an unsettling experience for the new civilian regime. As Steven Wright (1981, p. 1685) has suggested:

> Nigeria has "status" rather than "power", in that it has some of the major features of power, but at times cannot effectively utilize them to influence the actions of other states, whether at the global, continental or regional level.

Wright (1981, p. 1685) goes on to suggest an explanation for this gap between power and influence, suggesting that it is essentially a function of Nigeria's position in the world system, an issue raised later in the chapter: ". . . the neo-colonial nature of the Nigerian economy is a major constraint . . . the economy is open to manipulation by non-Nigerian forces, particularly the multinational companies." However, as Sonni Tyoden (1981, p. 20) and others have recognized, Nigeria is nothing if not dynamic – "we do not think that Nigeria the neo-colony of the sixties is the same as the neo-colony of the seventies" – so the character of the constraints continues to change; hence shifts in external relations.

The major aspect of Nigeria's development over the last decade is that it has begun to lay claim to a position at the semiperiphery of the world system. This elevation from the periphery remains tenuous but the combination of its natural resources and population with its energy production and industrial potential continues to support its claim (see Freund 1978; Gambari 1975). As Peter Evans (1979, p. 308) notes, from a comparative perspective, "Nigeria barely deserves to be considered part of the 'semi-periphery'." Nevertheless, "the international business community is beginning to discuss Nigeria the way they discussed Brazil at the beginning of the seventies – as a potential member of the 'semi-periphery'."

Nigeria's claim to being a semi-industrialized state at the semi-periphery is reinforced by recent shifts within its political economy; for, like Brazil the archetypical semi-peripheral state, Nigeria's political economy is characterized by "a complex alliance between elite local capital, international capital, and state capital . . . 'the triple alliance' " (Evans 1979, p. 11). Although this coalition of external and local social forces is not static but dynamic, its basic features are likely to continue into the future, particularly as the national bourgeoisie has begun to accumulate and so to reproduce (see Williams, 1977 and 1979).

This chapter does not restrict itself to an orthodox definition of foreign policy but rather seeks to place the interests and actions of Nigeria's bourgeoisie in global perspective. The focus, therefore, is on 1) debates over the nature and direction of Nigerian foreign policy; 2) the effects of its position at the semi-periphery on its status as a Newly Influential and/or Industrializing Country (NIC); and 3) tentative concepts and criteria by which to evaluate Nigeria's external performance. An attempt is made to put Nigeria's foreign policy (and so development strategy and political economy) into comparative perspective in the future as well as in the past and present.

This is especially timely given current criticisms reflected in Wright's article (1981, p. 1685) about two major foreign policy problems: "The first reason was the lack of planning and organization for foreign policy, while the second concerned the overtly rhetorical nature of policy, with its lack of action and effectiveness." Nevertheless, as Wright (1981, p. 1687) cautions, his intention was not "to paint too bleak a picture of the constraints and limitations on Nigerian foreign policy, because it is evident that the country does play a major role in the international system. The aim, however, was to point to some of the factors responsible for the apparent lack of success in foreign policy."

This chapter is divided into two parts: the first is more descriptive and the second more analytic. After examining some salient features of foreign policy intent and content under successive administrations both before and after the high price of oil, I turn to the growing debate over the constraints on Nigerian power and prosperity. In essence, this debate revolves around the inherently ambiguous character of a state at the semi-periphery of the world system in the final 20 years of the twentieth century.

I

CONTINUITY AND CHANGE

Although there may be some controversy over the degree of success of Nigeria's foreign policy, there is a greater degree of consensus over its continuity; for despite several changes in regime since 1967 – and an inexorable evolution in political economy – the overall orientation of Nigeria has remained quite consistent: the tenor has been cautious, conservative and continentalist. Interestingly, increments in Nigeria's power capabilities have not had a dramatic impact on its foreign policy direction, which has tended to revert to a decidedly *status quo* stance with the return of a civilian administration. Indeed, the only period in which Nigeria appeared to shrug off some of its caution was that of the Mohammed/Obasanjo interregnum (1975-79) (Akinyemi 1979), between the Balewa (1960-66) to Gowon (1966-75), and now the Shagari (1979-) eras. If the first civilian administration failed to mobilize Nigeria's potential in international affairs, the first military regimes were preoccupied with civil strife and then civil war: Gowon had little time for foreign policy except when it affected the outcome of the national conflict. Nevertheless, although the orientation has been characterized by a high degree of consistency and continuity, there has been some change in amount of activity, befitting an aspiring semi-peripheral state with a burgeoning, if still fluctuating, budget.

So if the sixties reflected passivity, the seventies were characterized by activity in Nigeria's African and global diplomacy. The new tempo of Nigeria's external affairs under the successive post-civil war Gowon and Mohammed/Obasanjo regimes was the result of an historic conjuncture at the beginning of the new decade: 1) the ending of domestic hostilities and internal crises (1970-71), and 2) the beginning of international energy and economic crises (1973-74) (see Mayall 1976). Both of these events enhanced Nigeria's external position and together constituted the backdrop to Nigeria's exertion of its capabilities and its transition into the second civilian republic. As Tyoden indicates in the above quotation: the "neo-colony" of the seventies is quite different from that of the sixties.

In the second half of the 1970s, then, Lagos emerged as the regional diplomatic and service center – headquarters of ECOWAS, site of global antiapartheid and continental economic summits, focus of mediation talks over Chad, location of many diplomatic and corporate regional offices, etc. – quite a contrast with the inheritance left by the first civilian republic of Balewa:

> when the military intervened in January 1966, Nigeria's foreign policy remained what it had been when the country attained its independence from Britain in 1960; it was openly pro-West and lacked any initiative, creativity, or leadership of any consequence in African affairs (Ogunbadejo 1980, p. 751).

By the time for the assumption of power by the second civilian regime, the widespread view of Nigeria's continental role was quite transformed:

> Nigeria is playing an increasingly influential role in the political and economic policies of other African countries. As a consequence of its oil wealth and OPEC membership, Lagos exercises considerable leadership in the OAU and dominates ECOWAS. Nigeria's resources and zealous commitment on Zimbabwe made it a mutual partner with the Front Line States at various stages of the negotiations for a settlement. Its diplomatic corps has been central to efforts by West African countries to resolve the conflict in Chad (Young 1981, pp. 655-656).

This periodization of Nigerian foreign policy is characteristic of the orthodox approach which examines diplomacy rather than economics, superstructure rather than substructure (see Shaw and Fasehun 1980). The widespread assumption that internal growth would generate external influence failed to look beyond aggregate data on national power capabilities either to the relevance or reliability of internal resources or to the perceptions of external targets. Moreover, subsequent changes in both political regime and economic fortune have produced a new caution in the 1980s, a fourth period to follow after the typical first three identified by Kirk-Greene and Rimmer (1981, p. 46):

> Nigeria's foreign policy during the first twenty years of her independence can be said to have been characterized by three different phases. These might be defined as the low-key conservative period of the 1960s, the bruised-and-withdrawn time during and after the civil war, and the assertive and interventionist period since the mid-1970s.

Despite the essential continuity of Nigeria's economic orientation – a basically dependent and capitalist system – its post-1975 activism in foreign affairs coincided with a shift in focus from world to African affairs: alignment in economics did not seem to exclude nonalignment in politics (see Anglin 1969). Over the last 20 years, however, the structure of Nigeria's political economy has not been entirely static. Because it has increased in both amount of production and degree of industrialization – at a time when many African economies have experienced either minimal or negative growth (see Shaw (ed.) 1982) – Nigeria has begun to achieve recognition as a part of the semi-periphery. As Evans (1979, p. 313) notes in his comparison between Brazil and Nigeria, despite considerable differences between these two countries at the semi-periphery:

> That the Nigerian case appears suitable to formulations of the triple alliance at all is impressive. In fact, the prospects for Nigeria moving successfully in the direction of the triple alliance seem good.

This ineluctable progress toward semi-peripheral capitalism – toward a more industrialized economy dominated by an ever-changing balance of fractional forces among national, transnational and bureaucratic bourgeoisies or capital – underlies Nigeria's evolving foreign and development policy.

Nigeria's new Afrocentric activism – which came to shape its attitudes toward other non-African interests and issues – was revealed most dramatically in its surprising recognition of the MPLA regime in Angola in 1976 and most consistently in its continuing concern for regional cooperation and integration in West Africa after 1975. These twin strands in its African policy – liberation in Southern Africa and integration in West Africa – are likely to continue into the future providing 1) its leadership is not changed suddenly, and 2) its national income does not go into a precipitous decline. Both of these conditions are likely to be met, at least in the short-to-medium term, given the character of Nigeria's political economy. As Ogunbadejo (1980, p. 765) concludes his own review of the soldiers' legacy at the end of the 1970s:

> Clearly, the record of the military in the field of the country's foreign relations is, in varying degrees, much better than that of the Balewa regime. But then, this could be explained to some extent by way of Lagos' increased capability for influence. Its oil wealth, particularly in the years after the civil war, provided Nigeria with the economic base, and thus the confidence to give more substance to its foreign policy of non-alignment.

There is growing evidence, however, that Nigeria's actual international influence remains quite circumscribed by the character of its inherited national political economy: it is more dependent than ever on one product and on capitalist countries and corporations. Nigeria was incorporated into the world system in the nineteenth century to provide raw materials for Europe's industrial revolution. Since the discovery of oil it has provided hydrocarbon feedstock to the world while trying at the same time to industrialize itself. But the switch from exporting palm oil to exporting fuel oil has led to new problems, not only of rapid expansion and inflation, but also to dependence on one commodity (at least until Liquified Natural Gas [LNG] is produced and exported) and on a few markets (the U.S. and the Netherlands primarily). Moreover, great expectations have been raised about a continuing flow of capital and consumer imports (see Shaw 1980 and 1981a).

Nigeria rapidly depleted its foreign reserves in the boom years from 1976 to 1978, but with military imposed restrictions its balance of trade surplus yielded foreign reserve holdings of more than ₦ 3 billion from 1979 onward, although these declined dramatically but briefly in the mini-oil slump of 1981. Dependence on oil revenue is important not only to cover imports but also to provide tax – of between ₦ 1 and ₦ 2 billion *per month* – for infrastructural development, the basis of Nigerian external capabilities or power. Petroleum profits tax and mining rents and royalties now constitute more than 50 percent of the federal government's revenue; company taxation and import/export duties cover most of the rest (see Shaw 1981a; Williams 1976). Income tax provides an infinitesimal amount of revenue. Nigeria is a very *laissez-faire* economy; its foreign policy can only reflect its capitalism as well as its nationalism (see Rimmer 1978; Williams and Turner 1978).

The contradiction between rapid economic growth and minimal diplomatic influence because of continued and intensified interaction with the major industrial powers – the U.S., Japan and the EEC – produced a period of economic nationalism during the Mohammed/Obasanjo period. But given 1) its inheritance of an essentially extroverted, capitalist and agricultural economy and 2) its determination to industrialize rapidly, there were distinct limits to Nigeria's indigenization strategy. Nevertheless, through a policy and period of economic nationalism – induced in part by external exchange imperatives rather than by internal demands – elements within the Nigerian state and bourgeoisie have bought into transnational branch plants: hence the prospect of semi-industrialization. For, as Evans (1979, p. 311) notes, "Despite external trade relations and an internal economic structure that resemble classic dependence more than dependent development, the Nigerian state is already thoroughly immersed in concrete alliances with the multinationals." So the "balance of power" within the "triple alliance" has changed in the postcolonial, especially post-1975, era – state and local capital are now on a more equal, albeit still asymmetrical, relationship with multinational capital – and yet the political economy is probably more, rather than less, integrated into the world capitalist system (see Joseph 1978b; Osoba 1978). For, as Claude Ake (1981b, p. 116) notes in his critique of indigenization in Nigeria:

> this approach . . . does not address itself to the fundamental causes of dependence. The approach concentrates on the redistribution of ownership and not on the widening of the resource base of the economy, nor even on changing the conditions and relations of production. Finally, the approach does not come to grips with the structural links of the economy to the metropole.

The essential feature of Nigeria's continuity is, then, that of capitalism rather than of nationalism. However, although capitalism at the periphery may not lead to development, it can lead to growth, especially within the semi-periphery. Hence, Nigeria's claim to be a NIC.

NIC: NEWLY INFLUENTIAL AND/OR INDUSTRIALIZING COUNTRY

Characteristic of Nigeria's continued conservatism is its attempt to contain supposedly radical movements in Africa in general and West Africa in particular. The post-military regime's efforts to limit the "contagion" of Rawlings in Ghana and Doe in Liberia – as well as of the Soviet Union in various Sahelian conflicts – are symptomatic of a very *status quo* orientation, one for which Balewa was criticized in the first years of independence. Nigeria's fear of military "intervention" from within as well as without the continent is, however, shared by its Western associates, albeit in differing proportions. Hence the tacit understanding apparent between, for example, Nigeria and the U.S. (see Aluko 1979; Ogunbadejo 1979) as articulated by Andrew Young (1981, p. 656): "The two countries will continue to share a strong interest in resolving African conflicts and in thereby minimizing the military role of outside powers in the continent. Thus, for the foreseeable future, the achievement of U.S. aims in Africa will require close cooperation with this African giant."

This prevalent Western attitude toward Nigeria as a Newly Influential Country is more ambiguous when Nigeria's industrial position and potential are considered. As Evans (1979, p. 299) indicates in his comparative analysis: "Nigeria is not only one of the least industrialized countries in the group but also one whose primary qualification for semi-peripheral status is its oil wealth. Brazil and Nigeria represent opposite poles within the range of Third World countries that might be considered members of the 'semi-periphery.'" Nonetheless, Nigeria can lay claim to being a NIC in both senses of the term precisely because of its *relative* level of both industrial and influential capabilities in West Africa in particular and in continental Africa in general. Although Nigeria is only just beginning the transition away from "classic dependence" its novel status seems to be assured already:

> To call Nigeria the "Brazil of Africa" underlines the difference between the two continents as much as it does the similarities between the two countries. In an African context the structure of the Nigerian economy may appear relatively advanced; in a Latin American context it would appear anachronistic. From the role of the state to the position of the multinationals, the structure of the Nigerian elite is in many ways more suggestive of the period of classic dependence than of the current period of dependent development in Brazil and Mexico (Evans 1979, p. 309).

Yet despite its relative power, Nigeria's affluence, even in Africa, is as limited as is its industrial production. Notwithstanding protests to the contrary, Nigeria's effective influence in controlling or resolving either the Chadian or the Saharan civil wars, or in the liberation of either Southern Africa from racist rule, or Equatorial Guinea (Osuntokun 1978) from tyrannical rule has been minimal. Awareness of this gap between aspiration and realization has been spreading in political and academic circles (but cf. Wayas 1979) particularly with the return of the soldiers to the barracks and with the revival of political debate, especially over the misplaced "macho" of some senior officers in the post-Gowon period. Appreciation of the limits of Nigerian power as a NIC has generated "growing unhappiness over the divergence between the expectations of foreign policy and the actual results" (Wright 1981, p. 1985). This gap may, in part, be a product of failure by policy makers and analysts to differentiate among regional, continental and global levels of interaction. But it is also the basis of a growing debate over foreign policy conceptions (see National Role Conceptions below), contradictions and projections in the post-military rule and post-oil boom era.

LEVELS OF ANALYSIS AND INTERACTION

A fundamental distinction can be made in the foreign policy of almost all Third World states between their global, continental and regional positions; this is so for those at the semi-periphery as well as for those at the periphery. In the case of Nigeria there is a basic tension between "dependence" at the global level and "interdependence" or "dominance" at the continental or regional levels (see National Role Conceptions, below). Clearly Nigeria's NIC status does not secure its particular influence in world forums (e.g., "global negotiations" for a NIEO) athough it may do so in African arenas (e.g., recognition of MPLA and Polisario). Nevertheless, because of its position at the semi-periphery, Nigeria may attempt to mediate between Africa and the world (e.g., its leadership role in EEC-ACP negotiations for Lome); likewise, extra-African actors may encourage it to represent them as a peripheral center in Africa (e.g., between the Front Line States and the five-power Western "contact group" over Namibia) (see Shaw and Aluko (eds.) 1982).

The constraints of global dependence, however, are hard to escape even when attempting to advance continental or regional interdependence. Hence the ambiguousness in, for example, the Nigerian-American "alliance" as Andrew Young (1981, p. 655) recognizes: "Nigeria will endeavor to foster its interest in economic development and stable trade relationships with the West while simultaneously continuing to use its leverage with Western nations and corporations in the interest of its political goals on the African continent – especially with regard to South Africa." Such national interests may transcend political changes. So the Carter-Obasanjo link created by Andrew Young over Zimbabwe has been superseded by a close Reagan-Shagari association over Chad.

Nigerian concern about exchanging its oil for imports of industrial, consumer and food products limits its leverage both globally (e.g., NIEO dialogue) and continentally (e.g., Namibia transition) (see Shaw 1981a; Turner 1976b). At both of the major levels at which Nigeria interacts in Africa – regional and continental – it collides with established Western interests. So attempts to exert influence over West African, Southern African and continental crises (e.g., Chad, Sahara, Shaba, Somalia) may be challenged by those countries and corporations with which it is closest in terms of global exchange:

> diplomatic successes in bringing ECOWAS into existence (over French hostility), Angolan independence (over American opposition) and the British Petroleum nationalization affair contributing to Zimbabwean independence all served to bolster the image of a dynamic and powerful foreign policy.
>
> It may be more accurate, however, to see these events as separate if sporadic successes rather than as linked events in a constant chain of political power. These successes were also partly assisted by favorable external factors. . . . Events over the last year or so, but particularly since the election of President Ronald Reagan, have to some extent made conditions less favorable for Nigerian foreign policy . . . the country does not possess the power to overcome Western intransigence (Wright 1981, p. 1685).

Like most states, Nigeria's global and regional relations are interrelated. Its efforts at 1) conflict resolution within the OAU system; 2) political liberation in Southern Africa; and 3) regional integration in West Africa cannot be separated from either its national political economy on the one hand or its global associations on the other hand. African activity and advocacy are interrelated with continuing issues at the national as well as global levels. Given the increasing Afrocentricity of Nigeria's foreign policy, Kai Holsti's (1972, pp. 121-27) typology of national role conceptions can be usefully applied to official policies and self-perceptions despite the constraint of global positions and connections. So at the continental level Nigeria has continued to be a *status quo* "mediator"; in Southern Africa it has become something of a "liberation supporter"; whereas in West Africa, despite a certain reluctance, it has maintained the role, in both formal and informal ways, of being "regional leader." Nevertheless, conflict resolution and political liberation in the African continent and regional integration and political cooperation in West Africa bring Nigeria up against a variety of extra-African interests and institutions: super- and great-powers (especially France's close ties with Ivory Coast and Senegal) and a range of international and transnational organizations are also involved in such issues. East-West conflicts and intra-Western tensions (including intra-EEC struggles) as well as corporate and religious (e.g., over Israel in the Middle East and Libya in the Sahel) concerns are all reflected in the range of such ostensibly "African" problems; and so they constrain Nigeria's own definition and implementation of its several African roles.

First, at the continental level, Nigeria's policy of supporting pan-African unity and diplomacy has led it into active involvement in a range of OAU questions. Its encouragement of an African Common Market was marked by the April 1980 economic summit and declaration in Lagos. Its concern over the festering civil war in Chad generated numerous meetings and proposals, including the dispatch of an ill-fated Nigerian "expeditionary force" to Ndjamena in 1979-80 which pitted Nigeria against Gaddafi's Libya. But with the ebb and flow of interrelated Sahelian struggles, Nigeria's often imagined regional security role was revived in late 1981 when 2,000 troops along with a Nigerian commander flew back to Chad to head up an OAU peace keeping force assembled to replace the Libyans after their "scuttle" which followed President Mitterand's implementation of a revisionist African policy. But Nigerian power is no less limited than that of Libya so the factional disputes both inside and around Chad may be expected to continue in both their parochial and global forms. Nevertheless, President Shagari has followed in the footsteps of Balewa, Gowon and Obasanjo in serving as a pan-African mediator. For example, he was one of the Wisemen and Implementing Committee members on the Western Saharan issue (1978-   ) just as his predecessors had been involved in Congo/Zaire/Shaba conflicts, Kenya/Ethiopia/Somalia tensions, and various Maghreb and Mashreq disputes.

Second, in the area of Southern Africa, Nigeria's support for anti-racist African nationalism has placed it more directly in opposition to various Western countries and corporations, although, once again, shared commercial interests moderate antagonisms between center and semi-periphery. Therefore, Nigeria's support of the liberation movements overall has been quite muted – especially in the comparable Balewa and Shagari periods – and it has emerged as a "helpful fixer" between the Western "contact group" and the Front Line States over a series of multilateral negotiations. In general it supports political rather than economic change (i.e., for nationalism rather than socialism) although its recognition of the MPLA regime in Angola was, probably mistakenly, generally taken to be a move toward a more radical stance (Akinyemi 1979). Its assistance in the Lancaster House negotiation and agreement over independence for Zimbabwe, however, revealed the essential continuity in Nigeria's Southern African policy: formal freedom without structural change. Yet the combined insensitivities of the Reagan and Thatcher administrations may further strain Nigeria's tolerance of Western perfidy, especially if the U.S. regime appears to enter into a tacit alliance with the South Africans to retard (or even reverse) change in Namibia (and hence in Angola too via the UNITA-Savimbi connection).

And third, at the West African level, Nigeria's advocacy of regional integration is based on a pair of interrelated concerns: 1) regional cooperation for development (ECOWAS and river basin development), and 2) regional cooperation to reduce extraregional penetration (aid to Ghana, Guinea and Liberia and plans for regional collective security). Clearly these two factors of development and vulnerability are interrelated. Nigeria's interest in its own economic, especially industrial, fortune since 1970 has coincided with its interest in reducing foreign, especially European, involvement in national and regional economies. Hence the careful balancing of attempts at regional self-reliance (e.g., ECOWAS and collective security) with efforts at global restructuring (e.g., Lome Conventions and inter-African peace-keeping capability, both involving revisions in EurAfrican linkages in favor of African interests). Nigerian diplomacy in West Africa – and hence its relationship with the EEC too – has come to reflect those national interests which favor such regional and global reforms, as Olatunde Ojo (1980, p. 601) indicates in his insightful analysis of the domestic and bureaucratic politics involved:

> Domestically, one of the factors in Nigeria's active role in the formation of ECOWAS was and is the country's desire to become the industrial heart of West Africa with all the political power that this may bring, not only within Africa but also in the world at large. A concomitant of this is the desire to undermine or erode French economic and political influence which has sometimes been inimical to Nigeria's interests in the sub-region. The need to utilize Nigerian petroleum revenue, while it lasts, and to provide alternatives to oil dependence later came to reinforce commitment to ECOWAS. As it became clear that this task of reducing dependence could not be solved in isolation, the commitment to the success of ECOWAS became irrevocable.

So much for the logic of the semi-periphery: the Newly Industrializing condition comes to affect the structural bases of diplomacy, the Newly Influential position.

Nevertheless, the status of intermediary is never certain. Particularly in the postmilitary, post-Bretton Woods period of pluralist politics domestically and protectionist politics globally, Nigeria's oil revenues and effective resources have both been unstable. Subsequent difficulties over independence in Namibia or over the roles of, say, Tanzania in Uganda, Libya in Chad or Senegal in the Gambia (all of which Nigeria opposed apparently out of fear of the three former states "annexing" the later trio in various "federal" arrangements) have revived worries about being either overcommitted or underpowered. As Wright (1981, p. 1686) indicates, Nigeria's grip on events has been uncertain even in relation to weak neighbors:

> The recent border clashes with Benin and Cameroon, the mistakes and failure to act effectively in Chad, and the refusal to intervene in Equatorial Guinea in the late 1970s, all are issues which have troubled Nigeria and which have not received the appropriate response.

In reaction to such apparent setbacks, Aluko (1981a, pp. 31 and 33) among others has called for a new calculus in foreign relations to avoid two particular errors based on economic and psychological miscalculations or misperceptions, namely:

> to cast for Nigeria a role in world affairs that is clearly beyond our means . . . [and] the psychological error made by most Nigerians in and outside government that because of the size, population, and the agricultural and mineral resources in the country we are destined to lead Africa.

On one level, this debate over foreign policy could be cast in terms of *scope* of the "national" interest:

> in the Nigerian context there has been some contention about whether the focus should be egocentric, that is to say purely Nigerian, whether it should serve the West African region, Africa as a whole, or at its broadest, the interests of the black people throughout the world (Wright 1981, p. 1685).

At another level, however, the debate is about the *bases* of the national interest. So in the second and more analytical part of this chapter, I intend to look at some of the limits on Nigerian "power," turning first to its own national role conceptions. Then I turn to some of the constraints on and contradictions in its foreign policy behavior, concluding with a more speculative look at its future orientations or direction.

II

NATIONAL ROLE CONCEPTIONS

The inclination shown by some of Nigeria's leaders to assume that Nigeria has a larger-than-life role on the world stage, reflected in the first opening citation about the latest development plan, cannot be deduced from the formal conception of foreign policy presented in the 1979 second federal constitution:

> The state shall promote African unity as well as total political, economic, social and cultural liberation of Africa and all other forms of international cooperation conducive to the consolidation of universal peace and mutual respect and friendship among all peoples and states, and shall combat racial discrimination in all its manifestations (Nigerian Constitution, Section 19, p. C66).

The earlier formulation of national interest in 1976 by the military appointed Adedeji Review Committee on Nigerian foreign policy is equally misleading because of its welcome but ineffective concern for self-reliance:

> i) The defence of our sovereignty, independence and territorial integrity;
> ii) The creation of the necessary political conditions in Africa and the rest of the world which would facilitate the defence of our sovereignty, independence and territorial integrity;
> iii) The creation of the necessary economic and political conditions in Africa and the rest of the world which would foster Nigeria's national self-reliance and rapid economic development;
> iv) The achievement of collective self-reliance in Africa and the rest of the developing world;
> v) The promotion and defence of social justice and respect for human dignity; and
> vi) The promotion and defence of world peace (cited in Aluko 1981a, p. 13).

Neither of these contemporary formulations really provides much of a framework either to guide Nigerian foreign policy makers or to enable non-Nigerians to predict Nigerian behavior. Nevertheless, the debate over Nigerian foreign policy is a lively one, especially among Nigerian scholars and practitioners (Shaw and Aluko (eds.), 1982): a considerable contrast to the rather moribund nature of foreign policy analysis in most of Africa (Shaw 1981b). This section attempts to capture (and, one hopes, to contribute to) the characteristic intensity of the Nigerian palaver over foreign policy.

Dependence on oil and associated dependence on Western corporations, investments, technologies and skills, constitute central features (albeit often forgotten ones) of Nigeria's political economy (see Shaw, 1980; Turner, 1976a). Together they constrain its range of foreign policy choices and roles and affect its performance in Africa and elsewhere. Nigeria has become an advocate of Third World collective interests in North-South and EurAfrican forums at the same time as becoming a relatively privileged oil exporter itself. Its position as a NIC within the global capitalist system – as well as fears of its dominance throughout Africa – constrains its leadership of the Non-Aligned coalition and presents ambiguities, if not contradictions, in its national role conceptions in Africa.

Before turning to some of these contradictions, I would like to note 1) the two major state visits that President Shagari has undertaken outside of Africa since assuming office – to the U.S. and the UK – and 2) the first major international conference to be held in Lagos under his auspices. Shagari's visits to the U.S. (October 1980) and UK (March 1981) symbolize 1) the renewal of Nigeria's traditional ties with these two central states in the Western alliance after a period of difficulties and 2) the recognition of growing interdependence among these three states, whether they be OECD members or NICs: the exchange of oil for food with the U.S. and markets for investment with the UK (with the prospect of a major £600m arms deal) although the UK may lose some of this major market following the president's late 1981 budget moves to reduce imports. Despite the election of conservative regimes in both countries, the Shagari administration (which is also quite conservative!) has reinforced these particular North-South ties, particularly in strategic and economic arrangements.

The military regime hosted two symbolic meetings in 1977: the lavish FESTAC spectacle and an OAU/UN anti-*apartheid* conference.

By contrast, in 1980, the civilian government hosted the first African economic summit from which emerged the Lagos Plan of Action on establishing an African Common Market before the end of the century. Like Nigeria's concern for political and racial decolonization in Southern Africa, the Lagos economic summit reflected its concern for economic decolonization. For Shagari the Lagos summit was

> the signal for the commencement of Africa's struggle for economic interdependence . . . without economic power political interdependence is meaningless, incomplete and insecure.

And when introducing the Lagos Plan of Action to the U.N. he warned that

> in spite of the enormous natural wealth and resources of Africa, our continent remains the least developed and our peoples the most deprived. These degrading disabilities mock our political independence . . . I call upon this august assembly to launch a decade of reparation and restitution . . . as a master plan for the economic recovery of Africa (*West Africa* October 13, 1980, p. 2011).

Meanwhile, Nigeria's own economy is quite distinguishable from the continent's generally unenviable condition (see Shaw (ed.) 1982): it is among the fastest growing in Africa, with an annual trade balance in 1979 of ₦ 3.3b on total external trade of $18 billion. However, the importation of food as well as of consumer and capital goods has accelerated once again and major infrastructural projects like the iron and steel complexes, nitrogen fertilizer factory and the proposed Bonny LNG plant remain incomplete. Yet the latest, fourth five-year plan is very optimistic, as befits a NIC: GDP is expected to rise over the period by 7.2 percent per annum to reach ₦ 51 billion in 1985, up from ₦ 36 billion in 1980. However, the balance of trade is projected to decline from ₦ 2,822 million in 1980 to a negative figure in 1985 as imports continue to expand (if the real price of Nigerian crude fails to rise from the lows of 1981 then a negative balance might occur well before 1985; hence the deflationary design of the December 1981 budget). And the new plan anticipates heightened not reduced dependence on foreign skilled (as well as unskilled) labor (see *Outline of the Fourth National Development Plan*, pp. 9 and 91). Such changing but continuing dependence not only affects national role conceptions; it also constitutes a major constraint on policy choices as indicated in sections "Contradictions and Constraints" and "Alternative Explanations and Projections" below.

DEPENDENCE AND/OR INTERDEPENDENCE

Notwithstanding massive oil revenues and development projects, Nigeria is likely to remain dependent on the world system in various ways into the next century as indicated in the concluding section, below. Although in ECOWAS in particular and in Africa in general it may come to achieve a position of "interdependence" (or even of limited dominance) in the global economy, its "dependence" may evolve but not be eliminated. As already indicated, Nigeria's position at the semi-periphery is still rather novel and tenuous; its foreign policy reflects the potential but also the problems of this intermediary status.

Nigeria's national economy still faces major difficulties in its transition from an oil-extraction and commodity-production base toward semi-industrialization (see Williams and Turner 1978). This process of "dependent industrialization" or "dependent development" (Evans 1979, p. 10) is traumatic for any social system. It is especially so in the Nigerian case because of the character of its inherited social and physical infrastructures: traditional values and communications failures complicate the process of change. Moreover, oil income though massive is not completely predictable or reliable over time.

Nigeria's new dependence on oil revenue is revealed by fluctuations in GDP over the last decade. National income grew dramatically in the seventies, after the war and before the slump of 1978/79. Revenue was again buoyant as oil prices continued to rise from mid-1979 to mid-1981 but the new dip of sales and prices in mid-1981 led to a rapid decline in both production – down from almost two billion barrels a day to 1.0 or 0.5 billion – and price – down from over $40.00 to $36.50 a barrel (see Shaw, 1981a). Given Nigeria's major commitments to its continental, Southern African and West African policies and roles, in addition to its ambitious development plans for industrial expansion and welfare satisfaction, the state cannot easily adjust to a more frugal lifestyle. In 1978 Nigeria reverted to the Eurodollar market to maintain its rate of expenditure and growth. The continued volatility of the oil market, despite the medium-term upward price trend, may force it to do so again in the amount of ₦ 2-3 billion in 1982: an uncertain base for activist or expansionist policies.

Nigeria's need to borrow foreign capital on occasion may be seen as characteristic of its continuing dependence on foreign investment, technology and skills, as well as on foreign supplies and markets. Because of the size and status of the country, however, few analysts consider Nigeria to be dependent in a classic, chronic manner; rather, they focus on its foreign and development policies: on the "output" rather than the "input," on diplomatic gestures rather than on political economy (Aluko, 1981b). Nigeria's essential *extra*continental structural dependence – which, to be sure, is not static but continually changing – is overlooked when scholars concentrate on its largely *intra*continental activist diplomacy.

However, extra-African dependence affects patterns of intra-African interdependence as indicated above. This is so both at the level of *interstate* relations – see, for example, difficulties with Western countries over various aspects of Nigeria's Africa policy – as well as at the level of *interclass* associations. The "triple alliance" among multinational, state and local capital is not fixed; rather, it is in a continual process of renegotiation and redefinition reflective of changes in global, regional and national conditions. Certainly, Nigeria's national bourgeoisie is increasingly influential within this transnational nexus, yet close relations with institutions in OECD states affect the effectiveness of Nigeria's diplomacy in Africa. This "conditioning" situation is likely to extend into the midterm future with the possibility that at least some elements of the Nigerian bourgeoisie will lose their "national" identity in favor of more "transnational" or cosmopolitan values. This is especially likely if, as Evans (1979, p. 312) suggests, local fractions have done rather well to date through the "indigenization" exercise:

> in Nigeria as in Brazil, the local bourgeoisie has not been left out. Given the objective weakness of local private capital in Nigeria and the low likelihood of its making a significant contribution to industrialization, it would be reasonable to expect a dualistic battle between the state and the multinationals rather than a triple alliance. But, far from being excluded, the local private sector has done extremely well for

itself. Relative to its resources, it has probably done better than local capital in Brazil.

Nevertheless, although local capital in Nigeria may have gained financial benefits from indigenization, it has not achieved organizational control perhaps because it was relatively disinterested in doing so: profit not decision making may be its primary criteria. Compared with other NICs, "Control over equity does not provide the Nigerian state with the same bargaining leverage within joint ventures that it does the Brazilian state, at least not at present" (Evans 1979, p. 312). Such constraints have generated a set of contradictions that underline Nigeria's foreign policy directions and debates. These are identified briefly before the concluding section on alternative explanations and projections; that is, how to resolve or contain such contradictions.

CONTRADICTIONS AND CONSTRAINTS

The above issues and concerns about Nigeria's position and potential as a NIC – semi-industrialization (substructure) and semi-periphery (superstructure) – can be brought together in a set of six tensions or contradictions. These are related to both its future policy and its future place in foreign affairs. They also range across the indivisible terrain of domestic and external policies. They constitute, then, the backdrop to the growing debate over alternative explanations and projections discussed in the concluding section.

First, Nigeria is becoming a very unequal society, with rapid urbanization, differentiation and alienation: is rapid growth going to continue to be sought at the expense of uneven development? And, if so, what social tensions are likely to emerge and how might they be contained: through reform, revolution and/or repression? Second, Nigeria is becoming very dependent on food imports, especially wheat, despite its history of feeding itself: is it able or willing to spend foreign exchange on wheat? If not, how will it revive its agriculture industry: peasant farmers or agribusiness? The present regime seems determined to introduce large-scale agriculture whatever the cost; the Outline of the *Fourth National Development Plan* (pp. 20-21) reveals that "the Federal Government would place emphasis on encouraging private entrepreneurs to establish large-scale farms . . . agricultural production and processing has been transferred from

Schedules II to III of the Nigerian Enterprises Promotion Act which means that foreigners can now own up to 60 percent of the equity in an agricultural enterprise."

Third, revealed in part by who owns land and capital, houses and shares, there is a growing tension within the Nigerian bourgeoisie between more "national" and more "transnational" fractions: are Nigerian industry, agriculture and services to be owned mainly by nationals or by multinationals? And if by Nigeria, then by individual citizens or by the federal or state governments? Fourth, many multinationals operating in Nigeria also have branches in South Africa, an *apartheid* regime that the Nigerian government is anxious to overthrow. Should Nigeria ignore or challenge those companies who "play both sides of the street"? Nigeria nationalized BP in July 1979 to put pressure on the British before the Lusaka Commonwealth meeting on Zimbabwe; but in February 1981 Nigeria compensated BP with $134m in oil and allowed it to resume its Nigerian operations at the same time as the U.N. was discussing oil sanctions against South Africa and actions against multinational energy corporations that supply the apartheid state.

Fifth, Nigeria is a country divided not only by region and tribe and class but also by religion: how should the officially nonsectarian Nigerian regime deal with, for instance, Libya or Israel? Senator Jaja Wachuku has called, at some personal cost, for the recognition of Israel. Meanwhile, an adviser to the Governor of Kaduna State, Dr. Bala Usman (1981) has lamented Nigeria's confrontation with Libya on the grounds that it advances French imperialism in Africa.

Finally, Nigeria's interests and influence tend to be concentrated at the regional level: is its role in West Africa to be that of regional leader or regional dominator? And if Nigeria has a decisive impact on regional cooperation and conflict is this exerted on behalf of itself or on behalf of extraregional interests; that is, is Nigeria a "sub-imperial" power (see Shaw 1977)? Nigeria is the only NIC in ECOWAS and, as has been noted already, it has been very active over political change in Chad, Gambia, Ghana, Liberia and Sahara. Does it advocate regional economic cooperation and conflict resolution for itself and West Africa or for Western countries and corporations? In short, is Nigeria's Afrocentric policy one it claims for its own national interests or a role it plays for extracontinental interests? Of course, there need not be any incompatibility between such interests (as indicated in the final section): they are all represented within the "triple alliance," especially if it is recognized that different elements within Nigeria and its external associates favor particular solutions at particular times.

Nigeria's several exercises in *status quo* mediation and regional leadership may not only reflect identifiable interests within its own political economy (e.g., military and entrepreneurial bourgeois fractions respectively); they may also be compatible or coincidental (but not necessarily conspirational) with Western strategic and industrial elements. Given the logic of the "triple alliance" some degree of conflict as well as cooperation may be tolerated among national and transnational fractions.

Notwithstanding this ambiguity or uncertainty – the very nature of complex interstate and interclass relationships tend to perpetuate these – let me conclude this penultimate section by citing two leading students of Nigerian foreign policy, both of whose comments are particularly relevant to changes and contradictions in Nigeria's African role but neither of which would accept the radical substructural mode of analysis of the triple alliance presented here. Overall, Ogunbadejo (1980, p. 763) remains rather optimistic and complimentary about the direction of Nigerian foreign policy:

> There is an element of continuity in Nigerian foreign policy in that all the various regimes subscribed to "non-alignment" at the international level and good neighbourliness in Africa. What varied was the way successive regimes interpreted these cardinal principles and the extent to which other intra- and extra-Nigerian events shaped the execution of these policies. . . . The Mohammed regime steered Nigeria's foreign relations onto a more militant path and redressed the lopsided nature of the country's non-aligned policy.

By contrast, in focusing on inputs rather than outputs, on constraints rather than rhetoric, Aluko (1981a, p. 30) remains pessimistic and critical, arguing that Nigeria both overestimates its power and overstretches its scarce resources:

> The catalogue of errors in our foreign policy is long. . . . The first is the failure of our leaders especially the post-1975 ones to appreciate severe external and internal constraints on their freedom of choice and therefore strike a foreign policy that will be Nigeria-centered; that is, it will be self-seeking in the sense that its primary preoccupation should be the promotion of the country's security and the well-being of the people.

Interestingly, both of these scholars fall largely within the dominant "realist" school of Nigerian foreign policy. They disagree, however, about how to calculate and employ its power capabilities. Moreover, Aluko is more prepared to express idealist as well as realist opinions than Ogunbadejo, reflective of a broader debate to which I turn in conclusion; for these distinctive perspectives also hold implications for different projections about the future of Nigeria's political economy and foreign policy, although neither advocates the third alternative of radical scholarship.

ALTERNATIVE EXPLANATIONS AND PROJECTIONS

There is, then, a growing debate in and around Nigeria about the character and direction of Nigerian external politics and policies. Given the notable growth of a "foreign policy community" inside Nigeria, this debate is more national than in other African states (see Shaw and Fasehun 1980). These alternative views about Nigerian politics, economics and foreign policy – about the bases, effects, and limits of Nigeria's political economy in the world system – can be categorized into three distinct types: the "idealist" versus the "realist" (disagreement over contemporary and future forms) and the "realist" versus the "radical" (disagreement over historical, current and projected structures). The majority of analysts of Nigerian internal and international politics – as befits its place of relative "power" at the semi-periphery – are "realists"; only a minority are either "idealists" or "radicals."

Characteristic of the dominant *realist* position, as well as reflective of differences within this paradigm, is the work of Bolaji Akinyemi (1978) and Olajide Aluko (1981b) (see Shaw and Aluko (eds.) 1982), at least until Aluko's inaugural lecture (see Aluko 1981a). Both of these leading scholars – it is not coincidental that they are Director-General of the Nigerian Institute of International Affairs and Professor of International Relations at the University of Ife, respectively – take it to be axiomatic that Nigeria is powerful and influential. They may be in disagreement about some of the causes of this power and influence – political direction, bureaucratic style or economic resources – but they express few doubts about the overall character of Nigeria's external stature and status. In this shared assumption they reflect the perspective of most Nigerian scholars and statesmen as well as that of most students of Nigeria: Nigeria is seen as a Newly *Influential* Country, as Africa's great power, and as a successful example of "development." If any scepticism about Nigeria's standing is expressed by realists it is usually about 1) how long oil (and gas) reserves will last; 2) how long civilian government will last; and 3) how long contemporary confusion and chaos in the infrastructure will last. In general, though, such difficulties are taken to be surmountable given Nigeria's financial and entrepreneurial resources. In short, the mood is very optimistic and rather heady.

By contrast, the two minority positions are considerably less optimistic and popular. The *idealist* view is less developed and debated than the radical one and is not identified with the work of any single scholar. Rather, there are elements of idealist views in some of the writings of several Nigerian scholars such as Mazi Ray Ofoegbu (1976) and Aluko (1981a): what should be the bases and directions of Nigerian foreign policy? For instance, the latter as indicated in his citation at the beginning of this chapter has recently lamented the deficiencies in Nigeria's economic, strategic and political structures and argued for greater attention being given to the national interest rather than to regional and/or continental affairs: for a careful balancing of means with ends rather than a reckless pursuit of grandeur (see Wright 1981). In general, the realist and the idealist perspectives on Nigerian foreign policy are not very far apart. Rather, the latter consists of redefinitions of or revisions to the former; that is, *if* Nigeria is to be influential in the future *then* it must reform its political economy and federal bureaucracy to make its goals more readily realizable. In some ways, the idealist position is preemptive of the radical one: it anticipates future (positive) relations as a way of responding to current (negative) criticisms.

By contrast, the other minority position – that of the *radicals* – is much less optimistic and idealistic. Instead, it sees Nigeria as a Newly *Industrializing* Country confronting all sorts of contradictions and constraints such as those suggested above: the future is less clear and more problematic – the working out of various contradictions – than in either of the other perspectives. Rather, both indigenous and foreign analysts in this genre see Nigeria as an essentially dependent state, albeit one at the semi-periphery rather than at the periphery: its place in the world system and its emergent class society – in Evans' terms the triple alliance – will constrain both its present and future influence, as suggested in Ake's opening quotation.

So, instead of an assured future, Nigeria's growth and influence are seen to be rather unstable and unsustainable: the favorable conjuncture of forces that generated the oil boom may not be repeatable. As a state at the "semi-periphery" (see Evans 1979, pp. 33-54), however, Nigeria did experience rapid, if uneven, growth in the 1970s. Nevertheless, the projection of the oil based boom into the future remains problematic because of both internal contradictions and external changes, particularly domestic tensions and international demand.

Such radical analysis clearly remains the minority school of opinion, yet one that is growing in its forcefulness as Nigeria's rapid growth generates further uneven development (see Callaway 1975; Osoba 1978). Moreover, its persuasiveness is reflected in the fact that the major debate now is between realists and radicals (see Shaw and Aluko 1982); the idealist perspective is usually mobilized only in defense of the realist position rather than in its own right. One positive and immediate result of this growing debate is that both realists and radicals have had to reconsider their assumptions and evidence, especially the political and economic bases of foreign policy.

This reevaluation has been stimulated not only by setbacks to Nigeria's foreign policy goals, brought about by either inadequate resources or overly ambitious intentions, but also by changes in the world system since the mid-1970s. Ironically, Nigeria has benefited significantly, at least in the short-term, from the high price of oil; but in the longer-term the shake-down resulting from the demise of the Bretton Woods system may yet retard its prospects. As already suggested, protectionist pressures in the North may come to disturb the close relationship between center and semi-periphery to the detriment of the latter: the logic of the semi-periphery may disappear as inflation and recession lead to pressure for "re-industrialization" wthin the OECD. If, however, sufficient global growth is generated, only the periphery and not the semi-periphery will suffer, especially if, as in the case of Nigeria, the semi-periphery produces petroleum products and consumes industrial products. In this case, the logic of the NICs may yet be extended as Evans (1978, p. 52) suggests in the case of Brazil:

> The present version [of dependent development] assumes no irreconcilable differences between local industrialists and the multinationals or between the state and the multinationals. The contradictions between the global rationality of the multinationals and the interests of the local bourgeoisie and the state are seen as potentially resolvable, provided the overall conditions under which the alliance operates are not too unfavorable to continued capital accumulation in the semi-periphery.

This scenario for the semi-periphery constitutes a modified *dependencia* projection within the "radical" mold. The realist-idealist critique has also been examined above, with the implications made that to be effective in the future Nigeria should 1) accumulate more power resources, such as, perhaps, nuclear capability, and 2) match resources more carefully to goals. As Wright (1981, p. 1687) concludes his own review of Nigeria's debates and choices:

> No real distinction has been made between the Obasanjo and Shagari administrations in the field of foreign policy because, in broad terms, none exists. If anything, the problems facing the Shagari government are greater because of the increasingly unfavourable external environment as well as the domestic pressures from the competitive and volatile party system. Given these increased constraints, it is even more imperative to define and reorientate Nigerian foreign policy in order to attempt to match rhetoric with action.

Given the previous realist and idealist projections, the following three scenarios are all based on developments within the more radical genre. Yet they also affect in different ways – balances of external exchange, bourgeois fractions and party politics, respectively – the "power" calculation on which more orthodox realist projections are also based.

First, until the 1970s, Nigeria could largely feed itself, even exporting considerable amounts of primary commodities. However, the oil boom, combined with population pressure, diverted attention away from the produce of the land and toward the flow from oil wells. The consequent rapid rise of income for some led to accelerated taste transfer, reflected in dramatic increases in the importation of rice and wheat, automobiles and electrical gadgets. OPEC prices for "sweet" and light Nigerian crude have usually enabled the country to extract premium "rents" for its accelerating oil output. But the "high-life" led to a new vulnerability: the government could hardly afford to stem the tide of imports in 1978 or 1981 when the oil market went soft. Moreover, the demise of agricultural production left the country more vulnerable to vagaries in the price and supply of food as well as of oil (see Hughes and Strauch 1982). Nigeria's balances of trade and payments now reflect Saudi Arabia's oil production and the United States' wheat production and oil consumption. NICs like Nigeria may have become increasingly "interdependent" in the world of OECD members yet they continue to be more "dependent" than most industrialized economies because their basic structures remain essentially outward-looking.

Second, competition within the "triple alliance" between more "national" and more "comprador" elements within the indigenous bourgeoisie is likely to intensify as the growth rate declines, land becomes scarce, and policy choices narrow (see Shaw 1982). The Mohammed/Obasanjo military regime encouraged more national bureaucratic fractions to expand their industrial and service activities, partially because they sought to encourage "southern" Nigerian entrepreneurs. The civilian Shagari administration, however, has returned somewhat to the traditional corporate-Northern (Nigerian) coalition in which managerial and comprador elements are encouraged. Some of the limits placed on foreign investors under the indigenization programs have been eased under the National Party of Nigeria (NPN) government so that Nigeria is now once again a more extroverted political economy than at the end of the 1970s. This trend toward renewed and enlarged transnational linkages, especially in the fields of agribusiness and manufacturing, is likely to continue under civilian rule unless 1) oil revenue declines significantly for a considerable period of time or 2) protectionist pressures in the U.S., EEC and elsewhere produce a withdrawal of foreign investment, technology and personnel.

And third, "radical" elements within some political parties, various state governments and certain trade unions may yet pose a threat to the established transnational nexus. Nigeria's indigenization policy represented one attempt to meet such "nationalist" pressures but "state capitalism" is unlikely to satisfy demands for more "socialist" measures. These demands may also intensify if the logic of growth at the semi-periphery is eroded by continued inflation and recession in OECD metropoles. As already indicated, protectionist pressures in the North might curtail foreign investment and involvement in the semi-periphery undermining the position of the managerial and comprador fractions within the bourgeoisie and reinforcing the claims of more nationalist and radical elements. Immanuel Wallerstein (1979, pp. 117-18) has cautioned about the tension in the semi-periphery between fractions favoring less versus more integration, a tension that is likely to be exacerbated by global trends in the 1980s:

> The semiperipheral states in the coming decades will be a battleground of two major transnational forces. One will be the multinational corporations who will be fighting for the survival of the essentials of the capitalist system: the possibility of continued surplus appropriation on a world scale. The other will be a transnational alignment of socialist forces who will be seeking to undermine the capitalist world economy . . . forcing relatively drastic redistributions of world surplus and cutting the long-term present and potential organizational links between multinationals and certain strata internal to each semi-peripheral country. . . .

Nigerian decision makers may be compelled in the 1980s, then, to revive or redefine "nonalignment" as an economic as well as a strategic doctrine, otherwise external pressures may affect internal class formations and relations. However, while the prospects for socialism in Nigeria are still slight, the balance between more national and more international capitalisms is likely to become more central and controversial (cf. Biersteker 1978; Schatz 1977).

The next decade is likely to be an exciting as well as a challenging one for Nigeria as its process of semi-industrialization proceeds. Crucial "macroeconomic" factors are the costs of food and capital imports and the value of oil and gas exports; salient "microeconomic" factors include the balance between national and comprador fractions within the indigenous bourgeoisie and the relationship between more (conservative) capitalist and more radical (socialist) forces within the domestic polity. It is such growing contradictions that have led to the "overpoliticization" that Ake (1981a, p. 1163) has lamented. Nevertheless, the treatment of apparently "internal" political paranoia will have fundamental implications for the direction of foreign policy and position in the world system:

> Our problems are rooted in our history and in the concrete economic and social structures which it has evolved. By the very nature of the problems they cannot be finally solved without, at the very least,

> breaking our exploitative dependence on the West, and doing away with the existing relations of production . . . the contradictions of the present system are creating the conditions that will change it.

As indicated throughout this chapter, these contradictions also pose challenges for scholars and statesmen concerned with Nigeria. The external effectiveness of this leading black power (see Herskovits 1977-78; Wayas 1979) will remain problematic in the future, until its political economy becomes more autonomous as well as affluent and thus able to sustain an innovative and distinctive foreign policy.

NOTE

The majority of references in this chapter may be found in the section entitled, "Current Works on Nigeria – Foreign Policy."

CURRENT WORKS ON NIGERIA AND SOURCES:

A Bibliography

Robert Mandersheid

POLITICS AND SOCIETY

Adedeji, Adebayo, ed. 1968. *Nigerian Administration and Its Political Setting* (London: Published for the Institute of Administration, University of Ife, Nigeria, by Hutchinson), 162 pp.

A collection of papers presented at a 1966 conference at the University of Ife. Nigerian civil servants and Nigerian and foreign scholars examine the interactions of Nigerian politics and administration.

Ake, Claude. 1973. "Explaining Political Instability in New States." *Journal of Modern African Studies* XI, 3:347-59.

——. 1981a. Presidential Address to the 1981 Conference of the Nigerian Political Science Association, published in *West Africa*, 25 May: 1162-63.

——. 1981b. *Political Economy of Africa* (London: Longman).

Akinsanya, Adeoye. 1973. *Nigerianization of the Western Nigerian Higher Public Service*. Doctoral dissertation, University of Chicago.

——. 1976b. "The Machinery of Government During the Military Regime in Nigeria," 43 *The International Review of Administrative Sciences*, 357-68.

——. 1977. "Federalism and Military Rule, 1966-1975," 23 *Indian Journal of Public Administration* (January/March), 34-53.

Akpan, Moses. 1977. *Nigerian Politics* (Washington: University Press of America), 165 pp.

Aliyu, Abubakar Yaya. 1978. "[Local Government] As Seen From Kaduna," in Keth Panter-Brick, ed., *Soldiers and Oil: The Political Transformation of Nigeria* (London: Frank Cass).

____. 1978-79. "The Nature and Implications of Local Government Reform in Nigeria." *Nigerian Journal of Public Affairs*, Vol. 8:131-43.

Almond, Gabriel A., and Powell, G. Bingham, Jr. 1978. *Comparative Politics: System, Process and Policy* (Boston: Little, Brown & Company).

Almond, Gabriel A., and Verba, Sidney. 1963. *The Civic Culture*. (Boston: Little, Brown & Company).

Awolowo, Obafemi. 1970. *The Strategy and Tactics of the People's Republic of Nigeria* (London: Macmillan). 135 pp.

The author outlines and then comments on the economic and political paths which he thinks Nigeria should pursue.

____. 1968. *The People's Republic* (Ibadan: Oxford University Press). 356 pp.

A case is made for a "clean break with the British administrative heritage." A blueprint for an independent Nigeria is sketched.

____. 1966. *Thoughts on Nigerian Constitution* (Ibadan: Oxford University Press), 196 pp.

After a close look at the debate on the appropriateness of unitarianism and federalism for Nigeria, Awolowo enumerates and comments on the "basic principles" that should be part of any Nigerian constitution.

Azikiwe, Nnamdi. 1974. *Democracy With Military Vigilance* (Nsukka, Nigeria: African Book Co.), 104 pp.

Writing in 1972, the author proposes an experimental civilian-military diarchy as a possible remedy to Nigeria's political woes. Included in the volume are responses to criticism of the author's views.

Babatope, Ebenezer. 1979. "UPN and the Emancipation of the Nigerian People," in *AWO at 70*. Unity Party of Nigeria, Lagos.

Baker, Colin, ed. c1975. *Ife Essays in Administration* (Ife: University of Ife Press, Published for the Institute of Administration), 187 pp.

Theoretical and practical aspects of Nigerian administration are the subject of this volume of essays. Some reforms (in tax administration and the P. and T., for example) are outlined.

Balarabe Musa, Abdulkadir. 1981. "Why They Fear Our Forces of Democracy and Social Progress," Statement to a World Press Conference, Lagos, June 22.

Bates, Robert H. 1974. "Ethnic Competition and Modernization in Contemporary Africa," *Comparative Political Studies* 6, 4:457-84.

Beckett, Paul, and O'Connell, James. 1977. *Education and Power in Nigeria* (New York: Africana).

Bienen, Henry. 1982. "The Nigerian Elections of 1979," in a forthcoming volume edited by Ergun Özbudun and Myron Weiner, to be published by the American Enterprise Institute.

Caldwell, John C., ed. 1976. *The Persistence of High Fertility, Part I* (Canberra: Australian National University).

Chukumerije, Uche, et al. 1980. "Report of the Committee of Inquiry on the Party's Problems." (Lagos: PRP) (16 July).

Daily Times of Nigeria. 1970. *Independent Nigeria* (Lagos: Daily Times of Nigeria), 98 pp.

A major Nigerian newspaper looks, in magazine fashion, at Nigeria's first decade of independence: the state of the economy, the Civil War, personalities, etc.

Dent, Martin. 1979. "Presidential Propsects." *West Africa*, 6 August: 1406-9.

Deutsch, Karl W. 1961. "Social Mobilization and Political Development," *American Political Science Review*, 55, 3.

Diamond, Larry. 1982a. "The Transformation of Political Conflict in Nigeria." Paper presented to the Annual Meeting of the International Studies Association, Cincinnati, Ohio.

——. 1982b. "Cleavage, Conflict and Anxiety in the Second Nigerian Republic." *Journal of Modern African Studies*, Vol. 20, No. 4.

——. 1983. "Class, Ethnicity and the Democratic State: Nigeria, 1950-66." Forthcoming in *Comparative Studies in Society and History*.

Diamond, Stanley. 1967. *Nigeria: Model of a Colonial Failure* (New York: American Committee on Africa), 88 pp.

A collection of those of the author's controversial "Africa Today" articles which deal with the First Republic. Commentaries on these articles are also included.

Diejomaoh, V. P., and Anusionwu, E. C. 1981b. "Education and Income

Distribution in Nigeria," in *The Political Economy of Income Distribution in Nigeria*, pp. 373-420.

Dudley, Billy. 1981. "The Nigerian Elections of 1979: The Voting Decision," *Journal of Commonwealth and Comparative Politics* XIX (3:276-98).

Eastern Nigeria, Ministry of Information. c1967. *The Problem of Nigerian Unity* (Enugu, Nigeria: Ministry of Information, Eastern Nigeria), 50 pp.

Eastern Nigeria's Ministry of Information explains its dissatisfaction with a northern and western dominated Nigeria. Includes appendix of important 1966 speeches and Nigerian newspaper editorials.

Ekpu, Ray. 1981. "The Coup in Akure," *Daily Times*, June 21.

Elaigwu, J. Isawa. 1981. "Federalism and the Politics of Compromise in Nigeria." Paper presented to the Bellagio Conference on State Coherence and Ethnic Self-Determination, June 8-12.

Eleazu, Uma O. 1977. Federalism and Nation-building (Ilfracome: Stockwell), 280 pp.

After reviewing the history of Nigerian federalism, the author focuses on the failure of certain aspects of political socialization (e.g., education, the party system) to promote national values.

Epelle, S. 1960. *The Promise of Nigeria* (London: Pan).

Etim, B. A., and Erontini, F. N. 1979. "Personal Income Distribution in Nigeria 1960-70 to 1971-72," in *Poverty in Nigeria* (Ibadan: Nigerian Economics Society), pp. 295-312.

Fagbemigun, L. 1970. *Yakubu Gowon: Soldier-statesman* (Ibadan: Nigerian Sketch Pub. Co.), 64 pp.

Fagbamigbe, Olaiya. 1981. "Need for Workers Wages and Welfare Commission," text of the contribution of the Honorable Olaiya Fagbamigbe on the Floor of the House during debate on the Minimum Wage Bill, *Nigerian Tribune*, 14 June.

Fanon, Frantz. 1963. *The Wretched of the Earth* (New York: Grove Press).

First, Ruth. 1970. *The Barrel of a Gun* (Baltimore: Penguin).

Focus. 1975. *Investment in Nigeria* (London: Focus Research), 68 leaves.

Looks at the politics of Gowon's Nigeria in order to assess the prospect for foreign business entry into Nigeria.

Governors of Bendel, Imo, Ondo, Rivers and Cross River. 1980. "Comments and Recommendations on the Federal Government's White Paper on Revenue Allocation." Document No. 12 of 1980. Calabar.

Great Nigeria People's Party. 1979. "The Great People's Charter, being The Manifesto, Aims and Objectives, and Programme of Action of the Great Nigeria People's Party."

Hannan, Michael T. 1979. "The Dynamics of Ethnic Boundaries," in John W. Meyer and Michael T. Hannan, eds., *National Development and the World System* (Chicago: University of Chicago Press).

Haruna, Mohammed. 1981. "The Impeachment of Balarabe Musa," *New Nigerian*, 5 July.

Herskovits, Jean. 1975. "Nigeria: Africa's New Power," *Foreign Affairs* 53(2), January, pp. 314-33.

____. 1977-78. "Dateline Nigeria: A Black Power," *Foreign Policy* 29, Winter, pp. 167-88.

Huntington, Samuel P. 1968. *Political Order in Changing Societies*. New Haven: Yale University Press.

Huntington, Samuel P., and Nelson, Joan M. 1976. *No Easy Choice: Political Participation in Developing Countries* (Cambridge: Harvard University Press).

Idang, Gordon J. 1973. *Nigeria: Internal Politics and Foreign Policy 1960-1966* (Ibadan: Ibadan University Press), 171 pp.

Examines the process of Nigerian foreign policy formulation, the link between domestic and foreign policy formulation, and the link between domestic politics and foreign policy.

Imoagene, Oshoma. 1976. *Social Mobility in Emergent Society: A Study of the New Elite in Western Nigeria* (Canberra: Australian National University).

Inkeles, Alex. 1969. "Participant Citizenship in Six Developing Countries," *American Political Science Review*, Vol. 63, No. 4, December: 1120-41.

____ and Smith, David H. 1974. *Becoming Modern: Individual Change in Six Developing Countries* (Cambridge: Harvard University Press).

Joseph, Richard. 1978a. "Political Parties and Ideology in Nigeria," *Review of African Political Economy* 13 (May-August): 78-90.

____. 1981a. "The Ethnic Trap: Notes on the Nigerian Elections, 1978-79," *Issue* XI, 1/2:17-23.

____. 1981b. "Democratization Under Military Tutelage: Crisis and Consensus in the 1979 Elections," *Comparative Politics* XIV, 1:75-100.

Kaduna State Government, 1980. "Building the Foundations of a New Social Order: The First Progress Report of the Government of Kaduna State," Kaduna.

Katsina, Lamis Ibrahim. 1981. "As the Struggle Continues," *Nigerian Tribune*, July 14.

Keay, Elliot. 1977. *West African Government for Nigerian Students* (London: Hutchinson), 271 pp.

The book was designed to instruct West African School Certificate examinees in the fundamentals of Nigerian government, precolonial institutions, and West African colonial history.

Kirk-Greene, Anthony. 1981. "The Making of the Second Republic," in Anthony Kirk-Greene and Douglas Rimmer, eds. *Nigeria Since 1970: A Political and Economic Outline*. New York: Holmes and Meier. (London: Hodder and Stoughton).

Koehn, Peter. 1981. "Prelude to Civilian Rule: The Nigerian Elections of 1979," *Africa Today* 28, 1:17-45.

Laitin, David D. 1981. "The Sharia Debate and the Origins of Nigeria's Second Republic." Paper presented to the Annual Meetings of the African Studies Association, Bloomington, Indiana.

Lerner, Daniel. 1958. *The Passing of Traditional Society* (Glencoe, Illinois: The Free Press).

Lipset, Seymour Martin. 1960. *Political Man* (Revised and updated edition, 1981) (Baltimore: Johns Hopkins University Press).

——— and Rokkan, Stein. 1967. "Cleavage Structure, Party Systems and Voter Alignments: An Introduction," in Lipset and Rokkan, eds., *Party Systems and Voter Alignments* (New York: Free Press).

Lloyd, P. C. 1974. *Power and Independence: Urban African Perceptions of Social Inequality* (London: Routledge and Kegan Paul).

Lubeck, Paul. 1978. "Labour in Kano Since the Petroleum Boom" *Review of African Political Economy*, No. 13:37-46.

———. 1979a. "Class Formation at the Periphery: Class Consciousness and Islamic Nationalism Among Nigerian Workers." Manuscript published in R. L. and I. H. Simpson, eds., *Research in the Sociology of Work*, Vol. 1 (Greenwich, Connecticut: JAI Press).

———. 1979b. "The Value of Multiple Methods in Researching Third World Strikes: A Nigerian Example," *Development and Change*, Vol. 10:301-19.

———. 1981-82. "Islamic Networks and Urban Capitalism," *Cahiers d'Études Africanes*, Vol. XXVI, pp. 2-222.

———. 1983. *Islam and Labor: The Making of a Muslim Working Class in Kano* (forthcoming).

Lubeck, Paul, and Walton, John. 1979. "Urban Class Conflict in Africa and Latin America: Comparative Analyses from a World Systems Perspective," *International Journal of Urban and Regional Research*, Vol. 3, No. 1:3-28.

Mackintosh, J. P. 1966. *Nigerian Government and Politics* (London: Allen & Unwin).

Melson, Robert, and Wolpe, Howard. 1971. "Modernization and the Politics of Communalism: A Theoretical Perspective," in Melson and Wolpe, above, pp. 1-42.

Murray, D. J. 1969. *The Work of Administration in Nigeria* (London: Published for the Institute of Administration, University of Ife, Nigeria, by Hutchinson), 153 pp.

Five case studies of Nigerian public administration (e.g., "An abattoir for Ibadan," "The appointment of a chief in Okemeta") which demonstrate the complexities facing the Nigerian administrator.

———. 1978. *Studies in Nigerian Administration* (London: Hutchinson, 1978), 342 pp.

The Nigerian and foreign contributors to this volume examine the changes in Nigerian public administration brought about by independence and evaluate a decade of Nigerian administration.

Nagel, Joane, and Olzak, Susan. 1981. "Ethnic Mobilization in New and Old States: An Extension of the Competition Model." Paper presented to the Annual Meetings of the American Sociological Association, Toronto, Canada.

National Party of Nigeria. 1979. "Manifesto of the NPN," in Chuba Okadigbo, *Mission of the NPN* (Enugu, Nigeria: Ejike R. Nwankwo Associates).

Nigeria, Cabinet Office, Administrative Adviser's Office. 1967. *Public Administration in Development and Decentralisation* (Lagos) 25 leaves.

The administrative problems accompanying Nigeria's 1967 regional decentralisation (four regions being broken down into twelve) is the subject of this essay.

____. 1967. *The Struggle for One Nigeria* (Lagos: Federal Ministry of Information), 59 pp.

A standard Federal Government analysis of the Civil War. The appendix includes some important 1966-67 documents.

____. Constituent Assembly, 1978. *Proceedings of the Constituent Assembly* (Lagos: Federal Ministry of Information, Printing Division), 1993 pp.

____. Federal Ministry of Information, Information Division, 1975. *Nigeria-Action, First Month, July 29th-August 29th, 1975* (Lagos: Information Division, Federal Ministry of Information), 35 pp.

This first official look at Nigeria's new military leaders introduces them and some of their immediate reforms to the public.

Nigerian Economic Society. 1975. *Nigeria's Indigenisation Policy* (Lagos: Nigerian Economic Society).

Nigerian Opinion. 1966. *Nigeria 1965: Crisis and Criticism* (Ibadan: Ibadan University Press), 130 pp.

Nigerian People's Party. 1979. "Manifesto, Aims and Objectives, and Programme of Action." (Lagos: NPP).

Nnoli, Okwudiba. 1978. *Ethnic Politics in Nigeria* (Enugu, Nigeria: Fourth Dimension Publishers), 289 pp.

Nwanko, A. A. 1969. *The Making of a Nation: Biafra* (London: C. Hurst and Co.), 361 pp.

Nwosu, E. J. 1980. "Rural Development as a Factor in National Development," in E. C. Amucheazi, ed., *Readings in Social Sciences: Issues in National Development* (Enugu, Nigeria: Fourth Dimension Publishers).

Obasanjo, Olusegun. 1979. *Foundation for Stability* (Lagos: Federal Ministry of Information, Federal Military Government of Nigeria), 52 pp.

The transcription of a 1979 two-day Nigerian television interview with Obasanjo. The General discusses a wide range of domestic and international issues.

Odetola, Theophilus O. 1978. *Military Politics in Nigeria* (New Brunswick, N.J.: Transaction Books), 179 pp.

The author's analysis of Nigerian military rule leads him to conclude that "coercion does not automatically imply dictatorship, but may serve the purposes of democratizing as well as industrializing a society."

Ofiaja, Nicholas D. 1979. *Stability and Instability in Politics: The Case of Nigeria and Cameroon* (New York: Vantage Press), 220 pp.

A comparison of national policies with respect to ethnic issues leads the author to conclude that Nigeria needs a truly national party with great regulative capacity.

Ofonagoro, W. Ibekwe (ed.). 1977. *The Great Debate* (Lagos: Daily Times of Nigeria), 718 pp.

Brought together are Nigerian contributors to the debate on the Draft Constitution. The Draft Constitution itself is in the appendix.

——. 1981. *The Story of the Nigerian General Elections 1979* (Lagos: Federal Ministry of Information). (As reviewed in *West Africa*, 28 September 1981: 2233-5).

Ohonbamu, Obarogie. 1969. *The Psychology of the Nigerian Revolution* (Ilfracombe: Stockwell), 224 pp.

These reflections on Nigeria's political problems are critical of the "empty rhetoric" of purported reforms. The author claims that the pre-independence dream of progress, freedom, and prosperity still has not become reality.

——. 1967. *Whither Nigeria?* (Lagos: Printed by M.S.P. Press), 106 pp.

After looking for lessons in independent Nigeria's short past, the author makes a case for federalism and a one-party system.

——. 1966. *Nigeria: The Army and the People's Cause* (Ibadan: Printed by the African Education Press), 54 pp.

After commenting favorably on the 1966 military coup, the author proposes a series of constitutional modifications designed to truly unify and "decolonize" Nigeria.

Ojigbo, Okion. 1980. *Nigeria Returns to Civilian Rule* (Lagos: Tokion (Nigeria) Company).

Ojo, Olatunde J. B. 1981. "The Impact of Personality and Ethnicity on the Nigerian Elections of 1979," *Africa Today* 28, 1:47-58.

Okadigbo, Chuba. 1981. *The Mission of the NPN* (Enugu: Ejike R. Nwankwo Associates).

Okeke, Godfrey C. 1968. *The Biafra-Nigeria War* (London: The author), 30 pp.

A short review of the causes of the Civil War, and some thoughts on resolving it.

Okonjo, I. M. 1972. *Some Aspects of Public Administration in a Developing Economy* (Benin City: Ministry of Home Affairs and Information, Information Division), 169 pp.

Various Nigerian senior administrators offer essays on the proper role of Nigerian civil servants.

Okoye, Mokwugo. 1975. *Politics and Problems of the First Republic of Nigeria* (Ile-Ife: University of Ife Press, Published for the Faculty of Arts), 30 pp.

This 1974 Faculty of Arts lecture derives lessons from the mistakes of Nigeria's First Republic and calls upon Nigerians to learn from these mistakes.

Okpaku, Joseph (ed.). 1972. *Nigeria: Dilemma of Nationhood* (New York: Third Press), 426 pp.

This volume of African contributors to the Biafran question stresses the conflict's basis in economic and social structures.

Okpu, Ugbana. 1977. *Ethnic Minority Problems in Nigerian Politics, 1960-1965* (Uppsala: University of Stockholm, Almquist and Wiksell International), 191 pp.

An investigation of the role of ethnic minority problems in Nigerian politics. The book discusses the origins of political stances based on ethnic minority problems and some of the ensuing political instability.

Ollawa, P. E. 1981. "The Nigerian Elections of 1979: A Further Comment," *Journal of Commonwealth and Comparative Politics* XIX, 3:299-308.

Olorunsola, Victor A. 1977. *Soldiers and Power* (Stanford, California: Hoover Institution Press), 168 pp.

Focuses on various Nigerian groups' perceptions of the Gowon regime's development performance. The military's perceptions of its own performance is included.

——. 1978. *Societal Reconstruction in Two African States* (Washington: University Press of America), 296 pp.

Author's analysis of the performance of Nigerian and Ghanaian military regimes leads him to conclude that despite their nonconformance to classic democratic models, military regimes can respond more effectively to their peoples' needs than some democratically elected regimes.

Onibonoje, G. O. 1965. *Civics for the Nigerian* (Ibadan: Onibonoje Press), 229 pp.

A much published civics text for Nigerian schoolchildren.

Osoba, Segun. 1978. "The Deepening Crisis of the Nigerian National Bourgeoisie," *Review of African Political Economy* 13, May-August, pp. 63-77.

Osuntokun, Akinjide. 1978. *Equatorial Guinea-Nigerian Relations: The Diplomacy of Labor*. NIIA Monograph Series no. 1 (Ibadan: Oxford University Press).

——. 1982. *Expansion of University Education in Nigeria*. Occasional publication of the Nigerian University Commission in Washington, Vol. I, No. 1.

Oyediran, Oyeleye. 1979. *Nigerian Government and Politics Under Military Rule, 1966-1979* (New York: St. Martin's Press), 319 pp.

Evaluations of the impact of military rule on Nigerian political life. The assessments are mixed, though the military gets almost universal approval for its foreign policies.

Oyinbo, John. 1971. *Nigeria: Crisis and Beyond* (London: C. Knight), 214 pp.

The author traces Nigerian history from independence's "conspiracy of optimism" through the Civil War. He reviews the lessons learned from the Civil War and sees the end of the Civil War as a chance for the nation to start afresh.

Panter-Brick, Keith (ed.). 1978. *Soldiers and Oil* (London: Frank Cass and Company), 374 pp.

Subtitled *The Political Transformation of Nigeria*. Collection of essays by Nigerian and foreign scholars. Analyzed are the performances of the Nigerian military in office, and the military's federal, local, and constitutional reform efforts.

____ . 1981. "Nigeria: The 1979 Elections," *Afrika Spektrum*, vol. 3 (January).

Peil, Margaret. 1976. *Nigerian Politics* (London: Cassell), 209 pp.

An empirical study of the Nigerian public's feelings on a variety of topics: civilian or military rule, constitutional questions, corruption, *inter alia*.

Peoples Redemption Party. 1979. "The Platform of the People: The General Programme and Election Manifesto of the Peoples Redemption Party," Lagos.

Phillips, Claude S. 1980. "Nigeria's New Political Institutions, 1975-9," *Journal of Modern African Studies* XVIII, 1:1-22.

Post, K. W. J. 1964. "Nationalism and Politics in Nigeria: A Marxist Approach," 6 *Nigerian Journal of Economic and Social Studies*, 167-76.

____ , and Vickers, Michael. 1973. *Structure and Conflict in Nigeria, 1960-1966* (Madison, Wis.: University of Wisconsin Press), 248 pp.

The authors seek to understand the structural reasons for the breakdown of constitutional government in 1966. They analyze in detail the events that led to the 1966 coup and propose a series of models that identify and help explain the causes of that coup.

Rimmer, Douglas. 1981. "The Economy Since 1970," in Anthony Kirk-Greene and Douglas Rimmer, eds. *Nigeria Since 1970: A Political and Economic*

Outline (London: Hodder and Stoughton; New York: Holmes and Meier).

Sahlin, Michael. 1977. *Neo-authoritarianism and the Problem of Legitimacy* [Stockholm: Raben and Sjogren (dist.)], 243 pp.

The example of General Gowon's Nigeria is used to illustrate the author's study of Third World authoritarian military regimes.

Sahota, Gian S. 1980. "The Distribution of the Benefits of Public Expenditure in Nigeria." Report for the World Bank.

Sanda, A. O. (ed.). 1976. *Ethnic Relations in Nigeria* (Nigeria, Department of Sociology, University of Ibadan), 216 pp.

Contains a variety of multidisciplinary contributions to the study of ethnic behavior. Subjects include the interaction of politics and ethnicity, ethnic identity, links between ethnic relations and change.

Sklar, Richard. 1963. *Nigerian Political Parties* (Princeton: Princeton University Press).

____. 1965. "Contradictions in the Nigerian Political System," *Journal of Modern African Studies*, Vol. 3, No. 2:201-13. (Reprinted in [Robert Melson and Howard Wolpe, eds.] *Nigeria: Modernization and the Politics of Communalism*, East Lansing: Michigan State University Press, 1971.)

____. 1967. "Political Science and National Integration – A Radical Approach," *Journal of Modern African Studies*, Vol. 5, No. 1:1-11.

____. 1979. "The Nature of Class Domination in Africa," *Journal of Modern African Studies*, Vol. 17, No. 4:531-52.

____. 1981. "Democracy for the Second Nigerian Republic," *Issue*, Vol. 11, No. 1/2, Spring/Summer: 14-16.

Stokke, Olav. 1970a. *Nigeria* (Uppsala: Scandinavian Institute of African Studies), 142 pp.

Subtitled *An Introduction to the Politics, Economy, and Social Setting of Modern Nigeria*. This overview pays particular attention to regional differences (e.g., a chapter on regional pre-independence claims for separate status, and one on "The Cultural Setting).

____. 1970b. *Integration and Disintegration: The Case of the Nigerian Federation Up to June 1967* (Uppsala: Scandinavian Institute of African Studies), 32 leaves.

The thesis is advanced that the "prerequisites" for support for secession were present in Ibo societies but that the conditions for a successful secession were not.

Tukur, Mahmud (ed.). 1971. *Administrative and Political Development, Prospects for Nigeria* (Nigeria: Conference on the Administrative and Political Development of Nigeria, Kaduna Baraka Press), 237 pp.

The result of a 1970 all-Nigerian conference on administrative and political development. Papers address, *inter alia*, constitutional issues, the civil service, and state stability.

Unity Party of Nigeria. 1979a. *A WO at 70* (Lagos: Directorate of Organisation, Unity Party of Nigeria), 78 pp.

A pamphlet in which the U.P.N. presents in a series of essays its strategy and programs.

____. 1979b. "Up Nigeria: Manifesto of the Unity Party of Nigeria," Lagos.

____. 1979c. "Policy Papers," Lagos.

Unongo, Paul I. 1968. *The Case for Nigeria* (Lagos: Town and Gown), 1963 pp.

Offers an emphatic yes to the question of a unified Nigeria; explains why Biafra should not be allowed to secede.

Uwanaka, Charles U. 1966. *The 1964 Federal Election Crisis and Battle for the West* (Lagos: Exeagwu Bookshop), 147 pp.

A history of Nigerian domestic politics is followed by a focus on events surrounding the 1964 federal election crisis.

Uwechue, Raph. 1979. *Reflections on the Nigerian Civil War* (New York: Africana Publishing Corp.), 206 pp.

The author's examination of the Civil War leads him to espouse a "supple federal union" as the most reasonable solution to Nigeria's internal differences.

Whitaker, C. S., Jr. 1981. "Second Beginnings: The New Political Framework," *Issue*, Vol. 11, No. 1/2, Spring/Summer: 2-13.

Williams, Babatunde A. 1965. *Political Trends in Nigeria 1960-1964* (Ibadan: African Education Press), 39 pp.

In this contemporary study, the author points out the growth of ideology in party politics and predicts that party alliance, through the inclusion of both North and South, will preserve the Nigerian Federation.

Yahaya, A. D. 1981. "PRP Crisis: The Truth of the Matter," *West Africa*, 15 June:1349-53.

Young, Crawford. 1976. *The Politics of Cultural Pluralism* (Madison: University of Wisconsin Press).

ECONOMY

Aboyade, O. 1973. "Income Profile," University of Ibadan Inaugural Lecture, 3 May.

——. 1974a. "Income Structure and Economic Power," Presidential Address to the 14th Annual Conference of the Nigerian Economic Society, April.

Adelman, Irma, and Morris, Cynthia. 1971. "An Anatomy of Patterns of Income Distribution in Developing Nations," (Washington: USAID).

Adeyoju, S. K. 1970. *The Timber Economy and the Landscape* (Ibadan: Department of Forestry, University of Ibadan), 64 pp.

The history of timber exploitation in southwest Nigeria is recounted, and the general effect of the timber industry on the Nigerian economy is analyzed.

Arrighi, G., and Saul, J. S., eds. 1972. *Essays in the Political Economy of Africa* (New York: Monthly Review).

Ayeni, Bola. 1981. "Spatial Aspects of Urbanization and Effects on the Distribution of Income in Nigeria," in *Political Economy of Income Distribution in Nigeria*, pp. 237-68.

Berger, Manfred. 1975. *Industrialisation Policies in Nigeria* (Munchen: Veltforum Verlag), 333 pp.

A detailed discussion of the basic objectives of post-independence industrialization.

Bienen, Henry. 1981a. "The Political Economy of Income Distribution in Nigeria," in Bienen, H. and Diejomaoh, V. P., eds., *The Political Economy of Income Distribution in Nigeria* (New York: Holmes and Meier), pp. 1-28.

——. 1981b. "The Politics of Distribution: Institutions, Class and Ethnicity," in *The Political Economy of Income Distribution in Nigeria*, pp. 127-72.

Biersteker, T. J. 1978. *Distortion or Development?* (Cambridge, Mass.: MIT Press), 199 pp.

The author sets up opposing theoretical propositions (one set critical to multinational investment vs. a neoconservative set of propositions), followed by a case study (Nigeria) in which these contrasting propositions are tested. His tentative conclusion is that multinational investment in underdeveloped countries can clash with host country development objectives.

Blitz, L. F. (ed.). 1965. *The Politics and Administration of Nigerian Government* (London: Sweet and Maxwell), 281 pp.

A portrait of Nigeria's early post-independence years. A variety of contributors explain the structure of the federal system, Nigerian political parties, the judicial system, and foreign relations.

British National Export Council, Africa Committee. 1970(?). *Nigeria* (London: BNEC), 37 pp.

The report of a construction equipment mission sent to evaluate sales prospects.

Callaway, Barbara. 1975. "The Political Economy of Nigeria" in Richard Harris (ed.), *The Political Economy of Africa* (Cambridge: Schenkman), pp. 93-135.

Clark, Peter B. 1970. *Planning Import Substitution* (Amsterdam: North-Holland Publishing Co.), 315 pp.

A model to evaluate the potential of import substitution is proposed. After looking at Nigeria, the author concludes that a faster GNP growth rate is possible for Nigeria if domestic investment patterns shift.

Conference on Institutional and Administrative Perspectives for National Development. 1972(?). *In Search of a New Political Community: The Nigerian Case* (Zaria Gaskiya Corp.), 339 pp.

The report of a conference held at the Institute of Administration, Ahmadu Bello University. The authors address the problem of designing institutions appropriate to national goals. Half the articles draw lessons from others' experiences (transitional government in Egypt; economic growth in Japan); the other half discuss Nigerian constitutional arrangements, executive organs, and economic institutions and policies.

Conference on National Reconstruction and Development in Nigeria. 1971. *Reconstruction and Development in Nigeria* (Ibadan: Published for the

Nigerian Institute of Social and Economic Research by Oxford University Press), 766 pp.

The results of a 1969 conference. The book consists of fourteen presentations on the direction of Nigerian economic development, with commentary.

Damachi, Ukandi Godwin. 1973. *Social Change and Economic Development in Nigeria* (New York: Praeger), 252 pp.

An analysis of the interplay between economic development and education, labor relations, domestic politics, and communications.

Dean, Edwin. 1974. *Plan Implementation in Nigeria, 1962-1966* (Ibadan: Oxford University Press), 294 pp.

An evaluation of the performance of the First National Plan. Both the theory of the Plan and its implementation command roughly equal attention. The author concludes his study with a balance sheet of the Plan's weak and strong points.

Diejomaoh, V. P., and Anusionwu, E. C. 1981a. "The Structure of Income Inequality in Nigeria," in *The Political Economy of Income Distribution in Nigeria*, pp. 89-126.

Eicher, Carl. 1970. *Growth and Development of the Nigerian Economy* (East Lansing: Michigan State University Press), 456 pp.

Various contributors provide a historical overview of Nigeria's economic development. The latter half of the book discusses the planning and implementation of development in the sixties and the economic prospects for the seventies.

Fajana, Olufemi. 1979. "The Distribution of Personal Income in Nigeria," in *Poverty in Nigeria* (Ibadan: Nigerian Economic Society), pp. 277-94.

——. 1981. "Aspects of Income Distribution in the Nigerian Urban Sector," in *The Political Economy of Income Distribution in Nigeria*, pp. 193-236.

Focus Research. c1975. *Investment in Nigeria* (London: Focus Research), 68 pp.

A presentation of several facets of the "political climate" for foreign investment that includes discussion of trade unions, industrialization, and foreign investment.

Frank, Charles R. 1967. *Employment and Economic Growth in Nigeria*, 51 pp.

This 1966 analysis of Nigerian unemployment concludes that, given continued rural exodus and no major policy change, Nigerian unemployment is likely to increase. Frank suggests that the rural exodus can be reduced by lowering urban-rural income differentials.

GATT. 1966. *Programme for Expansion of International Trade* (GATT: Geneva), 254 pp.

A GATT special committee studies the 1st National Development Plan (1962-68). Particular attention is paid to the Plan's effect on Nigeria's export capacity. Includes detailed commodity exports appendix.

Gowon, Yakubu. 1975(?). *Address* (Nigeria), 18 pp.

Gowon's inauguration of the 3rd National Development Plan. General remarks and a brief sector by sector review of the Plan.

____. 1970. *Nigeria's Forward March* (Nigeria: Associated Press of Nigeria), 30 pp.

In this speech to the Nigerian nation, Gowon inaugurates the 2nd National Development Plan. Goals and allocations are presented.

Hanson, A. H. 1959. *Public Enterprise and Economic Development* (London: Routledge & Kegan Paul).

Harris, John Rees. 1969. *Entrepreneurship and Economic Development* (Nairobi), 38 pp.

Offers an economic model of the role of Nigerian entrepreneurship in that country's economic growth.

Lewis, A. O. 1973. *Nigeria's Exports: Problems, Prospects, and Implications for Economic Growth* (Budapest: Center for Afro-Asian Research of the Hungarian Academy of Sciences), 51 pp.

The author suggests that Nigeria deal with its foreign exchange problem by building up her industrial productive capacity.

Lewis, William A. 1967. *Reflections on Nigeria's Economic Growth* (Paris: Development Centre of the OECD), 65 pp.

These reflections straddle pre- and post-independence economic development. Included are thoughts on Nigeria's "engine of growth," the problems of economic growth, and the future of continued economic growth.

Mabogunje, Akin L. 1971. *Growth Poles and Growth Centres in the Regional*

Development of Nigeria (Geneva: United Nations Research Institute for Social Development), 81 pp.

A study of the application of the theory of growth poles to Nigeria. The author identifies growth pole tendencies in the Nigerian economy and then applies them to the theory as a whole.

Matlon, Peter. 1981a. "The Structure of Production and Rural Incomes in Northern Nigeria: Results of Three Village Case Studies," in *Political Economy of Income Distribution in Nigeria*, pp. 323-72.

Melson, R. 1971. *Nigeria: Modernization and the Politics of Communalism* (East Lansing: Michigan State University Press), 680 pp.

Contributors to this volume explore aspects of intergroup conflict within the context of Nigerian nation building.

Morrison, Donald. 1981. "Inequalities of Social Rewards: Realities and Perceptions in Nigeria," in *The Political Economy of Income Distribution in Nigeria*, pp. 173-92.

National Management Conference. c1974. *Indigenisation and Economic Development* (Nigerian Institute of Management), 39 pp.

Publication of the proceedings of the tenth annual National Management Conference. Problems confronting Nigerian entrepreneurs are discussed and remedies proposed.

Nigeria. 1971(?). *Building the New Nigeria: National Development Plan, 1970-74* (Apapa: Printed by the Nigerian National Press), 66 pp.

The Nigerian National Press summarizes for the general public the implications of the 2nd National Development Plan.

——, Federal Ministry of Economic Development. 1966. *Guideposts for Second National Development Plan* (Lagos: Ministry of Economic Development), 16 pp.

The government sets forth some preliminary objectives for the Second National Development Plan.

——, Federal Ministry of Economic Development. 1962(?). *National Development Plan, 1962-68* (Lagos: CPO), 362 pp.

In addition to a general survey of the First Development Plan, the book also includes chapters on regional development programs.

____, Federal Ministry of Economic Development and Reconstruction, Central Planning Office. c1974. *Guidelines for the Third National Development Plan, 1975-1980* (Lagos: Central Planning Office, Federal Ministry of Economic Development and Reconstruction), 61 pp.

A synopsis of the Nigerian economy is presented along with remedies for economic ills.

____, Federal Ministry of Economic Development and Reconstruction, Central Planning Office. 1972. *Second National Development Plan 1970-74* (Lagos: CPO), 312 pp.

This first progress report of the Second Development Plan covers the first year of the plan in detail. Bottlenecks are identified in what remains a generally positive evaluation.

____, Federal Ministry of Economic Development and Reconstruction, Central Planning Office. 1974. *Second National Development Plan, 1970-1974* (Lagos: Central Planning Office, Federal Ministry of Economic Development and Reconstruction), 342 pp.

This second progress report on the Second National Development Plan discusses the first three years of the Plan. The generally "rosy" economic picture portrayed is qualified, particularly in its concern with the performance with the agricultural sector.

____, Federal Ministry of Information. 1966. *Six Year Development Plans* (Lagos: Information Division, Ministry of Information), 42 pp.

A primer of the First Development Plan, in the form of questions and answers. Illustrated.

____. 1970. *Second National Development Plan, 1970-74* (Lagos: Federal Government Printer), 344 pp.

The analysis is broken down by sector rather than by region. Among those sectors discussed: private, public, manpower, financing.

Nigeria (London: Collings, 1976), 226 pp.

A series of essays examines the oppressive effects of Nigerian development on different sociopolitical and socioeconomic groups (women, indigenous entrepreneurship, the Ibadan peasantry, etc.).

Obasanjo, Olusegun. 1976. *Call to Duty* (Lagos: Federal Ministry of Information), 70 pp.

A collection of 1975-76 speeches by Obasanjo, both as Chief of Staff and Head of State.

Odufalu, Johnson. 1981. "The Distributive Impact of Expenditures in Nigeria," in *The Political Economy of Income Distribution in Nigeria*, pp. 455-84.

Okurume, Godwin E. (n.d.) *Foreign Trade and the Subsistence Sector in Nigeria*

Develops a model for rural and agricultural development in an agricultural export economy. Advances the thesis that, because of small food markets, economic incentives for increased agricultural production do not exist in Nigeria.

Olaloku, F. A. (ed.). 1979. *Structure of the Nigerian Economy* (New York: St. Martin's Press), 270 pp.

Designed for Nigerian students in university economics courses. The book includes chapters on the economics of various sectors (mining, manufacturing, agriculture, etc.) and Nigerian balance of payments, capital formation, monetary and fiscal policy, and development planning.

Olaoye, S. Dayo. 1977. *Ramatism, A National Ideology* (Lagos: Bisco Communications), 48 pp.

A chapter of what was to be the author's book, *Towards African Economic Emancipation*.

The author defines and discusses Ramatism.

Olayide, S. O. 1976. *Economic Survey of Nigeria* (1960-1975) (Ibadan: Aromolaran Publishing Co.), 203 pp.

A team of Nigerian academics presents a general survey of the performance of various sectors of the Nigerian economy for the first fifteen years of independence.

Omorogiuwa, P. Ada. 1981. "Personal Income Taxation and Income Distribution in Nigeria," in *The Political Economy of Income Distribution in Nigeria*, pp. 421-54.

Oni, Ola. 1975. *Economic Development in Nigeria* (Ibadan: Nigerian Academy of Arts, Sciences and Technology), 262 pp.

The author's critique of aspects of capitalism in Nigeria is followed by his presentation of a socialist alternative.

Pearson, Scott R. 1970. *Petroleum and the Nigerian Economy* (Stanford, California: Stanford University Press), 235 pp.

The book discusses the effects of petroleum and petroleum related investment on the Nigerian economy. It offers an input-output model which projects future effects of the petroleum industry on the Nigerian economy.

Rimlinger, Gaston V. 1972. *Indigenisation of Industry and Progress of the Second Nigerian National Development Plan* (Houston, Texas: William Marsh Rice University), 16 pp.

An examination of the implementation of the Second Development Plan's indigenization. It is concluded that foreign industry has complied with Nigeria's initial requirements.

____. 1976. *Communalism and the Gains From Development* (Houston, Texas: Program of Development Studies, William Marsh Rice University), 55 pp.

The author stresses the Nigerian government's commitment to increase the level of communal equality and points out a series of government measures (universal primary education, a more equal distribution of national revenue) designed to implement this commitment.

Rimmer, Douglas. 1981. "Development in Nigeria: An Overview," in *The Political Economy of Income Distribution in Nigeria*, pp. 29-88.

Sada, P. O. 1981. "Urbanization and Income Distribution in Nigeria," in *The Political Economy of Income Distribution in Nigeria*, pp. 269-98.

Schatz, Ludwig H. 1973. *Industrialization in Nigeria* (Munchen: Weltforum Verlag), 262 pp.

An explanation of the spatial process of industrialization in Nigeria. The author applies geography to process in the industrial sector in order to determine industrial investment's optimal spatial structure.

Schatz, Sayre. 1977. *Nigerian Capitalism* (Berkeley: University of California Press), 294 pp.

The book begins with a discussion of the development of "nurture capitalism." The author then analyzes the "disappointing role" of Nigerian private enterprise in development and its interaction with government.

Seminar on the Second National Development Plan, 1971. *Report* (Lagos: Federal Ministry of Information, Print Division), 88 pp.

The details of a seminar dedicated to probing the difficulties of the Second National Development Plan.

Symposium on Financial Institutions and the Business Community. 1974(?). *Symposium on Financial Institutions and the Business Community* (Enugu: Nigeria, Economic Development Institute, University of Nigeria), 91 pp.

The published results of the symposium. For the most part, a look at the availability of capital (both domestic and foreign) to Nigerian businesses.

Teriba, O., ed. 1977. *Industrial Development in Nigeria* (Ibadan: Ibadan University Press), 388 pp.

Nigerian and foreign contributors present their views of Nigeria's industrial environment (ideology, entrepreneurship, development strategy), government policy, and the pattern of Nigerian industrial development. The final section suggests ways of improving Nigeria's industrial position.

____. 1981. "Financial Institutions, Financial Markets, and Income Distribution," in *The Political Economy of Income Distribution in Nigeria*, pp. 485-512.

____, and Phillips, O. A. 1971. "Income Distribution and National Integration," in *Nigerian Journal of Economic and Social Studies* 1.

Tims, Wouter. 1974. *Nigeria: Options for Long-term Development* (Baltimore: The Johns Hopkins University Press), 256 pp.

A World Bank country report. Economic activity in various sectors is examined, trends are established and future prospects discerned. A well-selected statistical annex is included.

Wey, S. O., and Osagie, E. 1976(?). *An Ideology for Social Development* (Lagos: Academy Press Ltd.), 112 pp.

The authors propose the implementation of a philosophy of "integratism" ("a movement . . . based on a universally acceptable belief or value system") to solve the problems of Nigeria and the world.

World Bank. 1978. *Report on Economic Conditions in Nigeria* (mimeo, Washington: World Bank).

____. 1981. *World Development Report 1981* (New York: Oxford).

AGRICULTURE

Clarke, J. 1979. *Agricultural Production in a Rural Yoruba Community*, Ph.D. dissertation, University of London.

Clough, P. 1979. *Indebtedness among the Rural Hausa* (mimeo, Oxford University).

D'Silva, B., and Raza, M. 1980. "Integrated Rural Development in Nigeria," *Food Policy*, Vol. 5, pp. 282-97.

Forrest, T. 1981. "Agricultural Policies in Nigeria 1900-1978," in G. Williams et al. (eds.). *Rural Development in Tropical Africa* (London: MacMillan), pp. 222-58.

Hill, P. 1977. *Population, Prosperity and Poverty: Rural Kano 1900 and 1970* (Cambridge: University Press).

ILO. 1982. *Nigeria: First Things First* (Addis Ababa: International Labor Office).

Jackson, C. 1978. "Hausa Women on Strike," *Review of African Political Economy*, No. 13, pp. 46-59.

Joseph, R. 1978b. "Affluence and Underdevelopment: The Nigerian Experience," *Journal of Modern African Studies*, Vol. 16, pp. 221-39.

Lagemann, Johannes. 1977. *Traditional African Farming Systems in Eastern Nigeria* (Munchen: Weltforum Verlag), 269 pp.

A detailed analysis of smallholder land use systems in highly populated areas of eastern Nigeria. The author suggests measures by which declines in soil fertility can be combatted.

Lapido, O., and Adesimi, A. 1981. "Income Distribution in the Rural Sector," in Bienen, H. and Diejomaoh, V. P. (eds.), *The Political Economy of Income Distribution in Nigeria* (New York: Holmes and Meier), pp. 299-319.

Matlon, P. 1981b. "Production and Rural Incomes in Northern Nigeria," in Bienen, H. and Diejomaoh, V. P. (eds.), *The Political Economy of Income Distribution in Nigeria* (New York: Holmes and Meier), pp. 323-72.

Mid-western State, Nigeria, Ministry of Finance and Economic Development. 1968(?). *Report of Pilot Sample Survey of Agricultural Holdings in Benin*

Division, 1966-67 (Benin City), 34 pp.

This survey was designed to help provide an agricultural data base suitable for future research in Benin Division. Included *inter alia* are estimated acreages of staples, size of farm holdings, and livestock numbers.

Netting, Robert. 1968. *Hill Farmers of Nigeria* (Seattle: University of Washington Press), 259 pp.

Subtitled *Cultural Ecology of the Kofyar of the Jos Plateau*. The author describes the traditional agriculture practiced by the Kofyar and then examines the Kofyars' shift in cultivation from subsistence agriculture to cash crops.

Nigeria, Federal Office of Statistics. 1972. *Methodological Notes on Rural Sample Surveys Carried Out by the Federal Office of Statistics* (Lagos), 25 pp.

An explanation of the methodology used in rural sample surveys (definition of the study, methods of data collections, dealing with sample errors) by the Federal Office of Statistics.

____, Federal Office of Statistics. 1976. *National Agriculture Sample Census of Nigeria 1974-1975* (Lagos: Federal Office of Statistics, Agricultural Census Division), 17 leaves.

Presents basic 1974-75 agricultural data obtained from national sample survey. The breakdowns are done for the most part in terms of crops and states.

____, Federal Office of Statistics. 1966. *Farm Survey 1963-64* (Lagos), 20 pp.

The results of a 1963-64 nationwide agriculture survey conducted jointly with AID. The breakdown is in terms of crops and regions.

____, Federal Ministry of Agriculture. 1980. *The Green Revolution: A Food Production Plan for Nigeria* (Lagos: Federal Ministry of Agriculture), 2 Vols.

Norman, David W. 1973. *Methodology and Problems of Farm Management Investigations* (Zaria, Nigeria: Institute for Agricultural Research, Samaru, Ahmadu Bello University), 41 pp.

Discusses some of the methodological problems of farm management surveys. Concludes, in part, that working intensively with fewer farmers can reduce sampling errors.

____, et al. 1976. *A Socio-Economic Survey of 3 Villages in the Sokoto Close Settled Zone* (Zaria: Institute for Agricultural Research, Ahmadu Bello University, Samaru Miscellaneous Paper no. 64).

Ogbonna, D. 1979. *Geographical Consequences of Petroleum in Nigeria*, Ph.D. dissertation, University of California, Berkeley.

Oluwasanmi, H. A. 1966. *Agriculture and Nigerian Economic Development* (Ibadan: Oxford University Press).

Stressing the links between modernization and greater agricultural production, the author argues for change in agricultural techniques and organization.

Oyenuga, Victor A. 1967. *Agriculture in Nigeria* (Rome: F.A.O.), 308 pp.

An overview of Nigerian agriculture. Included are chapters on cereals, pulses, livestock, tree and economic crop agriculture, and animal husbandry.

Palmer-Jones, R. 1980. *Why Irrigate in Northern Nigeria* (mimeo, Oxford University).

Sada, P. O. 1981. "Urbanization and Income Distribution in Nigeria," in Bienen, H., and Diejomaoh, V. P. (eds.), *The Political Economy of Income Distribution in Nigeria* (New York: Holmes and Meier), pp. 276-98.

Upton, Martin. 1967. *Agriculture in South-west Nigeria* (Reading: University of Reading, Department of Agricultural Economics), 115 pp.

This 1963-65 sample study looks first at agricultural production in Southwestern Nigeria. It then examines the relationship between agricultural production and the social and cultural environment.

Usoro, E. J. 1978. *Observed disparity in Nigerian rural poverty*. Proceedings of the Annual Conference of the Nigerian Economic Society, Ibadan.

Wallace, T. 1981. "The Challenge of Food: Nigeria's Approach to Agriculture 1975-80," *Canadian Journal of African Studies*, Vol. 15, pp. 239-58.

Watts, M. *Silent Violence: Food, Famine and Peasantry in Northern Nigeria*, University of California Press (forthcoming).

Williams, G. 1980. "Inequalities in Rural Nigeria," report prepared for the ILO, Oxford University.

BUSINESS

Aboyade, O. 1974b. "Closing Remarks," in *Nigeria's Indigenisation Policy*. Proceedings of the Symposium organized by the Nigerian Economic Society. Ibadan: University of Ibadan.

Akeredolu-Ale, E. O. 1976. "Private Foreign Investment and the Underdevelopment of Indigenous Entrepreneurship in Nigeria" in Gavin Williams (ed.), *Nigeria: Economy and Society* (London: Rex Collings).

____. 1975. *The Underdevelopment of Indigenous Entrepreneurship in Nigeria* (Ibadan, Ibadan University Press), 119 pp.

Stresses that problems of third world entrepreneurship must be analyzed through structures as much as through values. The author uses Nigeria as a case study for his theory.

____. 1972. "The 'Competitive Threshold' Hypothesis and Nigeria's Industrialization Process," 14 *Nigerian Journal of Economic and Social Studies* (March), 109-20.

Akinsanya, Adeoye. 1978. "Reforming a Public Enterprise Through a Management Audit: Many Lessons from the Western Nigeria Development Corporation," 24 *Indian Journal of Public Administration* (October/December), 1016-31.

____. 1979. "Permanent Sovereignty Over Natural Resources and the Future of Foreign Investment," 5 *Nigerian Journal of International Affairs*, 70-92.

____. 1980. *The Expropriation of Multinational Property in the Third World* (New York: Praeger).

____. 1981a. "The Former Western Nigeria Development Corporation: A Framework for Performance Evaluation," 1 *Public Administration and Development*: 30.

____. 1981b. "Host-Governments' Responses to Foreign Economic Control: The Experiences of Selected African Countries," 30 *International and Comparative Law Quarterly*.

____. 1981c. "The United Nations Charter of Economic Rights and Duties of States: International Protection of Economic Independence of Third World Countries," 3 *Annual of the Nigerian Society of International Law*.

____ . 1983. *Economic Independence and Indigenisation of Private Foreign Investments: The Experiences of Nigeria and Ghana* (New York: Praeger).

Asiodu, P. C. 1974. "Closing Remarks" in *Nigeria's Indigenisation Policy*. Proceedings of the Symposium organized by the Nigerian Economic Society. (Ibadan: University of Ibadan).

Bergsten, C. Fred. 1974. "Coming Investment Wars?" *Foreign Affairs*, Vol. 53, No. 1.

____ , Horst, Thomas, and Moran, Theodore H. 1978. *American Multinationals and American Interests* (Washington: The Brookings Institution).

Biersteker, Thomas J. 1978. *Distortion or Development? Contending Perspectives on the Multinational Corporation* (Cambridge: The M.I.T. Press).

Collins, Paul. 1975. "The Policy of Indigenization: An Overall View," *Quarterly Journal of Administration* (January 9).

Deutsche Bank. 1975. *Nigeria* (Frankfurt, Deutsche Bank), 52 pp.

A German bank's short guide to Nigerian economic prospects and investment opportunities. Includes disucssion of legal constraints.

Evans, Peter. 1979. *Dependent Development: The Alliance of Multinational, State and Local Capital in Brazil* (Princeton: Princeton University Press).

GATT. 1966. *Development Plan Studies: The First Six-Year Plan of Nigeria* (Geneva: GATT), 254 pp.

The GATT analyzes the 1962-1968 National Development Plan and predicts the Plan's impact on future Nigerian export capacity.

Gilpin, Robert. 1975. *U.S. Power and the Multinational Corporation* (New York: Basic Books).

Hakam, A. H. 1966. "The Motivation to Invest and the Location Pattern of Foreign Private Industrial Investments in Nigeria," 8 *Nigerian Journal of Economic and Social Studies*, 54.

Hay, Alan M. 1970. *Interregional Trade and Money Flows in Nigeria, 1964* (Ibadan: Published for the Nigerian Institute of Social and Economic Research by Oxford University Press), 245 pp.

A detailed study of Nigeria's interregional trade in 1964. Contains extensive agricultural tables and shipping and payment estimates for various commodities.

Hoogvelt, Ankie. 1979. "Indigenisation and Foreign Capital: Industrialisation in Nigeria," *Review of African Political Economy*, Number 14.

Jones, H. O. 1976. *Report on Markets in Nigeria, 1976* (London: Publishing and Distributing Co.), 94 leaves.

A general guide to a businessperson's Nigeria.

Lewis, A. O. 1973. *Nigeria's Exports: Problems, Prospects and Implications for Economic Growth* (Budapest: Center for Afro-Asian Research of the Hungarian Academy of Sciences), 51 pp.

The author suggests that Nigeria can best deal with her foreign exchange problem by building up her industrial productive capacity.

Metra Consulting Group. 1977. *Nigeria, Business Opportunities* (London: The Group), 144 pp.

A look at a) foreign business opportunities in Nigerian industrial sectors and b) problems foreign companies have in setting up business and trading with Nigeria.

Nafziger, E. W. 1977. *African Capitalism: A Case Study in African Entrepreneurship* (Stanford, California: Hoover Institution Press), 293 pp.

Underdeveloped entrepreneurship is viewed as a fundamental limitation to Nigerian development. After a series of case studies, the author suggests ways of strengthening Nigerian entrepreneurship.

Nigeria, Federal Ministry of Information. 1967. *Guide to Nigerian Exports* (Lagos: Published for the Federal Ministry of Trade by the Federal Ministry of Information), 69 pp.

An early attempt to supply foreign business with information on Nigerian exports. An overview of the Nigerian economy is followed by an export commodity description.

____, National Petroleum Corporation. 1978. *Progress of Public Sector Participation in the Nigerian Oil Industry* (Lagos: NNPC).

Obasanjo, Olusegun. 1977. *Nigeria and International Trade* (Lagos: Information Division, Federal Ministry of Information), 7 pp.

Obasanjo's address at the opening of the first Lagos International Trade Fair in 1977.

Onah, J. O. 1978. *Nigerian Cases in Business Management* (London: Cassell), 136 pp.

Twenty-one case studies of Nigerian business administration "illustrate the speed with which changes are taking place in the Nigerian economy."

Onoge, Omafume F. 1974. "The Indigenisation Decree and Economic Independence: Another Case of Bourgeois Utopianism" in *Nigeria's Indigenisation Policy*. Proceedings of the Symposium organized by the Nigerian Economic Society. Ibadan: University of Ibadan.

Oyebode, A. 1977. "National Participation and the Control of Nigerian Economic Activities," presented at the 15th Annual Conference of the Nigerian Association of Law Teachers, University of Lagos, Lagos, April 13-16.

Proehl, P. O. 1965. *Foreign Enterprise in Nigeria: Laws and Policies* (Chapel Hill, N.C.: University of North Carolina Press), p. 159.

Rediffusion International Ltd. 1975. *Advertising and Programmes Division, Nigeria* (London: Rediffusion International Limited, Advertising and Programmes Division), 29 pp.

This advertising market profile evaluates advertising media in Nigeria (radio, television, newspaper, cinema) and attempts to provide potential advertisers with a means of assessing potential sales in Nigeria.

Stepan, Alfred. 1978. *The State and Society: Peru in Comparative Perspective*. (Princeton: Princeton University Press).

Teriba, O. 1969. "The 1967-69 Banking Amendments in Nigeria – An Appraisal of Financial Adaptation in an Underdeveloped Economy," 11 *Nigerian Journal of Economic and Social Studies* (March), 43-64.

———, and Kayode, M. O. eds. 1977. *Industrial Development in Nigeria* (Ibadan: Ibadan University Press).

Turner, Terisa. 1976a. "MNCs and the Instability of the Nigerian State," *Review of African Political Economy*, Number 5.

United States, Bureau of International Commerce. 1976. *Nigeria* (Washington, U.S. Department of Commerce, Domestic and International Business Administration, Bureau of International Commerce for sale by the Supt.

of Docs., U.S. Government Printing Office), 190 pp.

Part of U.S. Commerce's "Country Market Sectoral Survey." This survey of the Nigerian economy identifies opportunities in various sectors for U.S. business.

Williams, Gavin. 1976. "A Political Economy" in Gavin Williams (ed.), *Nigeria: Economy and Society* (London: Rex Collings).

FOREIGN POLICY

Akinsanya, Adeoye. 1976a. "The European Common Market and Africa," I *West African Journal of Sociology and Political Science*, pp. 147-63.

Akinyemi, A. Bolaji. 1973. *Foreign Policy and Federalism* (Ibadan: Ibadan University Press), 217 pp.

The author investigates determinants of Nigerian foreign policy through analyses of case studies, including Nigeria's support of Lumumba and Balewa's break with the Ghanaian government.

____, ed. 1978. *Nigeria and the World* (Ibadan: Published for N.I.I.A. by Oxford University Press, Nigeria), 152 pp.

A series of lectures and commentary by members of Nigeria's foreign policy elite, on Nigeria's interplay with African states and institutions.

____, ed. 1979. *Foreign Policy and the Constitution* (Lagos: Nigerian Institute of International Affairs), 72 pp.

Five short essays explore the relationship between Nigeria's draft constitution and Nigerian foreign policy. By way of background, the history of the Constitution's drafts is sketched.

____. 1979. "Mohammed/Obasanjo Foreign Policy," in Oyediran Oyeleye, 1979.

Akinyemi, A. Bolaji, and Vogt, Margaret. 1978. "Nigeria and Southern Africa: The Policy Options" in Douglas G. Anglin, Timothy M. Shaw and Carl G. Widstrand (eds.), *Conflict and Change in Southern Africa* (Washington: University Press of America), pp. 151-68.

Aluko, Olajide. 1976. *Ghana and Nigeria 1957-70* (New York: Barnes and Noble), 275 pp.

After an examination of respective attitudes, foreign policy stances on important African events (Congo crisis, the Nigerian Civil War, etc.), and relations with the superpowers and the OAU, the author identifies and offers an explanation of the sources of discord.

____. 1979. "Nigeria, the United States and Southern Africa," *African Affairs* 73(310), January, pp. 91-102.

____, ed. 1979. *The Foreign Policy of African States* (Atlantic Highlands, N.J.: Humanities Press), especially Aluko's "The Determinants of the Foreign Policy of African States," and Aluko's "Nigerian Foreign Policy."

____. 1981a. "Necessity and Freedom in Nigerian Foreign Policy," Inaugural Lecture, University of Ife, 17 March.

____. 1981b. *Essays on Nigerian Foreign Policy* (London: George Allen & Unwin).

Anglin, Douglas G. 1964. "Nigeria: Political Non-alignment and Economic Alignment," *Journal of Modern African Studies* 2(2), July, pp. 147-63.

Coleman, J. S. 1963. "The Foreign Policy of Nigeria," in J. E. Black and K. W. Thompson, eds., *Foreign Policies in a World of Change* (New York: Harper & Row).

Evans, Peter. 1979. *Dependent Development: The Alliance of Multinational, State, and Local Capital in Brazil* (Princeton: Princeton University Press).

Freund, Bill. 1978. "Oil Boom and Crisis in Contemporary Nigeria," *Review of African Political Economy* 13, May-August, pp. 91-100.

Gambari, Ibrahim A. 1975. "Nigeria and the World: A Growing Internal Stability, Wealth and External Influence," *Journal of International Affairs* 29(2), Fall, pp. 155-69.

Holsti, K. J. 1972. *International Politics: A Framework for Analysis* (Englewood Cliffs: Prentice-Hall), pp. 121-27.

Hughes, Barry B., and Strauch, Patricia A. 1982. "The Future of Development in Nigeria and the Sahel: Projections from the World Integrated Model (WIM)," in Timothy M. Shaw (ed.), *Alternative Futures for Africa* (Boulder: Westview), pp. 179-99.

Joseph, Richard. 1978b. "Affluence and Underdevelopment: The Nigerian Experience," *Journal of Modern African Studies* 16(2), June, pp. 221-39.

Kadzai, Ayuba. 1976. *Nigeria's Global Strategy* (Lagos: The Nigerian Institute of International Affairs), 25 pp.

Noting with approval Clausewitz's dictum that war is an instrument of policy, the author advocates a fully modernized Nigerian Armed Forces "with an offensive capability."

Kirk-Greene, Anthony, and Rimmer, Douglas. 1981. *Nigeria Since 1970: A Political and Economic Outline* (London: Hodder & Stoughton).

Knapp, George. 1968. *Aspects of the Biafran Affair* (London: Britain-Biafra Association), 56 pp.

Subtitled: A Study of British Attitudes and Policy Towards the Nigerian-Biafran Conflict. Criticizes the Commonwealth Offices's decision to support (clandestinely) the Lagos Government.

Mayall, James. 1976. "Oil and Nigerian Foreign Policy," *African Affairs* 75(300), July, pp. 284-316.

Nweke, G. Aforka. 1976. *External Intervention in African Conflicts* (Brookline, Mass.: African Studies Center, Boston University), 77 pp.

Demonstrates that national self-interest rather than "justice" was the motivational force for outside intervention in the Nigerian Civil War.

Ofoegbu, Mazi Ray. 1976. "Towards a New Philosophy of Foreign Policy for Nigeria," in Bolaji Akinyemi (ed.), *Nigeria and the World* (Ibadan: OUP for NIIA), pp. 116-35.

Ogunbadejo, Oye. 1980. "Nigeria's Foreign Policy under Military Rule, 1966-79," *International Journal* 35(4), Autumn, pp. 748-65.

——. 1979. "A New Turn in US-Nigerian Relations," *World Today* 35(3), March, pp. 117-26.

Ogunsanwo, Alaba. 1980. *The Nigerian Military and Foreign Policy 1975-1979* (Princeton, N.J.: Center of International Studies, Woodrow Wilson School, Princeton, University), 86 pp.

A look at changes in foreign policy effected by the military government and an evaluation of their foreign policy performance (through a country-specific examination of Angola, South Africa, the U.S., and Great Britain).

Ojo, Olatunde J. B. 1980. "Nigeria and the Formation of ECOWAS," *International Organization* 34(4), Autumn, pp. 571-604.

Oyediran, Oyeleye. 1978. *Survey of Nigerian Affairs, 1975* (Ibadan: Oxford University Press), 347 pp.

A series of essays dealing with 1975 political issues commences the book; major government statements constitute the second section; a third section summarizes Nigeria's 1975 relations with institutions and selected countries; the last section lists individuals on important 1975 national panels.

Phillips, C. S., Jr. 1964. *The Development of Nigerian Foreign Policy* (Evanston: Northwestern).

Rimmer, Douglas. 1978. "Elements of the Political Economy," in Keith Panter-Brick.

Shaw, Timothy M. 1982. "Introduction: Nigeria as Africa's Major Power," in Timothy M. Shaw and Olajide Aluko (eds.), *Nigerian Foreign Policy* (London: MacMillan).

____. 1981a. "Dependence with Growth: The Political Economy of Petroleum in Nigeria," *Workshop on the Effects of Commodity Dependence on Development in African Countries*, Dalhousie University, March.

____. 1981b. "Class, Country and Corporation: Africa in the Capitalist World System," in Donald I. Ray et al. (eds.), *Into the 80s: Proceedings of the 11th Annual Conference of the Canadian Association of African Studies, Volume 2* (Vancouver: Tantalus), pp. 19-37.

____. 1980. "Nigeria's Political Economy: Constitutions, Capitalism and Contradictions," *ODI Review* 2, pp. 76-85.

____. 1977. "Kenya and South Africa: 'Sub-Imperialist' States," *Orbis* 21(2), Summer, pp. 357-94.

____, ed. 1982. *Alternative Futures for Africa* (Boulder: Westview).

Shaw, Timothy M., and Fasehun, Orobola. 1980. "Nigeria in the World System: Alternative Approaches, Explanations and Projections," *Journal of Modern African Studies* 18(4), December, pp. 551-73.

Shaw, Timothy M., and Aluko, Olajide, eds. 1982. *Nigerian Foreign Policy: Alternative Perceptions and Projections* (London: MacMillan).

Stremlau, John. 1977. *The International Politics of the Nigerian Civil War 1967-1970* (Princeton, N.J.: Princeton University Press), 425 pp.

Provides detailed coverage of African and international involvement (and noninvolvement) in the Civil War and, conversely, Federal and Biafran international efforts.

Turner, Terisa. 1976a. "Multinational Corporations and the Instability of the Nigerian State," *Review of African Political Economy* 5, January-April, pp. 63-79.

——. 1976b. "The Transfer of Oil Technology and the Nigerian State," *Development and Change* 7, pp. 353-90.

Tyoden, Sonni G. 1981. "State, Class and Capital Accumulation in the Periphery," *Nigerian Political Science Association*, Kano, April.

Unongo, Paul I. 1970. *Say It Loud: We're Black and Strong* (Lagos: Micho Commercial Printers), 101 pp.

Lessons are drawn from foreign involvement and tribal cleavage in the Nigerian Civil War.

Usman, Bala. 1981. "Debate on Libya Warms Up: Open Letter," *West Africa* 3318, 2 March, pp. 421-23.

Wallerstein, Immanuel. 1979. *The Capitalist World-Economy* (Cambridge: Cambridge University Press).

Wayas, Joseph. 1979. *Nigeria's Leadership Role in Africa* (London: MacMillan), 132 pp.

Reflections on how Nigeria can use its power to help liberate southern Africa, bridge Black African-Arab differences, make the OAU a more effective institution, and provide economic and technical assistance to other African countries.

Williams, Gavin. 1980. "Postface" in his collection on *State and Society in Nigeria* (Idanre, Ondo: Afrografika), pp. 10-21.

——. 1979. "Editorial: Nigeria," *Review of African Political Economy* 13, May-August, pp. 1-7.

——. 1977. "Class Relations in a Neo-Colony: The Case of Nigeria," in Peter Gutkind and Peter Waterman (eds.), *African Social Studies: A Radical*

Reader (London: Heinemann), pp. 284-94.

——. 1976. "Introduction" and "Nigeria: A Political Economy" in his collection on *Nigeria: Economy and Society* (London: Rex Collings), pp. 1-54.

Williams, Gavin, and Turner, Terisa. 1978. "Nigeria," in John Dunn (ed.), *West African States: Failure and Promise* (Cambridge: Cambridge University Press).

Wright, Stephen. 1981. "Limits of Nigeria's Power Overseas," *West Africa* 3339, 27 July, pp. 1685-87.

Young, Andrew. 1981. "The United States and Africa: Victory for Diplomacy," *Foreign Affairs* 59(3), pp. 648-66.

Zartman, I. William. 1971. *The Politics of Trade Negotiations between Africa and the European Economic Community* (Princeton: Princeton University Press).

Index

About the Editor and Contributors

I. WILLIAM ZARTMAN is Professor of International Politics and Director of the African Studies Program at the Johns Hopkins School for Advanced International Studies in Washington, D.C. He is the author of *International Relations in the New Africa*, *The Politics of Trade Negotiations between Africa and the European Communities*, *Ripe for Resolution: Conflict and Intervention in Africa* (for the Africa Project of the Council on Foreign Relations), and coauthor of *Africa in the 1980s* (for the Council on Foreign Relations), *Africa and the United States: Vital Interests*, *African Diplomacy*, and *Soldier and State in Africa*. Dr. Zartman is also editor of the series of SAIS African Studies published by Praeger, including *The Political Economy of the Ivory Coast* and *The OAU after 20 Years*. He received his M.A. from the Johns Hopkins University and his Ph.D. from Yale University.

ADEOYE AKINSANYA is a Senior Lecturer in Political Science at the University of Lagos and was Fulbright Scholar at the Johns Hopkins School of Advanced International Studies and the University of South Carolina in 1980-81. He is the author of *Expropriation of Multinational Property in the Third World and Economic Independence*, *Indigenization of Private Foreign Investment in Ghana and Nigeria*, and *Multinationals in a Changing Environment*, and coauthor of *Government and Politics in Nigeria*, *The Nigerian 1979 Elections*, *Development Planning and Priorities in the 1980s in the ECOWAS*, and *Southern Africa in the Eighties*. He received his B.S. from the University of Ibadan, his M.P.A. from the University of Pittsburgh, and his Ph.D. from the University of Chicago.

HENRY BIENEN is Professor of Politics and International Relations at Princeton University and Director of the Research Project in Development Studies at the Woodrow Wilson School. He is author of *Kenya: The Politics of Participation and Control*, *Tanzania: Party Transformation and Economic Development*, *Violence and Social Change*, *The Military Intervenes*, *Armies and Parties in Africa*, coauthor of *Authoritarian Politics in Modern Society*, and contributing editor of *The Political Economy of Income Distribution in Nigeria*. Dr. Bienen received his A.B. from Cornell University and his Ph.D. from the University of Chicago.

THOMAS BIERSTEKKER is Associate Professor of Political Science at Yale University. He has written *Distortion or Development: Contending Perspectives on the Multinational Corporations* and is coauthor of *The African Bourgeoisie*. He was a Fulbright research scholar in the University of Ibadan in 1981-82. He holds a doctorate from the Massachusetts Institute of Technology.

LARRY DIAMOND is Assistant Professor of Sociology at Vanderbilt University and Fulbright lecturer (1982-83) at Banyero University in Kano. His dissertation was on Nigerian politics, and Dr. Diamond has published articles in the *Journal of Modern African Studies* and *Comparative Studies in Society and History*. He received his doctorate from Stanford University.

PAUL LUBECK is Associate Professor of Sociology at the University of California at Santa Cruz and Fulbright research scholar (1982-83) at Banyero University in Kano. He is author of *Islam and Urban Labor: The Making of a Working Class in Kano*, contributing editor of *The African Bourgeoisie: The Development of Capitalism in Nigeria, Kenya and Ivory Coast*, and coauthor of *Research in the Sociology of the World*, *World System of Capitalism*, *Third World Urbanization*, and *The Development of an African Working Class*. He received his A.B. from St. Michaels College and his Ph.D. from Northwestern University.

ROBERT MANDERSCHEID is currently with the Mellon Bank, Pittsburgh, Pennsylvania. He received his B.A. from Oberlin College and his M.A. from the Johns Hopkins School of Advanced International Studies.

TIMOTHY M. SHAW is Professor of Political Science at Dalhousie University and has taught at the University of Ife in Nigeria, as well as Makerere University and the University of Zambia. He is coauthor of *Zambia's Foreign Policy*, and contributing editor of *Cooperation and Conflict in Southern Africa, Canada, Scandinavia and Southern Africa*, *Conflict and Change in Southern Africa*, *Politics of Africa: Dependency and Development*, *Alternate Futures for Africa*, *The Foreign Policies of Africa*, and *Nigerian Foreign Policy*. He holds an M.A. from Sussex University and Makerere University, and a Ph.D. from Princeton University.

MICHAEL WATTS is Assistant Professor of Geography and African Studies at the University of California at Berkeley. He has taught and conducted research at Ahmadu Bello and Ibadan Universities in Nigeria, as well as in Niger and Senegal. He is author of *Silent Violence: Food, Famine and Peasantry in Northern Nigeria*, and coauthor of *Life after the Drought*. He received his A.B. from University College, London, and his Ph.D. from the University of Michigan.

Alisse has integrated her East and West with simple exercises and empowering stories, to clear underlying blocks to your flow of money. I love that she tells women it is ok to be abundant and successful. More and more we are looking to solve our own problems, get to the underlying issues, take personal responsibility and look at how to be clear on our purpose. Honouring your business is so important, using the core principles of Feng Shui - to be clear in your life and your surroundings - to see patterns clearly - to have skills written in a way that are clearly explained and easy to implement. Alisse as a person - you amaze me - for your sheer determination to find strategies to handle the blocks in your own life and I love that you have applied that drive and determination to your work with Feng Shui.

Marguerite Louis Amor / Speaker, Facilitator, Kinesiologist and Family Constellations Therapist / www.creatingyou.com.au

Alisse's wealth of knowledge and experience absolutely shines through in her work. The depth of information she provides and the ease with which she transmits this into actionable steps for the layperson is a rare gift. I have thoroughly enjoyed reading Millionaire Feng Shui *and using the hidden science Alisse reveals to increase my own business success. If you are interested in making positive changes in your life and work, I would highly recommend starting with this book.*

Assisi Chant / Word Whisperer and Photographer, Energy Empath and Resonant Resource Builder / www.resourceswithresonance.com

Alisse operates from her heart in the most authentic and passionate way. Her knowledge of Feng Shui is stunning, as is the manner in which she lives and breathes this way of life. There is something truly special about Alisse, which you'll discover here on the pages of this life-affirming book.

Sue Papadoulis / Award winning Journalist, Author and Founder of Publicity for Profit / www.publicityforprofit.com.au

What others are saying about

ALISSE BRADLEY

Speaker, Author, Business Coach and Designer

Working with Alisse helped me 'unleash my power' that was lying dormant within me for years. Prior to working with her, I was confused as to my direction in life and lacked self-confidence. I was also unclear on what my destiny was, though after working with Alisse, she was able to bring forth my 'inner' desires that I didn't even know existed, which in turn gave me both the courage and stamina to move forward, and to bring these goals into fruition. It is an absolute pleasure working with Alisse; she has a heart of gold and is able to build a quick connection with all her clients, allowing for an amazing friendship to develop. I recommend Alisse to anyone wanting to find clarity in their life and for people wanting to take their life or career to the next level.

Katrina Kavvalos / TV Talk Show Host, #1 Best Selling Author / www.katrinakavvalos.com

Alisse has provided for me wonderful guidance on finding the right path to wealth in line with my passion and values. I always thought that I couldn't be a successful businesswoman because I didn't have the same gutsy attitude that others had. However, having spent quite a few sessions chatting to Alisse, she has helped me define who I am and the unique gift that I can share in a way that still gets me noticed and brings clients to my business – the kind of clients that I want to work with and who want to work with me. Not only have my personal and business finances improved, the relationship with my children has also improved. Thank you Alisse, you have been a wonderful friend and coach.

Karen Thomson / Business Development Management / www.pulseecommerce.com

After meeting Alisse at a Women's Seminar, we employed her services to completely rebrand our business. We have an online business with a natural organic skincare and skin clinic on the Gold Coast. We have not only increased our business over the past two months, but furthermore the feedback we are receiving from our customers is super positive. I highly recommend coaching with Alisse.

Debbie Majella Nolan / Founder of Door of Your Skincare / www.doorofyouth.com

Thanks to Alisse I am finally shifting the areas of my business and life I have been stagnant in. She has shown me how to keep the "FAITH" and "TO NEVER GIVE UP." This experience has not only enriched my life; it has also given me more understanding of how to achieve success in all areas of my life. Thank you Alisse, you are truly on your path of greatness. You are brilliant and I am so grateful of my time with you.

Sandra Campbell / Handcrafted Jewelry Designer / www.facebook.com/edenayadesigns

Before I met Alisse, I was floating along doing stuff but not moving forward. Now I am finally really happy with my branding and business; I have been to the United States twice and Canada for the first time to further my training and passion, have become recognized amongst my peers and network team as a leader, and facilitated some major expos in Queensland and New South Wales. I have the confidence to know that whatever I believe I can do, I will most surely achieve it. Alisse is a person who lives what she teaches. I give her my highest recommendation if you wish to bring balance, peace, and prosperity in to your life.

Barb Free / Founder of Live in Synergy / www.liveinsynergy.com.au

Alisse, whatever you are doing it is just amazing! When I turned my phone back on after our session I had a call from a fellow coach. She signed up with me immediately on my Big Coaching Pack. Synchronicity?? I am starting to think there is more to this. Not to mention I have been feeling amazing and have so much energy. I am even looking forward to exercising!! Thanx so much!! Love & Peace.

Carolyn Greer / Raw Food Nutritionist / rawvival@gmail.com

Alisse, you have reignited my confidence to move forward in a way that truly represents who I am, a confidence to trust my inner self, and a confidence that transcends into the lives of others. My sense of self is stronger than ever, and I am once again feeling happy. I am very excited for what lies ahead for me, my family, and my business. Thank you from the bottom of my heart.

Karen Mudie / Holistic Life Coach / www.karenmudie.com.au

I have been fortunate to have met Alisse about a year ago and continued to do her courses. I have found that Alisse gives much more than is usually expected. Packed with value from the time spent in her courses, the content, and her continuing support. Her great knowledge in a range of different areas and her intuition to just know how to help people make the changes they so want in their lives. I have finally made so much progress it is amazing, after going around in circles no matter how hard I have tried to move on for years. Now finally I have moved through in business, my relationships, and I have become who I am today. I am now in a place where dreams can come true! Thank you Alisse; I am so grateful for all of your support and guidance! It is exciting doing my own change. And fascinating watching those around me also moving through and finally making amazing progress! It has been an amazing time of learning! Thank you, Alisse!

Wendy Skene / Owner Operator at Fairy Dell Shop / www. facebook.com/fairydellbywendy

When working with Alisse, she makes sure that her strategies and principles are explained in plain English, and this demystifies the entire process so that you intuitively start to see for yourself what works and why.

Wendy Chamberlain / Buyer & Vendor Advocate / www.followwendy.com

Working with Alisse has been one of the greatest drivers in boosting my career success over the past four years. She has a wealth of knowledge to share with entrepreneurs and business owners who are ready to start making real money. If Alisse gives you a piece of advice, you can "take it to the bank!"

Daisy McCarty / Brand Messaging Specialist and B2B Copywriter / www.daisymccarty.com

One of the greatest gifts Alisse has is listening to you; what you want, need, and desire then using Feng Shui to create those opportunities for you. The most prevalent lessons I learned from doing Feng Shui with Alisse was to stop blocking my path. I'd leave boxes near doorways or chairs in the walkway area, creating unnecessary obstacles to where I wanted to go. It is simple logical Feng Shui lessons like this that allowed me to open my mind and human being-ness to creating less stress and allow myself more, and so give myself permission to succeed in whatever I choose to do.

Katey Shaw / Entrepreneurial Development Consultant